Missing **Persons**

William E. Gruber

Missing **Persons**

Character and Characterization

in Modern Drama

THE UNIVERSITY OF GEORGIA PRESS

ATHENS AND LONDON

© 1994 by the University of Georgia Press
Athens, Georgia 30602
All rights reserved
Designed by Betty Palmer McDaniel
Set in ten on thirteen Sabon
by Tseng Information Systems, Inc.
Printed and bound by Thomson-Shore, Inc.
The paper in this book meets the guidelines for
permanence and durability of the Committee on
Production Guidelines for Book Longevity of the
Council on Library Resources.

Printed in the United States of America

98 97 96 95 94   C   5   4   3   2   1

Library of Congress Cataloging in Publication Data

Gruber, William E.
    Missing persons : character and characterization
in modern drama / William E. Gruber.
        p.   cm.
    Includes bibliographical references and index.
    Contents: Gordon Craig's depersonalized stage—
Brecht and the social self—Character portraits/
portraying character : Krapp's last tape, Rockaby,
Catastrophe—Mental life in Thomas Bernhard's
comic types—The characters of Maria Irene Fornes.
    ISBN 0-8203-1630-X
    1. Drama—20th century—History and criticism.
2. Characters and characteristics in literature.   I. Title.
    PN1689.G78   1994
    809.2'04—dc20   93-38149

British Library Cataloging in Publication Data available

In memory of
Bessie Hartman Gruber, 1908–1992

This thing we name the individual, this piece of matter, this length of memory, this bearer of a proper name, this block in space, this whisper in time, this self-delighting, self-condemning oddity—what is it? who made it?

MICHAEL LEVENSON,
Modernism and the Fate of Individuality

The likeness we want is the likeness of the missing persons.

HERBERT BLAU, *Take Up the Bodies*

Contents

Acknowledgments

Part of chapter 1 was presented at the annual Comparative Drama Conference (the University of Florida, 1985) and subsequently published in *Within the Dramatic Spectrum,* ed. Karelisa V. Hartigan (Lanham, Md.: University Press of America, 1986); part of chapter 2 appeared in *Comparative Drama* 21 (1987); part of chapter 5 appears in *Public Issues, Private Tensions: Contemporary American Drama,* ed. Matthew Roudané (New York: AMS Press, 1993). I thank the editors of these publications for their permission to reprint this material. Much of the rest of the book was written during two leaves granted by Emory College and Emory University Research Committee. I am grateful for Emory's continuing support. I wish also to extend my thanks and deep gratitude to Ellen T. M. Craig, Executor of the Edward Gordon C. H. Estate, for her permission to reproduce copyrighted material.

Missing **Persons**

Introduction

This is a book about character and the representation of character in modern drama. Its objective, however, is neither to develop a theory of modern drama nor to attempt anything like a comprehensive historical account of the subject. Rather, it aims to address within broad literary contexts a number of specific questions about specific playwrights' dramatis personae: why mechanical actors or the abrupt dislocations of oriental acting styles meant so much to dramatists as different as Bertolt Brecht and Gordon Craig; why the figures in Beckett's late plays are so often flat, schematized, heraldic; and why such contemporary dramatists as Maria Fornes and Thomas Bernhard share a profound fascination with the mechanics of theatrical representation—quoting, reciting, reproducing, or impersonating an absent text.

My immediate goal in writing the book was frankly personal, to learn how to understand certain plays whose images of human beings were problematic, abstract, alien. The figures who move across these stages are frail, contradictory, occasionally mutilated or even dismembered—sobering reminders that the individual's place in the world is not as secure or as central as we imagine it once was. Yet character remains for these authors a crucial element of drama, even if it is more fragile, more ghostly, more enigmatic than ever before. I wrote the book, therefore, to see in what ways one might in principle restore character to the criticism of modern drama. In one sense, then, the book is conservative; my primary assumption is that the representation of character remains among the dramatist's most important tasks. In another sense, however, I intend the book to be innovative. I see little point any longer in debating whether certain characters are real or unreal, convincing or incredible, round or flat. Instead I want to examine some of the ways by which certain modern dramatists define (or redefine) subjectivity, identity, selfhood—in short, character—on their stages.

What I will attempt over the course of the book is to develop a vocabulary for discussing character in dramas where more conventional languages for character seem insufficient or irrelevant. In brief, I will combine close literary analyses of plays with psychological and social theory and often with comments on the visual arts. The focus will be sharpened by limiting the number of playwrights and plays I discuss to a relatively small number and by concentrating on authors who regard character with some degree of skepticism. For Craig, the relevant idea is principally aesthetic; he created the *Übermarionette,* the mechanical being who was to replace the human figure. For Brecht, the focus is political and ideological, and the significant facts about character are to be discovered in its instinctive (and regrettable) malleability. Beckett and Bernhard independently turn to the couple, to the idea of a *relationship* (as opposed to a single autonomous being) as "the last safeguard and testament of subjectivity."[1] And Fornes, like a number of other contemporary women dramatists, collapses distinctions between public and private notions of identity.

Of course I am still talking about character in some essential sense. There are good reasons to restore character to dramatic criticism, not least of which is that it is practically (hence theoretically) impossible to ignore it. For the most part, plays continue to have people in them; that is, in an age in which art has been dominated impressively by abstractionist experimentation, plays still include recognizably human figures represented by live actors before an audience. Hence, there runs through modern drama a contradiction between various modern theories that assert there are no such things as enduring personal qualities[2] and the continuing presence in texts (not to mention on stage) of people in whom we see glimpses of individual behavior. I want to see if one can assign to some of the most problematic characters in modern drama something like a coherent narrative identity. I am looking for self-constancy, in other words, if not self-sufficiency. Mainly I read plays to discover the nature of dramatic agency. Is character an identifiable subject or an interactive unit? Is the mind represented on stage a cohesive identity or a forensic construction whose dissection (as Hume long ago argued) merely exposes a manifold of sensations, volitions, and emotions?

The drama of the twentieth century offers a bewildering display of images of humans and human psyches. More than any other period in theater history, the twentieth century is a time of revolution and experiment in which the most influential playwrights have abandoned many elements long thought essential to drama, including plot, action, and character. Indeed a commonplace of criticism is that modern dramatists have little interest in representing character for its own sake. It was no longer possible, Joseph Wood Krutch complained several decades ago, to speak of dramatists' characters as if they were continuous, persisting, relatively stable individuals: "One of the most significant differences between the past which lies on one side of a chasm and the future which is presumed to lie on the other is simply that the past is dominated by egos, by actors who are assumed to be directed by a hard-core personality, while in the future there will be only states of consciousness—continuous only in the sense that they function for a time by means of a given brain, housed in a given skull."[3] Modern drama, Krutch wrote, was increasingly empty of characters. Some of these "missing persons" are the subject of this book.

The study of character as a crucial component of drama has been neglected for much of this century for two reasons. The first involves a general shift in criticism throughout the modern period from studies of character to studies of words.[4] Earlier formalist critics habitually ignored the figures populating dramatic works in favor of thematic or technical interests, while more recent scholars have read character primarily for its cultural or ideological significance. The second reason for declining interest in character studies in drama has less to do with changing literary fashions than with a problem long peculiar to drama criticism. As any stage history of any particular character proves, playwrights, unlike novelists, are not solely responsible for their characters. That stage performance in some way contradicts the text has long been recognized as an anomaly in the criticism of drama, and the difficulty of writing about multiple Hamlets cannot be minimized.[5]

But the task of describing plays without somehow addressing character seems at best difficult and at worst perverse. I do not mean to reduce criticism of drama to the rehearsal of case histories, but I think that attending to character leads to a simple yet accurate insight: that understanding drama, whatever its capacity for "psychic polyphony," depends upon treating its characters as persons. If our sense that literary characters are persons is (as Harold Bloom puts it) "a kind of fact,"[6] I would want to claim at least so much facticity for real bodies moving through real space. Herbert Blau puts the case for character in drama even more clearly:

> [T]he idea of character haunts us in the theater like the absence of some pictorial metabolism in a color field painting (no referent, no analogy, no nature, no mimesis). In the most advanced forms of theater, the missing character is felt like the absence of some primary level of articulation. In art, the techniques of rendering persist in giving witness to the remembrance of nature. They are not easy to do without. A line or a drip in what appears to be a completely abstract painting

will betray the dispassionate image or the action field and remind us that something is being drawn from somewhere else, *outside* the picture frame, not coextensive with it, even when the frames are stretched almost beyond the limits of peripheral vision. There is something in the field painting of a Pollock that still makes us think of a landscape, and in his case the particular virility of the tracings makes us know the artist is very much there. The image was not meant to be dispassionate. Depending on the immediacy of the image, we will feel through the serenest abstraction the presence of the activating person.[7]

To return character studies to criticism of drama, then, is not merely a nostalgic exercise. Far from it: studies of character are one of the elements of which dramatic criticism is made. (One cannot rule out even discussing characters on occasion as if they were people or even asking questions about their extradramatic lives. From the point of view of an actor feeling her [or his] way into the character of Lady Macbeth, for example, it may be useful to imagine oneself having a certain number of children.[8])

As my title suggests, I write about dramatists' characters as if the delineation of character were still central to drama. At the same time I acknowledge the hazards and the paradoxes inherent in that task. Even the term "character" itself is problematic and covers a spectrum of meanings. Once used to betoken expressly moral qualities (in *The Poetics*, Aristotle includes ethos, "character," as one of the essential components of tragic drama), nowadays "character" generally substitutes freely for "person." We speak, for example, of Shakespeare's characters, meaning Hamlet or Rosalind or Caliban, whereas Shakespeare uses the term only in its older senses, as referring either to a distinctive mark or style or to a personal quality ("I will believe thou hast a mind that suites / With this thy faire and outward character," *Twelfth Night*, 1.2.50–51). The idea of "character" as referring to a specific person or personality in the abstract (as distinct from a quality peculiar to a specific person) seems not to develop until the eighteenth century. Fielding in *Tom Jones* advises his readers "not to condemn a character as a bad one because it is not perfectly a good one," and Johnson (comparing Fielding and Richardson) distinguishes between "characters of nature and characters of manners."[9] "Character" for Fielding and for Johnson still denotes moral bent, but for both writers (as, increasingly, throughout the eighteenth century) the term refers clearly to persons as well as to their personalities. Over the course of the century the term acquires explicitly theatrical connotations, as if character—far from referring to an essential component of the person—were similar to a role that one assumed or discarded at will.

It is not until relatively recently, however, that "character" has come to refer directly to fictional beings themselves.[10] Yet so completely does "character" now substitute for the unitary "person" in literary criticism that even novelists conveniently speak of characters as chefs might speak of eggs. Thus André Gide condemns "characters in a novel or a play who act all the way through exactly as one expects them to," and Arnold Bennett wonders "whether a novelist want[s] his characters to remain in the mind of the reader." (Some do, he says, and some don't.) But the most surprising view belongs to D. H. Lawrence, who cuts character free from its literary history. "Somehow," writes Lawrence, "that which is physic—non-human in humanity, is more interesting to me than the old-fashioned human element—which causes one to conceive a character in a certain moral scheme and make him consistent."[11]

It is disconcerting to note that character can now apply contradictorily both to moral and amoral domains. But it is worthwhile to dwell for a moment on the paradox inherent in Lawrence's separation of character from ethics because it points clearly to the range of problems I wish to address in this book. Modern studies of character have been particularly vulnerable to misconceptions such as the following in Charles Walcutt's *Man's Changing Mask*. In defining his subject, Walcutt turns naturally to Aristotle's *Poetics:*

> He writes (in the Bywater translation) . . . Tragedy is essentially an imitation not of persons but of action and life, of happiness and misery. . . . In a play . . . they do not act in order to portray the characters; they include the characters for the sake of the action. . . .
> Aristotle notes two elements that contribute to characterization. . . . One is moral bent or ethos, the second is intellect. We note immediately that these two qualities are described in connection with action; they have to do with making choices in situations that require them—not with what the character is but with what he does.[12]

The modern reader coming to *The Poetics* and its interpreters encounters a confusing terrain marked by brilliant insights and distressing misobservations. In the above commentary, for example, the difficulties of rendering ancient Greek into modern English cause crucial discrepancies. Bywater translates freely ("I have accordingly not scrupled to recast many of Aristotle's sentences . . . in order to make the sense and sequence of ideas clearer"[13]), and in this case his translation is accurate but seems to be seriously misleading. Bywater translates *ta ethe* as "the characters," which makes it sound as if Aristotle in naming the components of drama refers (as we would) to "the characters" as the persons in the play. In fact Aristotle in these passages and elsewhere treats "ethos" not as synonymous with "person" but as an element of the person. Ethos is surely for Aristotle the crucial element of the persons of the drama, but it is not to be confused with the persons themselves.

Thus Walcutt compounds the confusion by assuming that ethos contributes to character. But "ethos" as Aristotle uses the term cannot "contribute" to character; it *is* character. It refers to a quality that when visible accurately distinguishes one person from another—but it is not always visible. Ethos manifests itself only in actions that result from certain kinds of choices. This is the reason Aristotle elsewhere in *The Poetics* maintains that tragedies can lack character (he does not mean that they can lack people) but not action.

Aristotle uses "ethos" to denote "character" in accord with then-contemporary usage. But the meaning of ethos as Aristotle seems to understand it goes back many centuries before *The Poetics*. The term has a fascinating history. Originally "ethos" designated "the places where animals are usually found."[14] Homer, for example, three times uses "ethos," always in reference to animals; for Homer, "*ethea* forms an arena or range in which the animal naturally belongs."[15] Ethos and its derivative forms (*ethea* and *etheios*, "one who is found in a certain place") seem to combine at least two basic meanings: first, the idea of belonging to a particular space and, second, the idea of behavioral predictability. To these denotations of ethos—animals' territoriality and their predictability—is added a third, related quality, the will to resist change. (As anyone who has ever kept animals knows, they are creatures of habit and resist vigorously any attempts to change their familiar habitats and behavioral patterns.)

The subsequent extension of ethos from animal habitats to the most essential qualities of human beings is surely one of the most remarkable metaphoric extensions in human affairs. Charles Chamberlain speculates that the transference was completed by the 4th century B.C., "no doubt the natural culmination of its development as the center of belonging."[16]

Just as the horse [*Iliad* 6.506–11] possessed some area of his own which was unaffected by attempts to change his feeding grounds, so too the "tricky" *ethos* of a false friend is unaffected by any of the pleasing surfaces which Theognis mentions. In time both reassert themselves.

What we have then . . . is an idea of *ethos* as the arena in which people or animals move; further, this essence, whether in an animal or a human being, resists the imposition of outside influences.[17]

Chamberlain's summary of the etymology of "ethos" (character) is the best concise definition I know of what today we might call a person's "nature" or "self":

> Like the pasturage which the horse calls its own, there exists a part of our being which is untouched by higher reasons of love or friendship or duty, and may come to light in a crisis. . . . *[E]thos* is a quality of animate beings which is like habit in that it prescribes predictable behavior, but something more in that it cannot easily be "re-habituated." It is an apparently irrational or unaccountable entity which nevertheless follows a rational principle or principles of its own. To put it more suggestively, the *ethos* has its own *logos* which is in a sense beyond the reach of *logos*.[18]

Ethos as described by Chamberlain stands in marked contrast with more recent views of character in literature. By contrast, consider a definition of character proposed recently by Seymour Chatman. According to Chatman, character consists simply of an aggregate of traits that are understood by convention to represent a "whole" being. The character's name itself functions as a receptor for his or her particular characteristics, so that the individual then exists, according to Chatman, as a "paradigm of traits."[19] The proper name (as in Plato's discussion of *eidos,* the way an object "appears" in speech) allows us to hold the absent person before us. It may be that Chatman's theory squares with our experience of fictive persons in narrative; it is always a little disconcerting to tally up what we know of memorable characters and find how much is missing and how eloquent are such absences. "Characters in fiction," writes William Gass, "are mostly empty canvas. I have known many who have passed through their stories without noses, or heads to hold them; others have lacked bodies altogether, exercised no natural functions, possessed some thoughts, a few emotions, but no psychologies, and apparently made love without the necessary organs."[20]

But dramatis personae cannot be understood only as imagined assemblages of parts. Characters in a play exist in the form of enacted persons, so that in theater the agents are not linguistic but physiognomic metaphors; the basis of theatrical performance is mimetic involvement, somatic as well as affective. In theater, in consequence, says Bruce Wilshire, "one becomes aware of what one's body already is: something modeled on others mimetically. One also becomes aware of one's possibilities as an individual. The shimmering fictional character is the locus through which the actor is given back to himself through the audience, and the members of the audience are given back to themselves through the actor. It is a play of mutual 'mirroring.' "[21]

Character as embodied by the actor differs profoundly from that constructed by way of prose narrative. In fact one might argue that drama provides a singularly clarifying site for discovery of character: "the body too," as John Locke long ago argued, "goes to the making the man, and would, I guess, to everybody determine the man in this case." [22]

To face honestly the problem of arguing for the centrality of character in modern drama, I will discuss the work of five theater artists whose diverse representations of character seem each in its own way to be hostile to character—at least as character has been understood in the individualist or private sense defined by Krutch and Chamberlain. I have not tried to write psychoanalytic exegesis but empathic description, and I certainly did not attempt to write a comprehensive history of character on the modern stage. I have tried instead to define various typical and innovative ways in which five different modern playwrights have represented persons or personality.[23]

In writing about character in modern and postmodern theater one faces a multitude of practical and theoretical considerations. Of course there are inevitable distortions in any study of drama based on the text only, but in modern drama it is often the case that before one studies a text one must first decide which of several to study. Which *Godot* takes priority? The French (which has "original" status) or the English? Which *Not I?* The play (the genre in which Beckett wrote) or the later film (which Beckett preferred)? Most of Beckett's plays exist in variant forms—in different languages or in different media—all equally authorized. Much the same problem occurs in Brecht studies, where one almost always confronts coexistent versions of the same work. Which *Threepenny Opera* is authoritative? The original or the "improved" Marxist text? As for the plays of Maria Fornes, they are often acknowledged collaborations rather than individual creations; their author calls them "works in process," as opposed to finished artifacts. At first glance this appears to be simple humility on Fornes's part, but in fact it is much more than that. In denying the stability of her texts Fornes underscores a philosophical problem: who controls the meaning of art? And what of Gordon Craig? In the case of Craig's work the task of "reconstructing" character is ironic because most of his "plays" typically exist as woodcuts or sketches.

I try to accommodate representational and refractive criticism by writing about playwrights whose work clearly articulates various modern attitudes toward mimesis.[24] The first two chapters are concerned with theoretical issues as well as with specific plays or productions. In them I discuss the work of Bertolt Brecht and Gordon Craig for contrasting but complementary reasons. The initial assumption is that Craig's notorious attacks on actors and logocentric theater might articulate more than his own idiosyncrasies—that Craig, in short, might set the standard for new orders of representation that subsequent playwrights, whatever their particular politics or aesthetics, might carry forward. I am less concerned with specific questions of influence than with the timeliness of Craig's deep antagonism toward the "realistic" characters who dominated the early modern stage.

Despite its chronological distance, Craig's depersonalized stage is expressly relevant to postmodern drama and dramatic theory. It is true that Craig's Übermarionette was a product less of logical aesthetics than of his own personal ambivalence toward actors and acting. But it is true also that Craig's condemnations of live actors—however much they confused his followers and critics alike—are part of a century-long artistic assault on representational poetics of character.[25] Take Kleist's essay on marionette theater, Strindberg's "characterless" characters, Craig's set designs, and Meyerhold's experiments with "biomechanical" acting as examples of the "depersonalization" of drama. Add Brecht's "alienation effects," Pirandello's *Enrico IV*, Beckett's "talking heads," or Richard Foreman's Rhoda, a persona whose chief characteristic is that she repeatedly comes apart. In various ways, all these writers challenge inherited Romanticist or individualist views of character. In response to inherited dramaturgies that locate personal identity *within* a discrete subject, modern and postmodern dramatists stage characters who sometimes lack "interiority," whose outlines and edges blur into the environment, and whose chief characteristic often turns out to be a collection of qualities not private but public.

Brecht, too, invented new ways to figure character, and, like Craig, condemned conventional imitative performances. In the half century since he first promulgated his arguments against "realistic" and "culinary" theater, his reformations for theatrical performance have in many cases become normative. Yet much of the subtlety of Brechtian dramatic theory has been ignored, especially by American writers who cannot easily accept Brecht's social view of art. But there are two reasons to include Brecht's theory as well as his theater in a study of stage characters and characterization. The first is that Brechtian theory is not strictly literary criticism but more like theatrical proxemics. Brecht's theory details the workings of an apparatus of representation, and thus it is extremely useful in addressing ethical questions of theater art.[26] Second, Brechtian theory for all its gaps and contradictions is consistently "anti-Aristotelian." Brecht's stubborn resistance to Aristotelian dramatic theory, therefore, makes his criticism a "negative aesthetic." As such it is ideally suited to many postmodern theaters that are "out of sync" with the classical (Aristotelian) critical discourse.[27] One of the arguments running through this book is that modern dramatists see mimesis as inextricably (and inexplicably) entwined with ethos, and Brecht, perhaps more than any other playwright of this century, was acutely aware of the dramatistic basis of character.

The remainder of the book is focused on representative works of three contemporary playwrights who, like Brecht and Craig, rewrite the grammars by which agents are understood to act: Samuel Beckett, Thomas Bernhard, and Maria Fornes. Their works exemplify some of the problems that Brecht or Craig dealt with on more theoretical levels, and in these chapters I treat these postmodern dramatists within the broad contexts established by Brecht and Craig. For example, Maria Fornes's work, like much feminist theater, continues Brecht's attack (though for different reasons) on "Aristotelian" dramaturgy. For the generation of women playwrights writing after World War II, conventional plots, illusionistic styles for acting, and heroic models for character seemed irrelevant or even deleterious. Similarly, the flat, self-conscious artificiality of Thomas Bernhard's dramatis personae, the sense that everything spoken is spoken as if by a third person—"I am speaking of myself only in quotation marks, as you know, everything I said is only in quotation marks," says the mad prince in *Gargoyles*—such an ironic awareness of the individual's provisional status, of the self's terrifying emptiness, of the ease with which others speak for us and through us, this sense of character as "heteroglossic" is Brechtian long before it is Bakhtinian. Craig is no less present on the contemporary stage. Broadly speaking, Beckett's late plays require "Übermarionettes" to act them, and his stark mise-en-scènes match in striking fashion—apparently unconsciously—Craig's surreal sketches and woodcuts.[28] As for Craig's denigration of speech, one need only think of performance pieces like *Quad* or *Breath* in which movement and sound and decor are the only elements that speak.

One last explanation may be helpful, this time concerning my choice of authors to include in this study. In writing about so broad a subject as character in modern drama I was challenged repeatedly to write about works from within their particular historical contexts and occasionally to discuss some of the familiar modern movements in literary and theater history as well as more encompassing relationships between drama and the visual arts as a whole. Inevitably, therefore, I was sometimes led to make the kinds of general comments and comparisons typical of comprehensive literary histories or period studies. But my aims on the whole are far more modest. I aim mainly to discuss in detail certain crucial representations of the human figure on the modern stage, though I hope that some of what I have to say about a limited number of works will be sufficiently interesting to readers who might want to consider the question of character in relation to other dramatists. But my involvement with theater history in this book is only tangential, and before we go further I should apologize to the reader who expects a more comprehensive survey of the major playwrights of the twentieth century. To such a reader, the five artists whom I have chosen to discuss must seem an odd collection, all the more so because so many of the familiar makers of modern drama are absent. What about characters in Strindberg and Ibsen? Or Chekhov, Shaw, and Yeats? Or Pirandello and O'Neill? Were not these playwrights just as much concerned with character as Craig, Brecht, and Beckett? And among contemporary dramatists, where is Peter Handke? Harold Pinter? Caryl Churchill? David Mamet? Why not write about Heiner Müller, Ntozake Shange, or the Mabou Mines? And so on.

Of course these (and countless other playwrights or acting companies) might well have been included in my discussion. I chose not to attempt to write a synthetic history of modern drama, however, for two reasons that I will explain briefly. First, to write a truly comparative literary history or interdisciplinary study would have prevented the extensive close readings of individual works that I feel ought to be the heart of any literary study. Hence, even if I had the knowledge and skill to write about the several dozen playwrights whose work is important enough collectively to be called the history of modern drama, I lacked the space. Second, in any book such as this, which explores a period by concentrating on relatively few authors, the choice of individuals and individual works to discuss poses a considerable dilemma. On the one hand, I was guided by my strong wish not simply to readdress the familiar half dozen or so "masters of modern drama" to see how their characters fit (or did not fit) into my conceptual frame. I did not purposely omit authors for intellectual or affective ends. My aim was not to shock readers by rewriting history or to degrade particular dramatists by omitting them. On the other hand, I was fully conscious that to omit some of the dominant figures of modernism such as Ibsen or Chekhov might well call the whole argument into question. In the end I tried to strike a balance between familiarity and novelty. Brecht and Beckett are surely major players in any history of modern theater, while Craig, Bernhard, and Fornes are relatively unfamiliar (but neither eccentric nor minor) figures. My selections are admittedly arbitrary, but I believe they are exemplary and reasonable. In grouping these five diverse artists, therefore, I am certainly not advocating that they acted somehow in concert, much less that they are the only figures in modern drama who matter. I do think it is worthwhile, however, occasionally to test the validity of such hardened period concepts as "modern" and "postmodern." As I hope to show, when it comes to representing character, little distinguishes the work of the "high" modernist Craig from Beckett's "postmodern" figurations. Similarly, recent feminist representations of character are in nearly every respect identical to the dramatis personae staged and theorized years ago by Brecht.[29]

Finally, then, why these five? Simply because they confirm (in my opinion) that criticism of character is an important part of criticism of drama, an activity (as L. C. Knights long ago proved)[30] fraught with perils and folly, but one that is still useful and necessary and finally inescapable. In grouping Craig and Brecht with Beckett, Bernhard, and Fornes, my most important goal is to suggest that character remains a defining ideal among modern dramatists, especially among those dramatists who seem deliberately to have forsaken it.

Chapter One

Gordon Craig's
Depersonalized Stage

Lest it seem perverse to begin a study of dramatic characters by focusing on the work of a man who wrote no plays, let me explain my motives. Certainly in terms of his influence on contemporary and subsequent theater artists and dramatists, the importance of Gordon Craig is entirely obvious: Yeats, Meyerhold, Reinhardt, Artaud, Brook, and a multitude of others freely acknowledge his presence in their work.[1] Nor was Craig's influence limited to material innovations involving architectonics and artificial actors. Craig is perhaps the preeminent dramatic theorist of the early modern period, and he lays claim (along with Brecht and Artaud) to being one of the few twentieth-century theater artists who believed theater was important enough to have its own theory.[2]

The common assessment of Craig is that his real contribution to theater lay in the profound changes he helped to bring to mise-en-scène. In this activity, even his detractors acknowledge his enormous influence. One of Craig's ideas—the moveable screens he tested in connection with his most famous production, the collaboration with Stanislavsky on *Hamlet*—has become central in twentieth-century stage design. But making scenes leads to making human figures to appear in them, and Craig also gained considerable prominence (many would say notoriety) for his plan to replace actors with marionettes. Other contemporary artists (for example, Kleist, Appia, Yeats, even Shaw) were fascinated by marionettes and wrote essays and occasionally dramatic pieces to promote them; indeed, as Julian Olf has observed, throughout the history of early modern drama there runs a "man/marionette debate" concerning the suitability of human actors in theater art.[3] But Craig alone committed himself passionately to a stage inhabited exclusively by artificial persons; he said as much publicly on numerous occasions. Quoting himself pseudonymously, for example, in "A Note on Marionettes," Craig wrote that, "as Mr Gordon Craig points out, it is just this passivity, obedience and responsiveness which renders the marionettes such valuable material for the artist of the theatre, which would make possible that which with the living material of the living actor's body remains impossible, . . . the creation of a work of art."[4]

Craig viewed actors with attitudes that ranged from hostile to ambiguous; there seems little doubt that he seriously intended that plays be performed by life-sized puppets. Yet when we look more widely across Craig's writings on theater, we discover an intense artistic interest in the human form. Craig selected as the frontispiece for *The Mask*, for example, a Leonardesque figure depicting a male body within a perfect circle. And the pages of *The Mask* throughout the decades of its production are full of stylized representations of human beings—not only Craig's own prints and woodcuts but also haunting multitudes of figures drawn from stages ranging from contemporary to ancient, European to oriental. A reader of Craig's journal cannot help but observe how those representations define Craig's attempts to maintain touch with the human figure without yielding to the temptations of realistic art. This commitment to representing the human figure is not so odd if we remember that drama requires the figural if not technically the living presence of human beings. To construe character in drama, in other words, means that we may consider it for its figural as well as psychic reality. If the latter, we read dramatic character primarily in terms of an individual agent's individual personality; if the former, however, we take a more distant, abstract, or symbolic view of character, and from such a perspective the concepts of individuality and personality can become less important variables.

Making a preliminary distinction, one can say that character in drama tends to move in two directions simultaneously. On the one hand, the word recalls (as I argued in the Introduction) the notion of one's "inner" or "true" self; on the other (and here Craig's utility and importance are surely obvious), it denotes a human reality that moves away from the psychological or individualistic and toward the material, the figural, or, in its extreme case, the mathematical. One detects character in the former sense in, say, Miss Julie's confessions of her childhood dreams. But character in the latter sense is at once more material and yet almost hopelessly inarticulate—one has the impression, for example, that Jean's coat (again in *Miss Julie*) is a sign that a crucial aspect of his character is not psychological but iconographic.[5]

Gordon Craig is therefore a particularly good artist to launch a collection of essays on character and characterization in modern drama. While the subject of character in drama has traditionally been studied in categories such as psychology, phenomenology, or literary aesthetics, today there is widespread interest in these and other theories of representation themselves, in the relation of self to body and body image, and in the iconographic significance of literature. In the following discussion I will try to show that Craig's nonhuman actors—precisely because they contrast with the experimental but essentially representational characters developed, for example, by Strindberg and Chekhov—throw questions of how to represent character fully into view.

It will be useful to begin, therefore, by examining some of Craig's writings in favor of mechanical actors (most of which can be traced to his curiously puritanical bias against illusionist acting) and also to consider his idea of character as it can be adduced from his sketches and directing experience. In part I want to show (even though there is no question of direct influence of Craig on any of the playwrights in this study) that there are important parallels between Craig's work and subsequent modern dramatists' portraits of people. In part I will be covering familiar historical material. Of course there are throughout the twentieth century numerous artists and, increasingly, playwrights who have been particularly attracted by the aesthetic promise of artificial acting styles or even puppets or marionettes. One thinks of Jarry's Ubu, of Yeats's experiments with Noh drama, of Artaud's fascination with the mechanized beings of oriental theater, or of Oskar Schlemmer's Bauhaus *Kunstfiguren* and Roy Lichtenstein's enormous cartoons.

But I also want to draw a more radical comparison. Many critics have pointed out modern dramatists' frequent interest in artificial actors or acting styles, but no critic as far as I know has pursued that interest in terms of its redefinition of character according to different languages or new lines. It is precisely because the artificial actor moves in accord with powers external to it that it is of such importance to the representation of character. As we shall see in the chapters that follow, the major part of the expressive words and gestures used to represent character can be shown to have their origins not within but without. The acts and words that are an individual character's most "characteristic," it turns out, are less like idiosyncrasies than symptoms—that is, not something they are entirely responsible for or able to control, and often something they seem unconsciously to "catch" or pick up from others around them. Such acts are no less expressive of character than the acts of other characters on earlier stages; as symptoms, they betray something important about their individual possessors. In many cases they are acts by which, in Dryden's words, the playwright "paints the hero's mind." Yet a careful analysis of these playwrights' works leads often to an altogether different picture of mentality than Dryden imagined. As we shall see in the chapters that follow, the primary source of character tends not to be private mental life, carefully observed and represented; it is rather those patterns of emotional and gestural activity that originate in "mimetic fusion"[6] with others or at large in the social world. Bruce Wilshire offers a fine analysis of why the familiar illusion that character comes from within may be seriously flawed: "To conceive of *a* consciousness almost inevitably involves the tacit attribution to it of self-identity and self-consciousness anterior to its mimetic involvement with others, and this vitiates the account of this involvement and begs the question of its significance for identity of self."[7]

I do not mean to say (as some have said) that the notion of a self that lies "within" is entirely a piece of cultural propaganda.[8] But a striking feature of all the authors represented in this book is the way in which they understand character within the domain of mimesis. Running counter to orthodox (naturalist) concepts of identity as self-centered, in other words, Craig (like all of the dramatists of this study) denied that character could be equated solely with private psychological states or that representing selfhood was mainly a matter of representing interior states of consciousness.

In the images of character drawn by the dramatists in this study there is, additionally, a distinctive archaism, deriving in part from their deliberate borrowings from primitive or alien theaters but also in large measure the result of their questioning the implicit humanist assumption that character exists apart from the pull of mimetic interactions. (I understand *mimesis* from aesthetic as well as psychological frames to combine imitation and identification.) As one example, one might cite a comment from Brecht's drama of character construction, *Mann ist Mann* (*Man is Man*, 1927): "one person is no person" (*einer ist keiner*), says Uriah, one of the four soldiers who over the course of the play manufacture for Galy Gay a new identity. Or one might for another example argue that the echolalic speech of Beckett's characters' monologues suggests intrapersonal (rather than individual) models for selfhood. By way of contrast, the concept of an identity permanently centered in an interior (subtextual) reality—which is, by the way, precisely the model for character made famous by Stanislavsky—holds that dramatic agents are most like life when they are constrained in their choices by unchanging habits of mind. At almost precisely the same moment in history that Stanislavsky was inventing what were to become definitive methods of impersonation for the modern actor, in other words, Craig invented the Übermarionette chiefly as a means to avoid impersonation in the first place. Lifelike "impersonations," far from being a principal goal of theatrical representation, were themselves deeply problematic. For Craig, conventional characters and characterizations in a devious and subtle way left unanswered fundamental questions about impersonation— its politics, its psychology, its relevance for art.

To approach the subject of character in modern drama by way of Gordon Craig, then, highlights the kind of theoretical problems with character that I wish to address over the course of this book. Craig's abolitionist intentions for actors paradoxically provide us with an ideal frame within which to examine character as it has been created by representative modern dramatists. That theoretical frame includes several distinct lines of development. As we will see, Craig was not at all interested in making theater a force for political change, but with Brecht (who was, of course, interested mainly in the politics of theatrical representation) he shares a profound mistrust of the psychology of mimesis. Brechtian theater (and much recent feminist theater) calls for openly "primitive" or estranged acting in order to avoid the politics of conventional illusionist representation. In fact Brechtian models for the production of character, which regularly split off the actor from the person he or she imitates, form the root from which much feminist drama and feminist dramatic theory develops.

Likewise Craig's work with stage space extends in terms of its significance far beyond his specific collaborations with Yeats or Stanislavsky, significant as these collaborations admittedly were.[9] Despite his denigration of contemporary painters (he claimed, for example, that cubism had been invented first by the ancient Egyptians and a second time by Dürer), Craig's sketches and woodcuts are indisputably the work of a gifted visual artist, and his imagined dramas and sketches of dramas look forward to Beckett's "visual poetry."[10] In both Beckett's and Craig's work one finds the same visual features: an emphasis on the single image or on recurring design over developmental process; a preference for sober (often classical) architectonic forms; a tendency to emphasize the figural (as opposed to the psychological) reality of character, along with a concomitant "vaguening" of place that brackets character as if phenomenologically; and, finally, a reliance on chiaroscuro so heavy that it flattens the scene artificially and makes it look almost theophanic. On Beckett's and Craig's stages characters become "lights" whose existence testifies to a supernatural (divine? artistic?) light that enables the intellect to perceive them.

Lastly, one can see in Craig's monodramas something of the same problematic subjectivity dramatized by playwrights such as Thomas Bernhard or Marguerite Duras. The characters in these plays are not activists but "highly self-conscious solipsists." [11] They turn obsessively around past events, idealize memory as visual image at the same time they sense its inadequate representation in language, or long nostalgically for some primal unity. No dramatist staged this moving vision of loss better than Gordon Craig; "it seems to me," he said in conversations with Stanislavsky about *Hamlet,*

> that during Hamlet's monologue a figure comes up to him, a bright, golden figure. And at one time it even began to seem to me that this figure is *always* with Hamlet. Of course it is not on the stage, not in the theatre, but in my mind I feel the presence of this figure. All the idea of this play is the struggle between spirit and material—the impossibility of their union, the isolation of spirit in material. And I think that this figure which appears to me near Hamlet is Death. But not dark and gloomy as she generally appears to people, but such as she appeared to Hamlet—bright, joyful, one who will free him from his tragic position. [12]

In Craig's theater and theater writings, then, we discover a field of aesthetics and aesthetic theory clearly relevant to modern and contemporary drama. The most discernible pattern initially is an extraordinary skepticism of the ethics of illusionist theater. Craig directs much of his criticism squarely against mimesis and its attendant psychology. We should by no means overlook the positive aspects of this negative attitude: its underlying distrust of representation and the imitative basis of character (indeed of all identity) is echoed throughout the twentieth century by a variety of modernist and postmodernist developments in theater which together constitute a powerful counterweight to the interior portraits of individual psychology that we habitually associate with dramatic representations of character.

The Actor and the Übermarionette

The actor must go, and in his place comes the inanimate figure—the übermarionette we may call him, until he has won for himself a better name. Much has been written about the puppet—or marionette. Today in his least happy period many people have come to regard him as rather a superior doll—and to think he has developed from the doll. This is incorrect. He is a descendant of the stone images of the old Temples—he is today rather a degenerate form of a God. (*The Mask* 1 [1908], p. 11)

Much has been made of Craig's notorious proposal to replace living actors with "super-puppets," and it has been suggested more than once that in attempting to rid the stage of real people Craig was merely exaggerating to make his point. Craig himself says as much in subsequent writings, backsliding with respect to his famous early declaration. In 1912, for example, he coyly denied that he had meant what he said (or seemed to have said) some years earlier (*The Mask* 5 [1912], p. 97): "And did you think when I wrote five years ago of this new figure who should stand as the symbol of man . . . and when I christened him the ueber-marionette . . . to see real metal or silken threads?" Craig retreated further from his original position in 1921, offering to retract entirely the Übermarionette essay "if the Western actor can become what I am told the Eastern actor was and is."[13] And by 1930 Craig had decided that at least one Western actor had measured up to Eastern standards: Henry Irving. Lest his praise seem belated—Irving had died in 1905—Craig declared that for Irving, death was a fiction: "If any one died, was laid to rest in Westminster Abbey, it was Brodribb [Irving's real surname]; for Henry Irving, that shadow of a coming event, the Übermarionette, is still living."[14]

But Craig's aversion to actors was real, and it went deeper than mere dissatisfaction with the styles of contemporary Western acting. As close examination of Craig's early essays and journal entries shows, he really intended, at least at first, to replace living actors with mechanical objects.[15] Avant-garde artists such as Meyerhold or the Bauhaus group also experimented with mechanical figures in their productions, but Craig's interest in marionettes differed from that of most of his contemporaries. However much he may have believed that actors could merge ideally with light, architecture, and sound—the other absolute elements of the mise-en-scène— Craig never entirely resigns his dislike for them. Over and over in his writings one senses a marked strain of puritanism, an instinctive aversion to the actors' sensuous presence. Bound up with his compulsion to exercise absolute control over persons and productions, his criticism of living actors was as much a part of his psychology as his aesthetic theories. In fact it would be fair to say that Craig's psychology and his aesthetics were analogues of one another. Craig was always a passionate and frequently undisciplined writer, but on the subject of actors he waxed to apocalyptic fervor. Acting he dismissed merely as "movement"; facial expression he declared "worthless." As for actors themselves, he liked to cite Eleonora Duse, who urged that the theater could be saved only if the actors all died of plague. In one issue (*The Mask* 4 [July 1911]), Craig published Duse's remark in four separate places: at the end of a sequence of poems by Walt Whitman, as an epigraph to an article by "John Semar" (one of Craig's pen names), as argumentative support in a note to which he signed his own name, and as a coda to an article on circus classics by "Adolph Furst" (which of course was another of Craig's pen names).

In truth Craig's attacks on actors amounted to a crusade, a crusade all the more surprising as the ambition of a man who lived in and for the theater. For example, Craig repeatedly and vigorously defended the British Censor, arguing that that office was needed to protect innocent theatergoers from the effects of watching actors portray "jealousy, ambition, hatred, meanness, envy, murder, torture, seduction, and riot" (*The Mask* 1 [1908], p. 148). Nor did Craig care whether in the course of the play wickedness was rewarded or punished; simply to stage it was sufficiently seditious. As to the general effect of playgoing on the public, Craig sometimes cited Nietzsche, who once wrote that *Macbeth* (and similar dramas involving murder or ambition) was as likely to pervert audiences as to educate them. Nietzsche's argument was literary and highly speculative, but Craig gave it a specific histrionic emphasis by distinguishing between the text of a play and its embodiment on stage. The latter, Craig insisted, was always more dangerous because of the volatile presence of the actors. "This fact," he stated, "has escaped most people. Yet if we consider it for a moment there is hardly any line in any play to which a *double entendre* cannot be given, and even 'How do you do, Mrs Jones' can be made positively indecent by the way in which it is said and the gestures by which it is accompanied" (*The Mask* 2 [1909], p. 50). Typically hyperbolic and polemical, Craig's argument is less interesting as an intellectual position in its own right than for its historical antecedents. It is the familiar objection to the contagious effects of mimesis raised by dour antitheatricalists from Solon and Tertullian to Stephen Gosson and Jeremy Collier.

Lest I leave the impression that Craig's diatribes against actors were idiosyncratic and unrelated to the question of character, let me suggest one clear parallel with postmodernist representations. There are good reasons to see a direct line of development extending from Craig's polemics to Brecht's theater politics to Beckett's stage figures, for all three men share an aversion to actors who represent the private psychological "subtexts" on which individual character is said to rest. Consider, for example, a conversation between Craig and Stanislavsky concerning how the actor playing Hamlet should speak his first real speech in the play, his impassioned outburst to his mother:

> Seems, madam? Nay, it is. I know not "seems."
> 'Tis not alone my inky cloak, good mother,
> Nor customary suits of solemn black,
> Nor windy suspiration of forced breath,
> No, nor the fruitful river in the eye,
> Nor the dejected havior of the visage,
> Together with all forms, moods, shapes of grief,
> That can denote me truly. These indeed seem,
> For they are actions that a man might play,
> But I have that within which passeth show—
> These but the trappings and the suits of woe.[16]

For most readers of Shakespeare (and certainly for Stanislavsky), Hamlet here draws a crucial distinction between being and seeming. In order to act these lines successfully, the player must perform as if character were determined by a mental reality that exists apart from any exterior manifestation of it, a reality that is in fact falsified by any "show" whatsoever. The text invites—in a way similar to that described by Peter Schroeder in his analysis of dialogue and characterization in Chaucer's and Malory's narratives—the construction of an impression of character as involving a buried mental life.[17]

But Craig's only concern is with the actor's physical expression of syllables; in representing the person, he all but rules out dianoia and ethos. As he commented to Stanislavsky, "In this monologue only the first two lines and, at the end of the monologue, the last two lines are important. These four lines express an important thought and must be spoken accordingly. All the rest of the monologue must be pronounced more as music, so that the thought becomes so much lost in the sounds that the audience simply *does not follow* the thought except in the above-mentioned four lines."[18]

Craig's ideas seem at first seriously impractical: how can actors create character if they know nothing about the characters they represent apart from their gross physical reality? Here is proposed not so much a narrative of individual development over time as the freezing of character as if in tableau, so as to ensure that gestural reality itself be considered Hamlet's primary characteristic. Reading through notes of an early conversation between Craig and Stanislavsky, one is struck by Craig's insistent attempts to replace the realistic details of Shakespeare's play (details in which Stanislavsky was keenly interested) with an entirely different set of aesthetic features.[19] In the foregoing scene (act 1, scene 2), for example, Craig insisted that the most important character was not Hamlet but the king. Stanislavsky suggested (as might have been expected) that the actor playing the king should approach the character realistically and build eventually to a more abstract style of portraiture. The character was to develop by way of psychological correspondence, said Stanislavsky, "[b]ecause while he [the actor] does not feel it in himself he can do nothing."[20] Craig's reply ("Oh, certainly, certainly") reveals both the disdain with which he regarded psychological portraiture as well as his own idea of theatrical representation: the actor, he said, first of all "must give the idea of an unearthly strength in the king."[21] How exactly to do that Craig did not specify. All we can say is that in Craig's scheme, there seems no real distinction between that which is "within" and that which is "without." But that is not to say that Craig's idea for kingship itself as character was incapable of realization. For Craig, trying to find ways to figure character without relying exclusively on signs of "internal" circumstances moved him increasingly away from psychology toward a more iconographic basis for character. There are modes of artistic representation perfectly able to achieve the effects of character that Craig intends, and it is to these visual parallels, rather than to psychological models for the representation of character, that I now want to draw attention.[22]

Deformations of Character and Space

One of Craig's early experimental dramas illustrates the way he redefines theatrical space in order to refigure character. In *The Steps* (1905), Craig turned from conventional mimesis in an attempt to create a purely abstract composition of figure and ground. *The Steps* (figs. 1–4) consists of four distinct parts (or "moods," as Craig described them), organized along the lines of a musical composition. The work was never performed, but, as is often the case with Craig's dreams for the stage, Craig's sketches and accompanying notes describe in great detail an ideal performance. Each "mood" (or act) of the play uses the same general set—a broad flight of steps rising slowly upstage between two massive walls. But colors and movements vary from scene to scene, and the resulting play of architectural repetitions and variations causes wide shifts in emotional effect. Over-

FIGURE I. Gordon Craig, sketch representing the first "movement"
from *The Steps* (1905)

FIGURE 2. Gordon Craig, sketch representing the second "movement" from *The Steps* (1905)

FIGURE 3. Gordon Craig, sketch representing the third "movement" from *The Steps* (1905)

FIGURE 4. Gordon Craig, sketch representing the fourth "movement" from *The Steps* (1905)

all the moods grow progressively somber: brightness yields to gloom and shadow, childlike figures are replaced by adults and then by solitary figures "heavy with unnecessary sorrow," and allegro gives way to a mysterious solemnity. The spoken word is superfluous and meaning results entirely from the interactions of light, movement, and space.

The Steps is a modern morality play, and it has been interpreted as a romantic allegory of life's journey.[23] Yet The Steps is not simply an allegory without words; the longer one studies these four haunting sketches and the accompanying notes, the less sentimental they become. While the expressivity of the play itself cannot be disputed, it is impossible to say what exactly it is about. Craig's bold simplification of conventional theater in a sense reduces the story line to the bare minimum, but the result not so much highlights plot (as in conventional allegory) as displaces or discounts it. Similarly Craig refigures character. The figures who appear in the play express a variety of emotions, and yet the basis of these deceptively simple psychological states is frustratingly elusive. The situation cannot be explained by reference to an identifiable reality, whether mental or situational. Craig's notes on his characters are frustratingly vague. In fact, the author comments on his play as if he were partly ignorant of its characters:

> In the first it is light and gay, and three children are playing on it as you see the birds do on the back of a large hippopotamus lying asleep in an African river. What the children do I cannot tell you, although I have written it down somewhere. It is simply technical, and until seen it is valueless. But if you hear in your mind's ear the little stamping sound which rabbits make, and can hear a rustle of tiny silver bells, you will have a glimpse of what I mean, and will be able to picture to yourself the queer quick little movements.[24]

Such ambiguity is typical of Craig—he sometimes falsified his drawings to protect them from his "enemies"—but Craig's coyness here cannot be attributed entirely to his persecution mania or to his private psychological strategy. Craig simply avoids describing his characters in illusionist terms. His exaggerated modesty, in other words, can be seen as a consistent effort to displace or discount psychological representation as the source of meaning in theatrical performance. There are no necessary connections, Craig insists, between the staged acts or emotions and a prior narratorial reality.

The descriptions of subsequent "moods" are equally circumscribed or cryptic. On the one hand, they offer an image of extreme authorial control over the text as it is to be performed: the *metteur-en-scène* eliminates dialogue and provides a full set of narratorial instructions. On the other, they consistently withhold information about the agents' motives for their acts:

> Something a little older has come upon the steps. It is very late evening with them. The movement commences with the passing of a single figure—a man. He begins to trace his way through the maze which is defined upon the floor. He fails to reach the centre. Another figure appears at the top of the steps—a woman. He moves no longer, and she descends the steps slowly to join him. It does not seem to me very clear whether she ever does join him, but when designing it I had hoped that she might. Together they might once more commence to thread the maze. But although the man and woman interest me to some extent, it is the steps on which they move which move me. The figures dominate the steps for a time, but the steps are for all time. I believe that some day I shall get nearer to the secret of these things, and I may tell you that it is very exciting approaching such mysteries. If they were dead, how dull they would be, but they are trembling with a great life, more so than that of man—than that of woman. (*Towards a New Theatre*, 46)

What is the point of such theater, and how does it work? The "message" of *The Steps* is clear, but the message is not the meaning. Craig clearly expects his audience to become involved with the performance and to experience deeply the sequence of moods. From the point of view of actors, however, his comments are likely to sound quixotic if not deliberately obscure. How does one tell two actors that it is "not clear" whether they join on stage or "commence to thread the maze"? Acting, as Craig surely knew, is never abstract; actors are trained to act *something*. Yet the text offers little grounds on which mimesis (let alone psychological reality) can rest. For Craig, character is not informed by the customary determinants of psychology and history but by formal and expressly visual elements such as the interplay of solidity and light. (We will see again, when we come to Beckett's dramas, what remains of character when it loses its customary orientation with respect to space.) Craig in effect makes the individual subject much harder to read. It is as if character were the result of material, variable compositional balances and tensions rather than a persistent, indivisible whole.

Craig reorganized character on stage almost as thoroughly as cubist painters reorganized subjects in painted space. Craig himself ridiculed cubist art; its famous geometries, he claimed, far from being new, were "as old as the pyramids" (*The Mask* 6 [1913], p. 97). But Craig's theatrical spaces share a number of similarities with the several phases of cubist or precubist reorganizations of represented space in pictorial art. Craig, for example, like Cézanne, believed that the subject could be represented without resorting to illusionist space. It is significant that almost as soon as he invented the Übermarionette, Craig invented a new theatrical space to accompany the new actor. This new space was named the "kinetic stage."[25] The intent seems to have been to devise a space that would contradict the expectation that the actors were to be imagined as somewhere other than where they were in physical fact. The staged space thus ceases to have a mimetic component and becomes an end in itself.

In insisting that the set be three-dimensional, therefore, Craig was not only calling for less objectionable forms of illusionism—for replacing the faithfully detailed sets of naturalism, for example, with stylized drops and flats or with architectural solids. Sometimes Craig's scenes seem "set" in some classical court; his heavy solids and sharp lines give the drawings the dignity and *gravitas* we associate with classical architecture. But these sketches are often foreboding or claustrophobic: rather than return to neo-classical spatial values, Craig seems to have created the illusion of a space subtly discordant with the figures who inhabit it. The classical set functioned with respect to actors in two complementary ways. First, because it was minimally detailed and clearly artificial, it provided actors a neutral but infinitely adaptable background against which to play. It could, chameleon-like, change color according to need: "as for me," comments the Prologue of Plautus's *Menaechmi,* "I will report the scene as being nowhere, save where, by report, the events occurred." Far more important, however, the classical façade and playing space invariably placed character within an environment where the marks that signified character could be made public. This is what Charles Lyons (following Kenneth Burke) means when he argues that "scene . . . is crucial to the development of an image of character," where "scene" is taken to mean not only the specific location of an event but also "the political, ideological, and psychological 'situation' in which an act takes place."[26] "In drama," Lyons continues, "scene encompasses situation through the representation of the characters' perception."[27]

Craig's figures cannot consistently define themselves by any such referential means. The most striking feature of Craig's kinetic stage is that as theatrical space it is "pure"—actual rather than virtual, hermetic rather than referential. But equally important with respect to character are the apparent psychological effects of his architectonics. In *The Steps,* for example, Craig's theatrical space is not fixed but animate: somehow, Craig writes, the stage is made to dance. Moreover, the steps and the walls that loom on either side cannot be viewed merely as a site for human action, for they have too potent a presence of their own. They are aggressive, even menacing, in the way they impinge upon the human figures.

At the same time, however, none of the elements within the stage environment of *The Steps* can be read as particular signs of nature or culture. Craig's sketches are powerfully evocative, but their emotional power derives almost entirely from Craig's artistic medium: a two-dimensional, perspectival rendering of space. The space defined by walls and steps opens and sweeps forward toward viewers, enveloping them in an expanding funnel of central perspective. The absolute symmetry of the architecture adds to the effect of depth and contributes also to the scene's formal dignity and solemnity. As for the various human figures who appear in Craig's sketches, even though the scene defines them as a function of their environment, the overall effect makes them seem unusually vulnerable. This occurs partly because they are dwarfed by the relative scale of the architecture. Were they to be reproduced on a real set (I deal subsequently with the question of Craig's "practicality"), the walls near the front would tower nearly thirty feet high.

Craig's designs often turn on such contrasts of scale between actor and architecture; as a result, the aesthetic of character here belongs more to the visual arts than to theater. Indeed Craig's stage is primarily pictorial, for its expressivity derives from painterly techniques of contrast, dissociation, dislocation, and deviation from a recollected standard. What strikes us when we examine Craig's sketches is how "incorrect" are the relative proportions of figure and ground. The exaggeration itself is a powerful source of meaning; as Rudolf Arnheim says, "when bigness and smallness face each other like Goliath and David in the same image, the contrast generates dynamics by relation."[28]

More important, sketches such as these possess a dynamism beyond that which can be attributed to the tensions of scale. Craig's pictorial rendering of stage space forces a perspectival distortion on the represented world in that it expresses that world exclusively in terms of a viewer; it is a world without history whose only distinguishing feature is that it is being sighted. As theater, *The Steps* is designed not for the actor but for the spectator. And on a stage such as this, as in the painterly tradition, "character" then becomes a function of vision, and the difficulty of reading character on this stage (as on Beckett's) arises because of its novel dependence on the visual arts.

We should note another feature that anticipates Beckett's theater, the progressive restrictions Craig imposes on his characters' ability to move within their space. The progression from childhood to age is reinforced by an apparent bodily deterioration. Whereas in the first two scenes the characters' movements are "light and gay" or dancelike, their movement in the third "mood," is slower, apparently failing. In the final scene the main figure is slumped lifelessly against the wall. The physical difficulties experienced by the characters as they attempt to move within the space they inhabit tends to reinforce their oppositional engulfment by it. They expend energy in an environment that will not yield to their efforts but only baffles them. They are, after all, transient; but the steps, Craig says, "are for all time." The continuing reality of the environment contrasts boldly with the characters' gradual diminution. By the time of the fourth "mood," character and space have become queerly estranged even as they physically merge. It is as if the set had somehow become an alien ground upon which the characters have nevertheless come to depend.

This ambiguity of spatial relations was for Craig essential to theatrical performance. In fact, on Craig's stage an apparent drama between character and environment grows to be a defining feature. As early as *Acis and Galatea* (1902) Craig experimented with scenery that partly obscured his characters. In that play Craig robed both set and chorus in flowing ribbons so that at times the human figures seemed to vanish in their environment. The effect was apparently magical, similar to camouflage; spectators witnessed a new definition of character as a function of the overall artistic environment. Here the blurred image of human presence resembles that diffusion of subject into background one finds in the paintings of Picasso and Braque. In Craig's and cubist art there is a suggestion that the relationship between figure and ground is both dynamic and problematic. *Acis and Galatea* distorts the treatment of human figures; background and figures seem to have no consistent spatial relationship, and at times the boundaries between the two are indistinguishable. Normally separate or opposed, figure and ground here "fit" one another; in other (more specifically dramatic) words, character and environment resonate in mimetic involvement.

Like the work of the analytic cubists, who attempted in their work to capture a fundamental incoherence of conventionally represented space, Craig's mise-en-scène suggests a profound reorganization of character and space. The merging of figure and ground in *Acis and Galatea* cannot be explained simply as a revolt against illusionist representations. Craig blends character with architectural elements in what seems an attempt to refigure human presence. In *Acis and Galatea* he creates an environment that obscures human presence by being visually consistent or continuous with it, but in *The Steps* Craig diminishes his characters by exposing them publicly in a space that cannot readily be integrated with quotidian sense experience. Just as the cubists rejected direct conventional representation of space and substituted for it the notion of space as animated by perception, so in *The Steps* Craig depicts space as active ("kinetic") so as to create an effect of the uncanny. Characters are not "real" on this stage but beings more on the order of ghosts or shades, beings who, like holograms, suddenly manifest themselves from without their background.

In order to clarify Craig's suppression of character, it is worthwhile to compare his illustrations with the spatial configurations of contemporary abstract works of drama or with some expressionist mise-en-scènes. For example, Craig's sets are often likened to Yeats's or to those of Adolphe Appia, and yet Craig's kinetic stage has virtually the opposite function.[29] Appia, for example, created a series of designs that he called "rhythmic spaces," but in Appia's sketches space and architectural elements enhance the presence of performers. "Whenever the pencil touched paper," he wrote, "it evoked the naked body, the naked limbs . . . the quality of the space rendered the presence of the body indispensable." [30] In these spaces figures are isolated in order to preserve (or to emphasize) their gestural expressivity and to define specific relationships between them and their surroundings. Furthermore, Appia insisted that the set, however real, be subordinated to the figures who inhabit it; on his stage a figure's isolation is consistent with its ability to master space, to dominate it as a piece of sculpture is said to command its immediate domain. In contrast, on Craig's stage the human figure seems belittled.[31]

Neither the sketches nor the commentaries for *The Steps* contain anything that can be used to locate the action in any specific mythic or symbolic space. Likewise, the links between Craig's work and that of expressionist dramatists are apparent at several points. Strindberg, for example, knew of *The Mask* and praised it enthusiastically. Craig also wielded considerable influence on German theater before the war, and in his outspoken criticisms of stage realism, German expressionist dramatists found a coherent and eloquent spokesman. Craig's visions of a theater without words and of the stage dominated by a flight of steps were echoed, respectively, in Hasenclever's *Menschen* and Leopold Jessner's "Spieltreppe" (play-stairs).[32] Even though Craig could not have known "expressionism" during the two years he worked in Germany—the term first appeared in Germany in 1910—his impact on German theater, according to H. F. Garten, was "crucial" and "gave a powerful impulse to the rise of expressionist drama."[33]

But if there are crucial similarities between Craig and the expressionists, there are crucial differences, and for our purposes these are most significant. Craig's sets are not usually (his Moscow *Hamlet* being an exception) physical expressions of his characters' imaginative or emotional experience. Like Craig and like many theater artists of the early modern era, expressionist dramatists avoided sets that depicted simple physical locations. But the unrealistic distortions that typify expressionist drama invariably intend to glorify the "inner" reality of their characters, not to deny it. Most of the writers who can reasonably be called "expressionist" simply removed mimesis from their stages only to install it at a higher order. That is to say, they flatly rejected mimesis insofar as it necessitated the representation of external appearance, but they depended on it nevertheless to depict "the pictorial equivalent of individual soul states."[34]

So frequently do German expressionist dramatists represent private experience (whether their own or that of their imagined characters) that their plays are occasionally termed "I-dramas."[35] As for more clearly textual forms of expressionist drama, one can see in Strindberg's late works much the same emphasis on interior states as well as (in John Willett's description of German expressionist theater) "a degree of self-dramatization bordering on narcissism."[36]

For all its violent distortions of the conventions of realistic drama, therefore, expressionist dramatics cannot really be said to have had much impact on psychological orthodoxies of character. To the degree that the life of the central character (and in expressionist drama there is often only one real character) was viewed as a kind of spiritual pilgrimage, the question of character remains essentially an interior one; to the degree that the central character undertook such a pilgrimage after making a break from society and family, there persists the belief that the individual is the source of all value and exists apart from social forces. This is true of the early expressionist experiments (for example, Hasenclever's *Der Sohn* [1916] or Kokoschka's *Mörder, Hoffnung der Frauen* [1917]) and of its subsequent derivatives such as O'Neill's *The Hairy Ape* (1922) or Miller's *Death of a Salesman* (1949).

The difference between Craig's stage and the stages of the expressionist dramatists is similar to the difference between purely abstract art and art which is merely "abstractionist." The latter art retains formal ties with the natural world so that represented objects may be severely distorted but never disappear entirely, while in the former objects are constructed so as to deny any referentiality whatsoever.[37] The question for Craig, of course, as for any dramatist who was obliged to include humans in the stage "picture," was more complicated than for painters who could simply dispense with figural representation altogether: how can a play with real people in it be abstract?

The remarkable thing about Craig's stage is that it gives the impression that the actors' primary task is not expressive but physical, to come to terms with an environment that mysteriously resists them. Craig's stage space seems to be endowed with actual power, and that power tends to contradict the performers' presence, to absorb it or screen it out.[38] Paradoxically, therefore, Craig was able to define his concept of theater more explicitly by way of his drawings than by actual productions. This paradox is important for two reasons. First, it explains the familiar objection to Craig's theater— its impracticality. As we will see, Craig's two-dimensional sketches almost always suffer losses when transformed into the three dimensions of a real set. It is ironic but not surprising, therefore, that the clearest view of the theater Craig envisioned can be obtained from his sketches rather than his productions. Second, it directs attention to a more fundamental matter— the constitution of a new kind of character whose identity depends less on his or her psychological distinctiveness than on an austere figural reality.

Craig typically introduces perspective contradictions into his architectural landscapes so as to estrange his human figures further from time and space. The sketch titled simply "Scene" (1907; fig. 5) at first looks like a straight perspectival representation, as if Craig had drawn an abstract rendering of a neoclassical set. The composition as a whole appears to be drawn in central perspective of space. The illusion of single perspective is further enhanced by the size differential between the large solitary figure in the foreground and the assembly of people (apparently women) who appear in the middle zone of the sketch. The women appear from behind the largest of the columns, and their placement and smaller size is consistent with the depth effect of perspectival representation. Finally, the principal figure faces rearward; his frontal position and orientation confirm the viewer's own impression of a world being sighted. Both he and we look into a world along lines of sight that converge at a horizontally located center.

FIGURE 5. Gordon Craig, "Scene" (1907)

FIGURE 6. Sebastiano Serlio, "The Tragic Scene" (1545)

But in fact the mysterious, foreboding quality of Craig's sketch is obtained not by following the rules of perspective but by misusing them. The illusion of depth produced by the converging bases of the columns is incompatible with the isometric mass that overhangs them. The difference between Craig's drawing and a true perspective set can be seen by comparison with a neoclassical sketch (fig. 6). Serlio's tragic scene extends the frontal verticals and horizontals with a system of oblique lines that together locate a single focus at rear center. Craig's sketch, on the other hand, defines no clear focal point. The figures in Craig's drawing inhabit a spatial framework whose apparent focus is located in the darkness at the center of the composition. At the same time, however, the overhanging solid, with its simpler isometric shape and its apparently unsupported mass, contradicts the space created by the steps and the receding columns. The space defined by this great mass is self-contained, and the pairs of parallel lines that define portions of its underside suggest a centerless continuum. It does not participate in the perspectival frame, therefore, but subtly violates it. Instead of inviting viewers to enter the pictorial space, the isometric solid excludes them; it makes the convergences in the lower parts of the sketch appear as distortions rather than as realistic extensions of the viewer's own position.

The opposition of two contrasting perspectives cannot be incidental or accidental, for it animates the entire composition.[39] Because of the conflict between two incompatible spatial systems the mass at the top looms ominously overhead. It looks uncanny, an entity that is within the pictorial space and yet cannot be contained by it. Meanwhile the rest of Craig's set provides an ambiguous contrast with the overhanging solid, mainly because its perspective looks impeccably correct.

Craig's bold assembly of solids and shades does not function as a coherent site on which to display the actor. This is another of the many points where Craig's work contrasts sharply with that of his contemporaries, many of whom were similarly engaged in creating new dimensional spaces for actors. Appia, for example, insisted that a variety of three-dimensional levels, steps, and slopes all be integrated "to establish the solidity and volume of the actor."[40] But Craig's set, in contrast, while visually stunning, cannot exist in this world. The effect is to transport viewers into a region of mystery where familiar pictorial illusion fails. The scene is inhospitable to character because it conforms to no consistent code of representation: the edges of the plaza meet on the horizon, but the extended inner and outer edges of the solid overhead converge at different points within the triangle

of darkness. Either the world ends abruptly at the edge of the plaza, beyond which is a sinister and infinite emptiness, or, if the inner and outer
edges of the upper solid are accepted as being drawn in perspective but
situated too near the viewer to show convergence, the columns and plaza
recede paradoxically. Viewed in isolation, the inner heights of the columns
appear quite regular, except that in their recession toward their own vanishing point they contradict the vanishing point defined by the inner edges
of the solid.

Granted, the sketch is not a finished set but the rough representation
of a set. Craig's work, therefore, must be understood as an attempt to
render in two dimensions the three dimensions of stage space. But in trying to resolve the perspectival contradictions of his design we discover the
paradoxes of his theatrical space. A number of apparent inconsistencies
within the sketch create a site that seems actual but remains indeterminate. Because the spatial systems contradict one another, the characters
who inhabit that space tend to become apparitions, shadowy figures who
exist within a space and yet remain weirdly detached from it. As with
the mechanics of dream, the spectacle is uncanny. Character is effectively
dematerialized, rendered improbable, ghostly. Such theater precludes contextual representation. This landscape and these figures cannot be true, yet
because Craig employs familiar elements of perspectival representations
we have the disquieting sensation of seeing what we think we have seen
before.

Similar uncanny effects can be found in many of Craig's designs for performances. "The Temple" (fig. 7), for example, hovers on the edge of dream.
At first glance the scene appears ceremonial, sacred. Yet the throng of robed
figures (priests? suppliants?) seems somehow imperiled, as if the darkness
in the foreground were about to overwhelm them. The landscape appears
mysteriously dangerous, as in *The Steps*. Here too Craig's scene haunts the
imagination largely because of the conjunction of contradictory perspectives. The eye looks inward along a plane that defines the horizon as lying
directly behind the multitude at the base of the narrow shadow, slightly
right of center. In this case the dark background masses loom threateningly
at supernatural heights. If, however, the horizon is located by the receding
edge of the dark mass on the right (it seems to cut behind the left-hand wall
as if it were situated at a greater distance from the viewer), the horizon lies
invisibly somewhere behind the picture, and the white figures and columns
suddenly seem to float within a sinister void.

Like surrealist art, Craig's sketches for scenes evoke the sense of mem-

FIGURE 7. Gordon Craig, "The Temple" (1911)

ory or dreams. Many of his drawings depict solitary figures who seem to be frozen in time or to traverse barren, alien landscapes. Again and again the figures seem less dramatic characters than human fragments or residues that have been weirdly disconnected from history. It is for this reason that human identity or "presence" in Craig's theater so often proves elusive, evanescent, ghostly. Grigory Kozintsev, the director of the Soviet films of *Hamlet* and *King Lear,* provides a vivid account of the powerful displacement of character effected by Craig's designs for theatrical space:

> While I was still only a boy, I was astounded by Craig's sketches: space, devoid of any recognizable landmarks, the unification of emptiness of night and the coldness of ice, sea mist in which anything can be imagined. Lonely figures in the midst of unfamiliar worlds of stone. There is not one detail, not one feature which you can grasp on to in order to find your way to that place, so strongly does the void beckon you. The rhythm of this structure, the shades of grey, the vertical and horizontal lines give it poetry in their own code—it is no longer heard but seen. Next to these engravings and sketches, the theatrical decor seemed mean, insignificant, on the level of provincial Shakespearean productions: wrinkled tights, drawers pulled tightly over them, declaimed speech and howling, and beards made of tow.[41]

Even when he worked with texts whose action was located explicitly in time and space, Craig physically or psychologically distanced the characters from their stage environment. An illustration drawn for *King Lear* (1908; fig. 8) depicts a traditional subject in a distorted and dreamlike manner. Three small figures are seen in silhouette within a great arching mesh that resembles concertina wire. Here again two different pictorial illusions interact to produce the powerful and enigmatic effect. The first illusion is that the sketch is done in perspective; consequently, the figures seem to be seen from a great distance, near the inner end of a long tunnel. Assuming as we must that this apparent stage space is three dimensional, we then interpret the converging black streaks as receding from us toward the distant horizon. Craig's monochromatic world looks like one of Beckett's symbolic sets—stark, ashy, lifeless.

But in the sketch for *Lear,* as in many of Craig's sketches for sets, the initial impression of coherent depth is complicated by a number of factors. For example, where is the white mass (is it a cloud? mountain? iceberg?) situated in relation to the action in the foreground? Craig's sketch invites us to consider it as situated on a remote horizon, but if so, its scale is dis-

FIGURE 8. Gordon Craig, sketch for *King Lear* (1908)

FIGURE 9. Gordon Craig, sketch for Ibsen's *The Vikings* (1908)

turbing, almost irrational. It looms threateningly large. The apparent size of Craig's "cloud" drastically foreshortens the perspective obtained by the illusion of looking through the weblike "tunnel." Depth of field is contradicted, and the radial lines now appear located on a frontal plane. In this case they emphasize the pictorial surface by appearing to disturb it. It is a little like looking at a scene through the cracks radiating from a bullet hole in a windowpane.

In a sketch drawn to illustrate the set from yet another historical drama (Ibsen's *The Vikings*, 1908; fig. 9), Craig depicts two warriors fighting at the base of high, sheer, white cliffs. Apparently Craig intended to convey the essence of armed combat rather than to represent specific events, but his sketch is no simple abstraction from Ibsen's play. Perhaps the cliffs can be explained as stylized fjords, but nothing else in the drawing is even remotely referential, and much of it is deliberately contradictory. Here Craig works like certain postmodern artists by cannibalizing various painterly traditions. The soldiers are not Norse but Greek, for they wear crested helmets and carry the long spears of hoplite warriors. Moreover, they are not "realistic" figures but stylized borrowings with their own aesthetic history. These "Vikings" are obviously classical soldiers, drawn in the black-figure style of ancient Greece. Meanwhile the sky above their heads is distinctly modernist. Its composition resembles *pointillisme,* and the innumerable tiny dots give the sky a separate emotional intensity as well as a patterned formality. The aggressive combination of styles removes Craig's landscape from reality. The picture defines no "moment"; depth is flattened by an insistent surface quality and the scene takes on a frozen, preternatural stillness.

Craig attempted to transfer his painterly aesthetic into his productions, but with mixed results. In 1926, for example, he distorted *The Pretenders,* Ibsen's colorful pageant of Norwegian political history, into a dematerialized fantasy. Craig specified for *The Pretenders* a mise-en-scène dominated by color harmonies and abstract shapes whose purpose was to repudiate historical authenticity. When the curtain rose on the first scene, for example, the audience saw "a forest of lances grow toward the sky, while behind them, projected on a cyclorama [was] a dream in yellow light and bluish shadow, a half dematerialized cathedral."[42] As for the events of the play, these took place in a theatrical environment at odds with the set implied by Ibsen's text and by the play's production history. In the final scene, for example, Ibsen's text clearly specifies a gothic courtyard; yet for this scene Craig designed a "twisting network of low picket fences . . . almost like the barbed wire on a First World War battlefield."[43]

Intending once again to sever the action from any recognizable context, Craig filled the interior at the episcopal residence with more than twenty-odd gray parallelepipeds. These resembled the looming architectural solids that appear again and again in Craig's sketches. The parallelepipeds were "high, block-like shapes" of various sizes, some colored "in a greenish light and one of them illuminated with blue."[44] Characters too were stripped of their individual psychologies and of their Scandanavian features. Skule (a Norwegian Hamlet) was dressed in a demonic red wig and beard, and his opponent Haakon was "a dark, short, robust figure . . . [with no] physical features of Ibsen's blond Nordic hero."[45]

Johannes Poulsen, who played Bishop Nikolas, spoke in favor of Craig's abstract set as enhancing the apocalyptic mood of the play, but numerous eyewitness accounts convey a different impression. Almost universally, reviewers commented on the disjunction between character and environment—a disjunction one might expect when transferring Craig's painterly aesthetic onto an actual set. Frederick and Lise-Lone Marker summarize these criticisms in their reconstruction of the production:

> "The Bishop's room, resembling a warehouse cellar in the dockyards, filled with packing cases, robbed [Johannes Poulsen's performance] of all its mystique, in spite of a violet spotlight on one of the packing cases," declared *København*. "Bishop Nikolas dies on a sofa that has been moved out into the open air—in Oslo!" exclaimed Cavling in *Politiken*. "The Bishop's moving death scene was acted in something resembling a churchyard, in which he breathes his last on a divan," grumbled *Aftenbladet*. "The strange blocks among which the Bishop dies were," Valdemar Vedel stated categorically in *Dagens Nyheder*, "among the most unfortunate elements in the production."[46]

Part of the critics' disenchantment can be attributed to their bias for conventionally mimetic drama. They seem unable to cope with a set in which objects are not expressly referential; their criticisms surely would have been scorned by Craig. But their objections cannot be entirely discredited because they point to a deeper contradiction between Craig's two-dimensional sketches and three-dimensional sets. The problem is not that the cubes and screens "represent" nothing or that the presence of real actors is incompatible with the artifice of the set. Rather, there is a singular incongruity between the surreal distortions of Craig's preliminary sketches and the final material reality of the stage. No audience can separate what it sees from what it knows to be true. Perspective on a real stage must be read consistently, and it is difficult if not impossible to introduce incompatible perspectives on an actual set. Whether or not they are predisposed to look for "realism" in the theater, in other words, spectators see the characters and objects on stage within a perfectly coherent spatial setting. That space can be material or hieratic (as, say, on the medieval stage), and it may sometimes prove difficult for spectators to see where the stage ends and the painted backdrop begins (as might occur in Serlio's classical sets). But no set can change the spectators' lines of sight. As Vaughan Cornish long ago observed, viewers "instinctively regard an object as extended in the plane at right angles to the line joining the object to the eye."[47] The shapes within Craig's sketches for theater scenes, however, complete the illusion of a precarious and dreamlike world. The visual contradictions and mutual interferences give the drawings an uncanny effect, as if the scene were in the process of dissolving before one's eyes. In this respect Craig's ideal theater is strikingly cinematic; it can be compared to a fade or dissolve that replaces the illusion of pictorial space with the flattened superficiality of the screen.

To say that Craig's sketches cannot easily be transformed into working sets raises the issue of his "practicality." The charge of impracticality was often made against Craig, and it is certainly an accusation he would have rejected. But the claim of impracticality carries greater weight when it refers not to Craig's personality or his limited experience in working with actual productions but to the peculiar distortions of his pictorial space, distortions which in many cases cannot possibly be carried out in the real space of the theater. Photographs of the production of *The Pretenders* seem prosaic and unevocative (in contrast to Craig's drawings, which are stunning), and the relative crudeness of the real thing cannot be attributed entirely to photographic diminutions nor even to the presence of human actors in an otherwise uniform artistic world. Quite apart from the actors, the set itself is equally disappointing. Craig's drawings evoke scenes that are irrational and remote, but the ambiguity inherent in his sketches vanishes when the mysterious "solids" acquire a real third dimension. In a way, the discrepancies between Craig's drawings and the actual set confirm a familiar paradox of pictorial representation, that it is easier to mistake art for reality than to see it purely as art.[48] Being forced into actual juxtaposition on a stage, the twenty-odd cubes cannot deny their own solidity or offer viewers contradictory perspectives. Their spatial interrelations instead appear rational and orderly, and they are seen as what they are—abstract architectural solids in a perfectly coherent space.

Craig's designs for theater are studies in the attrition of individualized characters. Certainly he did not "invent" his new stage style solely for the purpose of suppressing actors and their lifelike representations. In a broader context, however, Craig responds along with his contemporaries to what has been called the pervasive modern anxiety about the importance of the individual in theater art. ("Individuality is an arabesque we have discarded," proclaimed Hugo von Hofmannsthal in his well-known prologue to the first Viennese performance of Brecht's *Baal* [1926]. "I should go so far as to assert that all the ominous events we have been witnessing . . . are nothing but a very awkward and long-winded way of burying the concept of the European individual in the grave it has dug for itself."[49]) Viewed in this way, Craig's dazzling paintings are in a sense elaborate denials of the possibility of representing individual experience. To a stage tradition that located character securely within a narrative framework, or that situated identity solely within the mind, or defined personality in terms of individual psychological states and that required actors to imagine those subtextual realities in order to produce a coherent image of character—to that tradition Craig responded with an extreme archaization of the body. Craig depicts a world peopled not by minds or personalities but by figures whose principal reality is geometrical or monumental. To the extent that literally making figures of the dramatis personae effectively "kills" the conventional subject, Craig's characters appear to behave autonomously but without apparent innerness. Character takes on a nervous and distinctly figural expressivity; as a consequence, character on this stage is largely visual, as if bodily configuration were the sole meaningful reality. Craig's environments, in turn, vie with his characters for prominence, and it becomes difficult if not impossible to identify the sources of behavior in his works, the feeling that a distinctive ethos guides these acts. The key concept is painterly: "to establish man" (in a reversal of the famous surrealist program) "as anatomy instead of psychology."

The problem Craig created for himself, therefore, was not simply to dispose of an outmoded, realist theater, but to replace individualist ways of representing character with more purely iconographic modes of representation. It is not that Craig denies the validity of inner experience; his ideas for *Hamlet* occasionally depend on making Hamlet's inner world visible. It is rather that Craig sees the mind as no more valid than the body as the sign of human character. Craig puts forward with impressive authority the view that character is little more than a mysterious appearance of the body in space. Craig's drawings and his descriptions of ideal performances substitute rigorous order for spontaneity; unvarying geometry for the accidents of natural form; and an illusion of individual character that perpetuates its absence, like the remembered persons of a dream.

The argument of the remaining chapters is that some of the most difficult characters of modern drama are shaped (as were Craig's characters) according to modes of representation in which individuality is less a given to be discovered than a quality displayed through the interactions of language, society, or physical environment. The drawback to typical mentalistic approaches to character, whether older Freudian psychoanalysis or more recent discussions of a language-generated subjectivity, is that at best they offer an impoverished account of the various engulfments and undeliberate (or empathic) involvements that define many modern characters. Character here is more often than not a reflexive phenomenon—the product of an open-ended sequence of fusions (sometimes confusions) rather than the articulation of a unique personal being. In the next chapter I discuss the "non-Aristotelian" theater and theater writings of Bertolt Brecht. An investigation of Brecht's lifelong criticism of the empathic and illusionist Aristotelian theater offers a different language for reading characters on modern stages.

Chapter Two

Brecht and the Social Self

Among critics writing in English, Brecht's art (like Craig's) has long been regarded as superior to his criticism, and only comparatively recently have Brecht's theories been taken as seriously as his theater. As recently as 1983, for example, the reviewer for the *Times Literary Supplement* asserted that "the poet Brecht is superbly subversive of every orthodoxy—including his own."[1] Virtually overnight, however, Brecht has reappeared at the center of contemporary dramatic criticism. Paradoxically, Brecht's plays have in most cases become "classics" and therefore harmless, while his critical materials, in contrast, attract considerable interest.[2] Brecht's theoretical writings now influence much criticism of theater art, whether classic or contemporary. Jonathan Dollimore uses Brecht's terminology to expose the covert politics of Renaissance drama.[3] Patrice Pavis discusses Brecht's notion of *Gestus* from a semiological point of view and shows the close relationship between Brecht's Marxist poetics and supposedly formalist aesthetics.[4] And in the last few years feminist playwrights and scholars have discovered a productive fit between Brecht's non-Aristotelian theater and their own revolutionary programs.[5] As for film criticism, there Brechtian theory has long been central: the influential *Cahiers du Cinéma,* for example, has taken a Brechtian approach to representation in the cinema for more than thirty years.

The particular history of Brecht at *Cahiers du Cinéma* is instructive as a general index of Brecht's standing. As a matter of fact, Brecht's theater writings proved to be readily extensible to film theory. They are not strictly speaking literary criticism but a theory of modes of representation, and *Cahiers* in the 1970s developed extensions of Brecht's theories in the concept of the *lecture* (the "reading" of a film) and also by promoting such films as Jean-Marie Straub's *Othon* (1969), *History Lessons* (1972), and *Moses and Aaron* (1975), all of which deconstructed filmic art. Straub's approach to filmmaking (and *Cahiers'* defense of his work) was conceived against filmic illusionism, just as Brecht's theater attacked conventional stage performances.[6]

What is true of *Cahiers* is now true of drama criticism generally. Brecht's concepts of alienation and *Gestus,* his fondness for mixed styles and genres, and his stubborn refusal to separate art from economics and politics seem in retrospect more postmodern than modern. Moreover, Brecht alone among theorists of drama provides a vocabulary sufficient to discuss important contemporary questions of the politics of theater and theatrical performance.[7] In this chapter I want to examine Brecht's plays and theoretical writings on theater as they contribute to the apparent eclipse of character on the twentieth-century stage. If Craig sees character mainly in terms of its figural reality, Brecht sees it more conventionally as an ethical reality but one that is fragile, secondary, derivative. Hence in his dramas Brecht decenters or destabilizes the notion of character, replacing essential images of persons with dialogic, multivoiced or multivalenced personae. Brecht's works for the stage repeatedly confirm his attempt to redefine character as a variable of particular social or political environments.

The objections to reading Brecht's plays mainly as character studies are real, and I do not intend to minimize them. They rest in part on Brecht's own intense aversion to what he thought were the deleterious consequences of empathic stagings of individual personalities.[8] ("[Y]ou can wipe my ass with 'characters' " [*Charakterköpfen,* literally, "character-heads"], says one of the machine gunners in *Mann ist Mann.*) But they also have to do with Brecht's historical situation as an artist in the Weimar Republic. It is this factor that seems to point to a general turning away from the representation of individuals in art. In Germany in the decade following the end of World War I, personal sensibility as a subject for art seems to have been all but eliminated, and Brecht could hardly have avoided being swept along with the currents then in motion in art. "Everything combined," writes John Willett,

> to make this culture a consciously impersonal one. First and foremost there was still the revolutionary sense of belonging to a huge community, whether this was "the masses," the proletariat or the Communist party. This, combined perhaps with some realization of the powerlessness of the artist in any such vast social context, was what gave men like Grosz their conviction that individuality was outdated and must be "discarded." Then there was the concern with the object . . . and the objective art which would deal with such things. By defini-

tion, subjectivity, the personal viewpoint, was very largely ruled out; nor was much room left for the human being, even as a theme for art. He had already been intuitively mechanized by the Italian Metaphysicals . . . and much the same marionette-like interpretation of the human figure can be seen in Goll's farces, Schlemmer's ballets and Meyerhold's neutrally-clothed "biomechanical" actors; these too are on their way to being animated robots, objects on legs.[9]

Masks and impersonal acting styles are central to a number of Brecht's productions and theoretical dramatic writings, for example, the white-faced soldiers in his version of Marlowe's *Edward the Second,* the masked figures in *Antigone* or in *The Caucasian Chalk Circle,* or the influential essay "Alienation-effects in Chinese Acting." Still, one might argue that Brecht's apparent disregard for individualized "character studies," if it means anything at all, applies mainly to his belief that conventionalized and coherent psychological narratives could not fully account for the acts and thoughts of his dramatis personae. For example, Brecht defended Peter Lorre's acting in *Mann ist Mann* against criticism that he had played Galy Gay inconsistently. In part, Brecht argues that Lorre's acting had to be interpreted as a means rather than an end. "The speeches' content was made up of contradictions," Brecht wrote, "and yet the actor had not to make the spectator identify himself with individual sentences and so get caught up in contradictions, but to keep him out of them. Taken as a whole it had to be the most objective possible exposition of a contradictory internal process."[10]

Brecht's defense of Lorre's acting is interesting because it implies that he wants actors to maintain a visible split (or inconsistency) in their representations of character. What for Lorre's critics was evidence of incompetence was for Brecht the theoretical grounds of successful performance. The actor, in other words, was to abandon decorum as well as psychological ballast because both acting traditions—classical as well as naturalistic—tended to produce seamless illusions of individual behavior. Brecht's actor, in contrast, by treating the character as something external, something to be temporarily put on or "quoted," was to imply the existence of an ideological subtext that spectators had to decode rationally. This is the reason, for example, for Brecht's fascination with oriental acting. Brecht sensed in the highly formal performance of Chinese actors a "transportable technique" that could be employed profitably in a "realistic and revolutionary theater."[11] Unlike many other modernist playwrights—Yeats, for example, or Craig or Artaud—Brecht did not favor oriental acting styles because any relatively stylized performance tradition promoted an awareness of aesthetics at the expense of a credible illusion of reality.[12] Inasmuch as the Chinese actor divorced himself from the character he played, his acting carried out visibly the kinds of extrinsic ideological contradictions that Brecht saw as the source of character in the first place. In the well-known essay "Alienation-effects in Chinese Acting," for example, Brecht condemns the representation of character as if it were independent of historical or social determinants: "Bourgeois theater worked out the timelessness of its subjects. The representation of humans depended on the so-called eternally-human. Through the arrangement of the plot were created such 'universal' situations that simple Man, Man of all times and skin colors, could express himself." [13]

In the last analysis, there is in Brecht's enthusiasm for "inconsistent" or austere performances more than can be attributed to a desire to distance art from life or to exclude emotion from theatrical performance. Modes of acting such as these are not necessarily impersonal or cool, but they do commit the actor to a style that walls off the elements of character as objects of attention in their own right. The kind of performance Brecht here envisions separates the person playing from the person produced by that playing, making character in effect the obvious result of a semiological process, a matrix of signs and signals.

The productive dissonance between actor and character that Brecht sought was (and is) difficult for Western actors to achieve, but something like it, Brecht discovered, could sometimes be forced mechanically. A visible separation between actor and role can be achieved, for instance, by transvestite performance. Brecht himself sometimes favored an approach one might call "antitype" casting to rehearsals, writing, for example, that having men play women (and vice versa) not only challenged the actor imaginatively but, more importantly, brought into view the various codes and signs by which masculinity and feminity were represented in the first place. Transvestite performance might expose certain aspects of character, for example, as cultural fictions: "played by a person of a different sex, the *representation* [my emphasis; Brecht's word is *Figur*, i.e., representation, illustration, or character] of the sex will be more clearly revealed." [14]

It is instructive in this case to test Brecht's theories about acting and the production of character with some recent experimental productions whose sponsors initially were not at all interested in Brechtian theater or Marxist ideology. For example, during rehearsals for productions of medieval mystery plays at Lancaster Grammar School (1982–83), productions that attempted for historical reasons to duplicate the performance conditions of medieval drama, Peter Norton observed that men playing the parts of women were necessarily split off from their characters:

> [T]he men were more detached from the content of the script: rather than acting a character and "getting under its skin" they were presenting a situation. When we went to the Salford conference I took the part of Elizabeth, and I was aware of a distance between myself and the part I was playing: at no stage did I identify with the part of Elizabeth. I felt comfortable with John [an actor playing the Virgin Mary], but I did not relate to him as I would have if he had been playing a man, or if his part had been taken by a woman.[15]

Transvestite acting depends in part, it was discovered, less on representing character than on representing the codes on which character depends. Instead of the seamless blending of actor and role that is at the center of realist performance, one finds an inbuilt structural insistence that appearances are deceiving. The male actor in these circumstances, writes Meg Twycross, "takes on the costume and mannerisms of a woman in order to represent a woman: not in order to deceive the audience into thinking that he really is a woman, but so as to give the audience material to create their own perception of the role."[16] By deliberately forcing a split in the representation, in other words, the actor becomes in effect a demonstrator. He "hands over" (I use Brecht's term for the actor's function) "femininity" to the audience "as a concept rather than as part of a real person."[17]

My aim in this chapter is to avoid the widespread polarization that has typified discussion of Brecht's characters in recent decades. On one hand are those scholars who see in Brecht's dramatis personae an unintentional but ennobling humanism; on the other are those who view Brecht's characters as purely ideological signifiers or as sites upon which are written expressly political texts.[18] It seems fair to say that for Brecht, the crucial task with respect to character was to expose its relative fragility, or, alternatively, its peculiar absorbability. Brecht's well-known comment— "Character is not like an ineradicable stain of grease in a pair of trousers"— is a reminder that human behavior depends more on circumstances and less on the continuing subject than one likes to believe.[19] Mother Courage, for example, is presented dialectically rather than psychologically: we are given a selection of apparently contradictory acts (Mother Courage is brave, Mother Courage is cowardly, she is a good mother, she is a poor mother, and so on) that we must try to resolve for ourselves.

A predictable result of such dramaturgy is that Brecht's dramatis personae are not thought to be coherent characters at all (recall the criticisms of Lorre's acting), or they are perceived to become genuine characters in spite of their author and his ideology. This view is popular especially in the English-speaking world: Brecht's strategy of representing Mother Courage, for example, is dismissed by Ronald Hayman as "fortunately . . . self-defeating."[20] Another result is that characters like Mother Courage, because their behavioral inconsistencies are not normally rooted in a consistently maintained psychology, lend themselves poorly in the eyes of modern audiences to credible representations of intense feeling.[21] This view, as is well known, is one partly encouraged by Brecht's early claims (subsequently modified) that in the new epic drama emotion or feeling ought to be subordinated to reason.

Yet one naturally wonders why the depiction of behavioral contradictions on stage constitutes an incredible divergence from human behavioral norms. As a matter of speculative interest, one would expect the opposite. Standards for defining character vary considerably, of course, but in general many modern critics use inconsistencies as a kind of litmus test to separate "round" (i.e., realistic) characters from flat ones. Trying to specify why some inconsistencies are lifelike and others are not can be endlessly frustrating and lead ultimately to reducing art, in T. S. Eliot's phrase, to "deserts of exact likeness" to reality. But it is not an utterly fruitless exercise to focus on closely restricted acts such as seem to display themselves simply and without disguise. In discussing the notion of character as Gordon Craig construed it, I used comparisons with pictorial art to show how Craig's dramatic representations of character might be read mainly for their figural significance. I want now to introduce a comparison with narrative art to demonstrate the depths and perplexities that constitute character on Brecht's stage.

"The test of a round character," says E. M. Forster, "is whether it is capable of surprising in a convincing way. If it never surprises, it is flat. If it does not convince, it is a flat pretending to be round. It has the incalculability of life about it."[22] The emphasis for our purposes must fall on Forster's qualification: round characters must surprise "*in a convincing way*" (my italics). Concerning what makes an act surprising yet "convincing" Forster is brief but emphatic. Any character by Jane Austen, says

Forster, is ipso facto round: "All the Jane Austen characters are ready for an extended life, for a life which the scheme of her books seldom requires them to lead, and that is why they lead their actual lives so satisfactorily."[23] Even minor characters—by Forster's definition, characters about whom we know relatively little—can seem to lead real lives. To be convincing, in other words, it is not necessary that a character reveal (or appear to reveal) very much about the contents of his or her mind; all that is required is the illusion that the character be "novelized" by being situated (or seeming to be situated) within an extratextual frame.[24] When, for example, in *Mansfield Park*, Lady Bertram discovers that one of her daughters has eloped and the other abandoned her marriage for a lover, she behaves in a way that (according to Forster) suddenly extends the "formula" for her character: "Lady Bertram did not think deeply, but, guided by Sir Thomas, she thought justly on all important points, and she saw therefore in all its enormity, what had happened, and neither endeavoured herself, nor required Fanny to advise her, to think little of guilt and infamy."[25]

It might be objected that the cohesiveness here attributed to Lady Bertram is only illusory, an inevitable consequence of human habits of creating an illusion of subjectivity by clustering diverse acts under the aegis of the personal name. But the umbrella effect attributed to the individual's proper name in itself only partly explains the sense of personal coherence and credibility that Forster here describes.[26] Lady Bertram's reaction to the vicissitudes of her daughters' lives is not really uncharacteristic or psychologically revealing so much as it is causally ambiguous. *Why,* one asks, does Lady Bertram respond to the news of her daughters by shunning "comfort" and dwelling on "guilt and infamy"? Is it because, contrary to her characteristic aversion to deep thought, she followed Sir Thomas's direction on certain moral points? Not entirely: Austen has in fact not complicated Lady Bertram so much as pointed to part of her being that is beyond analytical discussion. "Her affections," writes Austen, "were not acute, nor was her mind tenacious. After a time, Fanny found it not impossible to direct her thoughts to other subjects, and revive some interest in the usual occupations; but whenever Lady Bertram *was* fixed on the event, she could see it only in one light, as comprehending the loss of a daughter, and a disgrace never to be wiped off."[27] Lady Bertram's melancholy,[28] that is, results not from a surprising though ultimately intelligible response to circumstances but from an animal core of mentality that remains essentially unfathomable.

Why does Austen do this? If we look again at the description of Lady

Bertram's response to her daughters, we see first (as Forster long ago discerned) that Lady Bertram suddenly behaves in a new and uncharacteristic way. As readers, therefore, we are challenged to integrate that new behavior as the expression of a single coherent character. We are drawn, in other words, not just to enlarge our view of Lady Bertram but to speculate about her mental life, and the only conceivable way for us to do that is to imagine her as having a mental life in the first place. Even if only temporarily, even if against our best critical sense, we test this flat character's behavior the only way we know how—against what we know of real people in real situations.

Viewed from this perspective, Lady Bertram's acts as Austen describes them seem to be the products of inarticulable but psychologically credible emotions. The scene seems in fact to be a miniaturized account of the mechanics of grief. Loneliness, consolation, guilt, the need for constant companionship, mental fixedness, the rituals of a "talking cure"—all are directly or implicitly stated in the text, and as a result we sense this particular behavior legitimately extends this particular character. By challenging readers to form for themselves a conception of Lady Bertram's mental life—it does not matter if different readers guess differently—Austen gains for her character the illusion of a complex narrative identity. That identity becomes formed, as Paul Ricoeur suggests, because it (or the conception of it) provides the answer to a single question: Who? This does not make Lady Bertram a realistic case study—the question Who? as Ricoeur notes, is one that cannot be answered with the description of a single stable identity because the self so identified "becomes the name of a problem at least as much as it is that of a solution." [29] But it does ensure the creation by (though not necessarily in) the text of the marks by which we identify character—the traces or vestiges that remain of living beings after their passage.

In discussing the subject of character in Brecht's theater, then, I will be asking similarly after a network of possible narratives that both express and shape character. The difficulties of coordinating the inner and outer persons in Brecht's theater can be circumvented if for "identity" understood in the sense of self-constancy or psychological depth we substitute Ricoeur's concept of an identity that is narrative. For the strictly psychological identity posited for Mother Courage, in other words, we substitute a character who may be, in Ricoeur's words, "refigured by the reflexive application of . . . narrative configurations. Unlike the abstract identity of the Same, this narrative identity, constitutive of self-constancy, can include change, mutability, within the cohesion of one lifetime. . . . [T]he story of a life continues to be refigured by all the truthful or fictive stories a subject tells about himself or herself. This refiguration makes this life itself a cloth woven of stories told."[30]

Brecht seems to disallow psychological frames for his characters while regularly inviting novelistic scrutiny of the workings of their minds. To begin to address the question of character in Brecht I would like to examine a small part of a single scene in which an illusion of real individualized behavior seems most apparent. For example, consider the following well-known scene near the end of *Mother Courage and her Children*, the scene in which Kattrin saves a town from destruction by drumming loudly on a rooftop to wake the sleeping citizens:

THE OFFICER: See, she's laughing at us. I can't stand it. I'll shoot her down before it's all over. Fetch the shotgun.

Two soldiers run away. KATTRIN *continues to drum.*

THE PEASANT WOMAN: I have it, Captain. Over there stands their wagon. If we smash it, she'll stop. They have nothing except the wagon.

THE OFFICER *to* THE YOUNG PEASANT: Smash it. *Upwards:* We'll smash your wagon if you don't stop hammering.

THE YOUNG PEASANT *aims a weak blow against the covered wagon.*

THE PEASANT WOMAN: Stop it, you cow!

KATTRIN *pauses, staring in despair at her wagon, making pitiful noises. But she continues drumming.*

THE OFFICER: Where are those shitheads with the shotgun?

FIRST SOLDIER: They can't have heard it yet in the town, otherwise we could hear their cannon.

THE OFFICER *upwards:* They can't hear you. And now we'll shoot you off. One last time: throw the drum down!

THE YOUNG PEASANT *suddenly throws the board away:* Keep drumming! Otherwise it's all over! Keep drumming, Keep drumming . . .

The soldier throws him down and stabs him with a lance.

KATTRIN *begins to cry, but she keeps drumming.*

THE PEASANT WOMAN: Don't stab him in the back! For God's sake, you've killed him!

The soldiers come running with the gun.

SECOND SOLDIER: The colonel is foaming at the mouth, Captain. We'll be court-martialed.

THE OFFICER: Stop it! Stop it! *Upwards, while the gun is being placed on its mount.* For the very last time: stop drumming!

KATTRIN, *crying, drums as loud as she can.* Fire!

The soldiers fire. KATTRIN, *hit, drums a few more beats and then slowly collapses.*[31]

In addition to Brecht's stage directions, we have available for study some of Brecht's comments to one of his actors during rehearsals of the foregoing scene. For the most part they are not a gloss on how to represent character; they seem more like an author's viewpoint rather than a director's, since they specify an attitude without explaining to the actor how to achieve it. But his description accords perfectly with a naturalistic (as opposed to stylized) approach to acting. To one of the actors sent to fetch the gun, Brecht gave the following account of the soldier's behavior; the man, Brecht said, trots out "with the well-known kind of tardiness that cannot be proved."[32]

Such reluctance would be a fairly easy attitude for an actor to represent in a naturalistic fashion; one does not even have to historicize the action, only to support it (or reference it) in terms of a recognizable or recoverable personal motive. One sees precisely the same kind of attitude, for example, in the behavior of small children told by their parents to perform some unpleasant task: eat peas, apologize to a sibling, go to bed. The idea is to perform the task slowly enough to indicate not just that the activity is disagreeable but to convey as well a clear sense of personal opposition to authority. The trick is to act slowly enough to indicate to the person giving the command that his or her authority is being questioned but not so slowly as to seem actually to challenge it. Presumably the actor would accomplish this task by locating his behavior within some analogous personal affective frame.

The character as Brecht writes it is not self-sufficient, in other words, and so he encourages the actor (and so the reader) to search below or beside the text for an appropriate motivational basis. In performance, as a result, the moment does not lack significance for the portraiture of character. Despite the smallness of his part, the soldier's tardiness appears at a crucial gestural moment in the text; he need not be emphatically defiant in order to appeal to the spectators' sense of justice or to their unspoken wish to intervene on Kattrin's behalf. By delaying shrewdly in responding to the order to fetch the weapon, the soldier seems to act according to an individual psychology of resistance to dubious authority.

But the truth Brecht is after here is more political and more complicated than a sentimental view of human behavior allows for. Brecht's interest is not merely in eccentricities of behavior—the surprises that Forster identified as the basis of "round" or lifelike characters—and spectators may well interpret the soldier's motives as less admirably motivated. The action perhaps forms the basis of a social gest; it distills in a single moment, for example, the antagonistic relations between officers and enlisted men. What moves this soldier, after all, may possibly be less human fellow feeling than the frictions of military class relations. Typically (one could even say stereotypically) officers and enlisted men do not readily get along.

I do not mean to say that Brecht substitutes caricature for human psychological complexity. But many of Brecht's most effective portraits render character as a problematic assembly of parts. However carefully Brecht creates an image of ethical behavior, his skepticism with respect to the genuineness of those motives remains uncompromising. What is more, it appears that Brecht cannot keep ethical distinctions from being tainted by material realities. The scene further includes a moment when character dissolves into a chilling insubstantiality, which Brecht defines clearly (and "realistically") with an additional instruction concerning behavior. When the officer gives the order to shoot, Brecht's comments are brief but bitter: "Nevertheless he fires."[33]

Does it matter that the soldier who fires the gun is the same one who moments before had seemed so slyly insolent? Indeed it does. "Nevertheless he fires": Brecht's terseness forces an ironic comparison of motives, and it effectively decenters the apparent character of the soldier. The gun explodes precisely at the climax of the scene, smashing to pieces the humane (and humanist) identity assigned only moments before to the man who now pulls the trigger. It is not a question of identity that has been distorted or suppressed; we are not to be made aware of a separate self glimpsed obscurely beneath the role of the assassin who is forced to shoot Kattrin. Rather Brecht's skepticism goes so far as to envision the open-endedness of subjectivity, the relatively limitless numbers of masks that can stand in occasionally for the person. Instead of ethical consistency, in other words, the scene demonstrates the larger material realities that often provide the frames within which character appears—militarism, class, professionalism, even "business as usual," however appalling that business might be.

Perhaps spectators do not fully comprehend how the single word "nevertheless" complicates even the simplest of dramatic characters. But Brecht's production note illustrates perfectly the playwright's attitude toward individualism in the theater. Behind the single word lies Brecht's conviction that the being we call the individual is less the independent agent we think he or she is and more the accidental product of material context.

The notion that humans sometimes act heroically by acting out unheroic agendas is precisely the feature of Brecht's poetics that makes it attractive to contemporary dramatists and literary theorists. For Brecht, characteristic acts flow not invariably from an inner personal core but instead vary according to the roles a person inhabits. An enlisted man cannot help but respond unenthusiastically to an officer's order, just as he cannot help but carry it out. In the scene under consideration, the circumstances of behavior are the same for the officer, for whom the appearance of being in command is integral to the role he expects others to expect him to play. The scene is more than a little reminiscent of a situation described by George Orwell in "Shooting an Elephant." Orwell shot a rampaging elephant, he said, not because he wanted to or because it was particularly dangerous to the Burmese village population but because his position as a police officer obliged him to appear in the eyes of the villagers as a conventionalized figure of authority. In Brecht's scene, the officer's acts seem to be precipitated (as were Orwell's) by the desire to avoid being publicly ridiculed: "See, she's laughing at us," says the officer; "I can't stand it"; "My whole life, every white man's life in the East," Orwell wrote, "was one long struggle not to be laughed at."[34]

The effort to discover a consistent inner nature by way of outward behavior or speech, fundamental to conventional realistic depictions of character, here results only in indeterminacy. It is not that Brecht's soldiers (and certainly not Orwell, for that matter) lack psychological depth or credibility. But something indeed new has complicated the picture of character. Conventional dramatic representation assumes no necessary connection between the most intensely personal acts and the roles the world obliges one to play. But both the officer's authority and the enlisted man's tardy compliance are "characters" made evident by way of mimetic investment in the only roles available to them in their immediate situation. The two mens' characters are not really forced on them by their independent situations so much as they are mutually derived; officer and enlisted man create each other by synthetic interaction, each being what the other needs him to be.

The episode is sobering to contemplate, but the point (like so much of

Brecht's poetry and drama) is broadly satiric and distinctly humorous. That character rests on role (rather than individualistic actions) in fact suggests the basis of Brecht's essentially comic dramatic talent. One of Brecht's best illustrations of the humorous vagaries of character can be found in a brief poem ("Wheelchanging") about a passenger who waits while the driver repairs a flat tire:

> I sit by the roadside.
> The driver changes the wheel.
> I do not like the place I am coming from.
> I do not like the place I am going to.
> Why do I watch the wheel changing
> With impatience?
>
> (*Werke* 12, p. 310)

Brecht's poem clarifies with great precision an inescapably humorous quirk of personal behavior. The funny thing about being a passenger is that one inevitably behaves like a passenger, even if that behavior runs counter to one's best interests. Even when we have clear knowledge of the discrepancy between our wishes and our values, in other words, we seem powerless to act on that knowledge. It is precisely the contingency of character that is most mystifying and likely to remain so—not necessarily because capitalist ideology compels one to fret over the loss of time and services that have been bought (there were presumably passengers who thought like passengers long before the rise of bourgeois capitalism), but because of the more broadly mimetic principle that people are inclined to play the roles that happen to be offered them.

Ostensibly, then, one ought not to suppose that in Brecht's passenger poem we see a victim alienated from himself, a character whose true inner cohesiveness has been suppressed by ideological forces. Brecht's formula for character as a phenomenon of surfaces or appearances is less directly tied to specific ideology than is sometimes thought. Just as in the foregoing poem being a passenger is ethically discontinuous from one's apparent likes and dislikes, so in *Mother Courage* the agent who pulls the trigger is in some sense discontinuous from the agent who delays in fetching the gun. Character, insofar as it is depicted in the poem and in Brecht's play, does not give us a sense of self-expression, nor even the sense that somewhere selves exist to which both men can return. Brecht disallows the possibility that character exists apart from its singular (and frequently contradictory) manifestations.

In both poem and play we see enacted a drama of behavior according to type, and if there were not a war in progress the situation depicted in *Mother Courage* might, like the passenger's ironic reflections, be quite funny. In this special sense Brecht's scenes display in miniature a humorous world. The officer and the enlisted man, like the anonymous passenger, behave distinctly as characters, and yet that distinctiveness is wholly based on their conforming to the expectations of the type; we know nothing more about them except that in some ironic sense they need one another if they are to exist at all. Like a pair of cartoon characters, they are locked into mutual dependence, and what identity they have depends on their continuing to enact this particular gestural (and political) pas de deux.

To stress that individualism was a fiction, that character was subject to a host of relationships and circumstances extending over one's life, is a motive present in Brecht from the very beginnings of his career. Brecht has long been recognized as an anti-individualist because of his Marxist politics, but the skepticism with which he views individualism has broader consequences for his drama than making it into a platform for socialist ideology. The broad implication of the two situations I have so far examined is that the production of character cannot occur except in terms of the "character-effects" called for by the presence of others in a specific situation. *Baal* (1918), for example, seems as much a definition of a generalized sociological self as an express anticipation of Brecht's subsequent orientation toward Marxism. Brecht's anarchic hero is no mere decadent, writes Keith Dickson; instead his brutality "ceases to be wilful exhibitionism and becomes a desperate search for a new kind of identity, totally independent of the moribund society of which individualism was a decadent product."[35] *Baal* and several other early works—*Drums in the Night, In the Jungle of Cities*—were written not to glorify egoism but to write its epitaph. But perhaps Brecht's first play to attack individualism openly is *Mann ist Mann*. The play was published under that title in 1926, but its history can be traced to the very beginnings of Brecht's literary career. According to John Willett, Brecht had worked on a manuscript ("the Galgei project") involving a hero with multiple personalities as early as 1918.[36] Brecht asserted that in *Mann ist Mann* he had introduced a new human type, and, indeed, the work treats character as if it were not fixed or essential but variable and manipulable like clay. Perhaps Brecht credits himself with more inventiveness than is his due—comic drama from Aristophanes through Shakespeare often centers on a hero with many faces—but his dramaturgy is consistent and clear. Character is changeable, and growth or development of character results from an osmotic process that makes it hard to say where individuality ends and collectivity begins, and vice versa.

Outwardly the protagonist of *Mann ist Mann* resembles a version of the Soviet collective hero, but in fact Brecht's play is by no means doctrinaire. Neither (like the comedies it resembles) is it unambiguously happy. It is true that Brecht at first defended his hero's apparent spinelessness as a form of strength through collectivity. In a radio preface to *Mann ist Mann* in 1927, he insisted that the audience were not to disparage Galy Gay's apparent spinelessness: "I suppose you are used to regarding a man who cannot say no as a weakling, but this Galy Gay is no weakling, on the contrary he is the strongest. . . . To be sure, he is only the strongest after he has ceased being a private individual, he only becomes strong as part of the mass." [37] This sounds like straightforward Marxist theory, as well it might. "It is surprising" (as Dickson writes) "how close he had come to the Marxist position without knowing it." [38] Nevertheless, as Brecht saw toward the end of his life, the play can seem deeply pessimistic. Its theme, Brecht wrote in 1954, "is the false, bad collectivity (the 'gang') and its powers of attraction, the same collectivity that Hitler and his backers were even then in the process of recruiting by an exploitation of the petty-bourgeoisie's vague longing for the historically timely, genuinely social collectivity of the workers." [39]

To see *Mann ist Mann* accurately, therefore, we need to separate its official Marxism from Brecht's broader belief in the social construction of identity. Individuals produce themselves (or are produced) only in the sense that they cooperate with other persons in society. It will be seen that character for Brecht very closely approximates the model for identity proposed by twentieth-century social psychologists, and in truth the connections between the characters in Brecht's plays and modern sociological views of selfhood are apparent at several basic points. "Selves can only exist in definite relationships to other selves," wrote George Herbert Mead, in a succinct description of the social basis of identity.[40] More recent sociologists (for example, Peter Berger and Thomas Luckmann) echo Mead's ideas with terms that repeat precisely if coincidentally Brecht's own ideas: "the relationship between man, the producer, and the social world, his product, is and remains a dialectical one." [41] Identity (or character) is neither present from birth nor continuous throughout life; it results from continuous engulfment within society and history.

The picture of character that emerges from Brecht's play, therefore, is dialogic, expressly mimetic: "one man is no man; another must address him" (*einer ist keiner, es muss ihn einer anrufen; Gesammelte Werke* 1, p. 362). *Another must write him,* one might add, for *Mann ist Mann* dramatizes psychological as well as political answers to the question of human identity. For Brecht, it was crucial to remain aware not only that "*all* social reality is precarious,"[42] but that character itself could become little more than a mask for the perpetuation of repressive ideologies. The successive transformations of Galy Gay can be seen as attempts by Brecht to supply an anti-Aristotelian aesthetic for character. Aristotle dismisses the actual unity of the subject as irrelevant to art—"infinitely various are the incidents in one man's life, which cannot be reduced to unity"[43]—but for Brecht the question of individual coherence is both problematic and crucial. The self is complex, malleable, and open, and character, in turn, demonstrates a continued susceptibility to exterior forces. The play proves that in literature, as in life, character lacks the unity or centeredness traditionally attributed to it. Galy Gay is a composite, and his successive metamorphoses deconstruct the idea of a subject who coheres throughout time.

Brecht replaces psychological (or Romantic) concepts for the individual with an expressly theatrical or dialogic language. It is not surprising in this respect that *Mann ist Mann* often figures importantly in recent theoretical discussions of postmodernism and the postmodernist self. Galy Gay's transformation from individual to member of a collective raises questions about the ultimate authorship of human identity and the relations between language and power that perhaps structure us all. Who wrote Galy Gay? What political, economic, or personal forces contribute to his remaking? And should we mourn his loss of individuality or celebrate his successful socialization?

We can obtain deeper insight into Brechtian characters by extending the discussion to include those works written specifically to dismantle traditional theatrical representation, the *Lehrstücke*. Written around 1929–30, none of these nine works is a play in the conventional sense; "performance piece" is a more accurate term for these remarkable dramas. But in them Brecht continues to renounce individualism and to stage "collective" characters. The *Lehrstücke* often take their form from music rather than from plot—*The Flight of Lindbergh* (*Der Flug der Lindberghs*, 1929, originally *Der Lindberghflug* and later [1949] renamed *Der Ozeanflug*), for example, was written for performance either as a concert or radio broadcast. The score for *Der Ozeanflug* includes tenor, bass, and baritone solos as well as choral singing. In the text, Brecht stresses the interconnectedness of The Flier with his machine and with all those who assembled it:

Seven men have built my machine in San Diego
Often working for twenty-four hours without pause

From a few meters of steel pipe.
What they have made must be sufficient for me.
They have worked, I
Work further; I am not alone, we are
Eight, here flying.

(Gesammelte Werke 1: 571)

In *Der Ozeanflug*, as in all the *Lehrstücke*, Brecht pressed for a new dramaturgy and for politically useful theater. All the *Lehrstücke* were written for nontraditional staging (usually environmental or platform), and all were expressly didactic. Most important, their didactic purpose depends less on ideological content than on a reorganization of mimetic performance. Not intended to be performed by professional actors before an audience, they were written instead to involve amateur actors (students or groups of workers) in mimetic activity. Even when they were staged in the traditional manner, Brecht tried to make spectators into active participants. The set for *Der Flug der Lindberghs*, for example, included in the background a large sign asking spectators to sing along loudly with the cast. Similarly, *The Measures Taken* (*Die Massnahme*, 1930) was written expressly for participants (which in its original production numbered in the hundreds) rather than for performance before a conventional audience. Brecht reluctantly tolerated spectators but insisted that only those who joined in the production would learn from it.[44]

For this reason the *Lehrstücke* differ from conventional theater in more than one respect. Rainer Steinweg summarizes these differences as follows:

1. *Lehrstücktheater* is a theater without audience.
2. The *Lehrstücke* work with negative, that is, asocial models of behavior, shown via attitudes, modes of speech, and gestures.
3. These plays are not out to show development of character, but work up from a variety of angles contradictory interpretations of situations deriving from a given problem, rather like a musical theme and its variations.
4. They are not to be taken as proving points by means of illustrations in the text.
5. The texts are rather to be regarded as experimental models, provoking criticism and adjustments by the players in the course of their stage practice.[45]

These features of the *Lehrstücke* follow directly from Brecht's conviction that mimesis is the principal means by which the individual becomes integrated within the social context. His emphasis in the *Lehrstücke* on experiment and progressive repetition makes no sense unless it is understood to provide an analytical frame for mimetic activity. That is, the *Lehrstücke* abolish traditional modes of performance in order to force all participants to repeat preexisting acts and statements—the roles they have been offered—with the assumption that there was something unsatisfactory about the original that had better be reconsidered. Theater performance is dismantled, revealed to be theater-like; it becomes more like a rehearsal, save that the point here is not just for individual actors to stand in temporarily for their assigned characters but to expose the mechanics of mimetic involvement as the preconditions for the construction of character in the first place. Within a single play, for example, the participants (no distinctions are made between actors and spectators) imitate a number of different characters so as to experience their different points of view. As the various roles are tried out, as questions are asked and characters exchanged, the minds of the individual actors are stretched in order to comprehend the machinery of representation.

In other words, Brecht seems to have intended the *Lehrstücke* to eliminate unconscious or undesirable aspects of mimesis in the theater. As such, they are important keys to understanding that aspect of Brecht's theater theory that is most frequently misunderstood: empathic involvement. The *Lehrstücke* do not eliminate empathy but inscribe it carefully within cognitive thought. Eliminating the spectators' gaze from theater does not entirely eliminate the dangers of mimesis, in Brecht's view. The participants in *Die Massnahme*, accordingly, were enjoined to take precautions to avoid full involvement with their roles. Thus mimesis in this theater does not permit identification with others to become an end in itself. Rather empathy becomes an instrument of further understanding, much as, for example, the empathic responses of an analyst to a patient may be considered part of a critical methodology.[46]

Other aspects of the *Lehrstücke* shed additional light on Brecht's ongoing redefinition of character, and it is worth considering them briefly for this reason. The *Lehrstücke* deconstruct and reconstruct the individual in more than one way—indeed, individual characters in these works prove elusive. And these works manifest one final irony of the missing subject: as the *Lehrstücke* lack characters in the traditional literary sense, so they lack an author. That is to say, one cannot meaningfully speak of "Brecht's" *Lehrstücke,* for substantial portions of the plays were written by Elisabeth Hauptmann. They are Brecht's plays only because of an accident of naming. That Brecht's work during this period was not quite his own seems to have been widely known; John Fuegi retells what was then a standing joke in Berlin: " 'Who is the play by?' 'Brecht.' 'Then, who is the play by?' "[47] Fuegi adds that "there is no major text of the period 1924–33 that does not contain considerable parts written by Hauptmann."[48] The collaborative history of the *Lehrstücke* makes it difficult (if not theoretically impossible) to speak of these texts as reservoirs of Brecht's intent. And what if one then acknowledges the many artists who contributed to Brecht's other plays of this period—Kurt Weill and Caspar Neher, not to mention John Gay and Christopher Marlowe? Finally, what of the theoretical question of the actors' collaborative effort in the production of character? In Brecht's case the question of individual authorship takes on a profoundly ironic meaning. Brecht's cannibalistic attitude toward other writers is well known—"In literature as in life," he is said once to have remarked in response to accusations of excessive borrowings, "I do not recognize private property." Brecht's quip is less defensive wit than a statement that demystifies art and the artist. There are no privileged intentions or interpretations with regard to texts, Brecht implies, and the *Lehrstücke* bear him out. A more radical decentering of the individual can scarcely be imagined. Yet the individual is not therefore radically dismembered. From every angle, one might say, Brecht's work illustrates how difficult it is to distinguish those acts out of which individual character arises from those, alternatively, in which agency is distributed across a cultural network.

In the *Lehrstücke* Brecht tries to make a political virtue of an institutional shortcoming, namely, undeliberate mimesis, the tendency of theatrical performance to induce spectators to fall passively in step with the characters they see enacted before them. It is surely no accident that these plays are his most explicitly political, his most radical formally, and those works that have attracted the most recent interest among dramatists and dramatic theorists who consider mimetic fictions less as imitations of real life than symbolic (and therefore culturally biased) structures of desire. Brecht seems at the time he created them (and toward the end of his life) to have believed that the *Lehrstücke* were forerunners of the theater of the future. He may well have been right. Latent in all Brecht's early works, as Herbert Blau observes, "are dramatic prototypes of the more radical agenda of recent critical thought, which moves through the deconstructed text into an analysis of sexuality, the historicizing of gender, and, transgressively beneath it all, to a sense of the relations between language and power that extends in the tradition from Nietzsche and Rimbaud to Genet, Foucault, and Deleuze."[49] It is to these materialist aesthetics of character that I would now like to turn.

One Person Is No Person: Brecht and the Social Self

Individuality on Brecht's stage is always being invented. Brecht's characters are truly multiple, for their identities at any given moment are always in the process of being defined or passing away. As if to stress the point, Brecht was fond of staging characters whose identity was doubled or somehow multiplied. This does not mean, however, that Brecht was interested in dramatizing the psychology of split personalities.[50] Instead Brecht's characters tend to be presented as discrete individuals who function without any clear interiority whatsoever. Characters do not lack individualizing qualities, in other words, but their individuality is compromised because the lines of mimetic fusion with the actor are so clearly illuminated. And this relation of actor to character models (according to Brecht) is the relation of self to society. As Craig's actors tended to be overwhelmed by the mise-en-scène, so Brecht's characters cannot remain separate from their material environment or historical forces. Only in cooperative or transactional relationships, in other words, does character appear.

Brecht sensed keenly the compounded identifications that produce character in real life, and his characters cannot, therefore, readily be described by the conventional metaphors of inside and outside. It is true that a subtext accompanies the texts of most of Brecht's characters, but it is not the kind most commonly associated with the Stanislavskian system of psychologically realistic acting, in which the actor makes available to the audience the individual psychological truths that are for the most part inaccessible to the character. Stanislavskian acting is based on a narrative of psychological truths that give both stability and continuity to the notion of character. But the narrative subtexts for Brecht's characters are not exclusively psychological but social as well; hence Brecht's characters may at first appear contradictory (by comparison with characters whose acts are grounded in psychology), but their contradictions tend to disappear when they are exposed by their actors as answering to their social exigencies. Their mode of self-definition suggests a mimetic interpenetration of self with environment that is political in the broadest possible sense of the term. Brecht's most fascinating characters exist in an arena in which bodies and minds are open to the world in a continuous (self-consuming, self-producing) encounter.

A number of Brecht's plays contain such disappearing (and reappearing) characters, but surely *The Good Person of Szechwan* (*Der Gute Mensch von Sezuan*, 1940–41) is his most extensive examination of the mimetic self. The play is so well known that it needs little introduction. Like many of Brecht's works, the plot resembles a parable. On hearing a rumor that goodness and success have become irreconcilable in the world, three gods visit the province of Szechwan to investigate matters for themselves. They encounter Shen Te, a prostitute with a reputation for benevolence, and reward her handsomely for her virtue. Yet the money brings only misfortune. She buys a tobacco shop—selling tobacco being presumably more respectable than selling sex—only to be overrun by parasites who take advantage of her generosity. In order to protect herself, she imitates her cousin, Shui Ta, a shrewd businessman who ruthlessly evicts the parasites. The two identities compete for much of the rest of the play, Shui Ta gradually effacing Shen Te, and near the end Shui Ta is accused of the murder of Shen Te. The play ends with the unmasking of the multiple persons and Shen Te's explanation to gods and audience alike:

> Your prior commandment
> To be good and yet to live
> Tore me like a lightning bolt in two halves.
> (*Werke* 6: 275)

Shen Te/Shui Ta is sometimes diagnosed as suffering from the schizoid consequences of capitalism, "the internal contradictions of which," according to Keith Dickson, "force the individual to adopt two mutually antagonistic attitudes." [51] But the schizophrenia Brecht here dramatizes is more complex than this explanation suggests. Certainly Brecht is not at all interested in dramatizing abnormal psychology, but even as metaphor "schizophrenia" cannot fully express the mentality of this character. "Schizophrenia" in the popular as well as the clinical sense refers to important splits or disjunctions in the various personality functions of individuals.[52] The psychology that explains schizophrenic personalities, in turn, depends upon concepts of the self as whole or discrete or inner, notions that (as the *Lehrstücke* suggest) hardly correspond to Brecht's representations of character. The location of the self "within" presupposes an internal hierarchy of mental operations, some public, some covert, the overall effect of which expresses the subject. Thus even acts that might seem illogical or out of character can be demonstrated to be intelligible and goal-oriented: for example, one may speak of a schizophrenic's impulse to mask with aggressive behavior a need to love and be loved.[53]

The schizoid model for character thus presupposes an expressive view of behavior. A person's self, in other words, exists prior to or in some sense apart from the various gestural and verbal acts that dramatize it, or it remains somehow distinct from the various roles or masks that it assumes in order to meet life's changing situations successfully.

Such de facto existence of the self at once differentiates Brecht's view of character from the view common to various modern theories. Character for Brecht is never simply expressive of inner mental life; it is always expressed as behavior that one adopts for one's own reasons, whether of pleasure or necessity. In a sense, character is expressly theatrical, but without the hint of self-betrayal normally ascribed to mimetic acts. Consider, for example, the "Interlude" in *The Good Person of Szechwan* where Shen Te first becomes Shui Ta:

Shen Te enters, the mask and clothes of Shui Ta in hand, and sings
"The Song of the Defenselessness of the Gods and the Good People."
In our country
A useful person needs luck. Only
If he finds a powerful helper
Can he prove himself useful.
The good
Cannot help themselves and the gods are powerless.
    Why don't the gods have tanks and cannons
    Battleships and bombers and mines
    To destroy the wicked and spare the good folk?
    Matters would doubtless improve with us and with them.
She puts on Shui Ta's suit and takes a few steps in his manner.
The good
Cannot remain good for long in our country.
Where the plates are empty, the diners are soon fighting.
Ah, the commandments of the gods
Help nothing against need.
    Why don't the gods appear in our markets
    And divide laughing the bounty of stores
    And permit those who have been strengthened by bread and wine
    To behave warmly and kindly toward one another?
She puts on Shui Ta's mask and continues to sing in his voice.
To get dinner
Requires the ruthlessness of one who has built empires.
Without trampling on twelve
No one can help a wretched man.
    Why can't the gods shout from on high

That they once again will make the world good for the good
people?
Why can't they stand by the good people with tanks and with
cannons
And order: Shoot! and suffer no suffering?

(*Werke* 6: 220–21)

Brecht wrote in a note to an earlier draft of this scene that the protagonist's metamorphosis was "not in any way mystical but merely a technical solution in terms of mime and a song."[54] The absence of explanatory motivation for the transformation may prove disconcerting, and indeed many readers still interpret Shen Te's act in terms of practical psychology or politics. Shen Te feigns Shui Ta, say, as Hamlet feigns madness. Alternate explanations attribute Shen Te/Shui Ta to capitalist economics. According to Elizabeth Wright, for example, Brecht's split protagonist "is the visible image of the objective contradictions of man/woman in the bourgeois capitalist world, an image of an alienated condition."[55] In this view, the ruthless Shui Ta becomes more than a useful fiction; he is a sobering reminder that capitalism splits individuals into private moral selves on the one hand and public business selves on the other.

Such readings are not wrong—Brecht himself described his play as "a plain story about how *li gung* [an early name for his protagonist] masquerades as her cousin and to that end makes use of the experiences and qualities which her gutter existence has brought out in her."[56] But they distort the image of character that Brecht here stages. The foregoing scene, for example, frames questions of gender psychology and politics within the metaphor of theatrical performance. When Shen Te puts on Shui Ta's costume and walks and sings in his manner, her acts do not reflect a hidden psychic interiority. They indicate simply a mimetic response to a situation: Shen Te becomes Shui Ta by performing him. The replication of characters from a single character, in other words, is allowed by mimetic reciprocity; it is as if the bad cousin inhabits Shen Te's body and she his in a continuous act of empathic exchange.

The performative nature of character reveals itself in *The Good Person of Szechwan* in numerous ways. Perhaps the most obvious instance concerns gender, for, as the play's title suggests, the protagonist is curiously unsexed. It is unfortunate that English lacks an equivalent for the German *Mensch* because, as John Willett notes, "the play . . . lends itself too easily to a prettified, sentimental interpretation, particularly when the neutral

'Mensch' of the title is rendered 'Woman,' with its ensuing temptation to play the heroine as that hackneyed figure, the good-hearted prostitute."[57] Certainly Brecht endows his character with greater complexities than the stereotype suggests. The real danger in this mistranslation, however, is more subtle, and, as far as Brecht's representation of character is concerned, more pernicious. The substitution seems harmless enough—the protagonist *is* a female. But to translate *Mensch* as "woman" instates an essentialist view of character. According to this view, certain kinds of acts express a gender identity while other kinds contradict it. This suggests in turn that gendered behavior constitutes one of the hallmarks of character because it expresses that which lies within an individual. The question of identity then becomes largely a matter of psychological interiority. The private self splits off from behavior, and the "I" expressed whenever Shen Te or Shui Ta speaks becomes a mask brought into existence by the various necessities of public life.

In fact Brecht's word choice comments ironically on how even so "natural" or intrinsic an element of character as gendered behavior may be rooted in cultural politics. Shen Te must replace her nurturing femininity with masculine aggressiveness in order to survive; she is caught in a set of contradictions, therefore, that compromise her character. Yet Brecht's parable does not simply depict a society in which women must abandon their true selves to gain power. The "Mensch" of the title captures what for Brecht may well be the social ground for gendered identity. Continuous with Shen Te's transformation into Shui Ta is an instinct for imitation that transcends gender. Her transformation into Shui Ta, for example, is not an extemporaneous invention. Long before Shui Ta appears on stage he has been created as a role by the old couple:

> THE WIFE (*shaking her head*): She cannot say no. You're too good, Shen Te. If you want to keep your shop, you must be able to refuse a request now and then.
> THE HUSBAND: Say it doesn't belong to you. Say it belongs to a relative who demands a strict accounting from you. Can't you do that?
> THE WIFE: One could do that if one didn't always have to play the benefactress. (P. 187)

In becoming Shui Ta, then, Shen Te matches herself to a model of identity that already has been created for her:

THE WIFE: My dear Shen Te, why don't you turn the whole matter over to your cousin? (*To the carpenter*) Write your bill up and Miss Shen Te's cousin will pay it.

THE CARPENTER: I know these "cousins"!

THE NEPHEW: Don't laugh like a fool. I know him personally.

THE HUSBAND: A man like a knife.

THE CARPENTER: Fine, he'll get my bill. (*He tips the stand over, sits down on it, and writes out his bill.*) (P. 189)

The identity here manufactured exists only within social discourse; it is a publicly defined and publicly sanctioned fiction. Before becoming Shui Ta, Shen Te joins with others in his creation:

MRS. MI TZU: So. (*To Shen Te*) And otherwise you have no one else from whom I receive information about you?

THE WIFE (*prompting*): Cousin. Cousin.

MRS. MI TZU: You must have someone who can guarantee what I am to take into my house. This is a respectable house, my dear. Otherwise I certainly can't give you a lease.

SHEN TE (*slowly, with downcast eyes*): I have a cousin.

MRS. MI TZU: Oh, you have a cousin? Local? Then we can go straight there. What is he?

SHEN TE: He doesn't live here, he lives in another city.

THE WIFE: Didn't you say in Shung?

SHEN TE: Mr. Shui Ta. In Shung!

THE HUSBAND: But I know him! A tall, lean man.

THE NEPHEW (*to the carpenter*): You too have done business with Shen Te's cousin! About the stands!

THE CARPENTER (*grumpily*): I'm just now making out his bill. There it is! (*He hands it over*) I'll be back tomorrow morning. (*Goes out*)

THE NEPHEW (*calls after him, peeking at Mrs. Mi Tzu*): Please rest assured, her cousin will pay.

MRS. MI TZU (*with a sharp look at Shen Te*): I'll be very glad to meet him. Good evening, miss. (*Goes*). (Pp. 190–91)

This is the essence of individuality according to Brecht. To be named as the recipient of a bill constitutes irrefutable proof of one's existence. Brecht's satire on the socioeconomic creation of an individual is not farfetched; utility bills are commonly accepted as proof of individual identity, and generally speaking there is considerable evidence that people happily conform to whatever roles happen to be created for them.[58] As soon as a bill is made out in his name, Shui Ta is effectively produced by an economic structure as an identity that Shen Te can assume. The effacement of Shen Te by Shui Ta occurs as comedy, and yet her metamorphosis clearly recapitulates Brecht's view of character as external. The identity of the cousin is literally manufactured in full view of the audience. This does not mean that Shen Te necessarily lacks interiority, but it does mean that interiority for Brecht is essentially separate from character and largely irrelevant. It is only by means of publicly regulated identities that individual character manifests itself.

Put in this form, Brecht's politics of identity is by no means outdated by the worldwide collapse of socialist economics. For example, Brecht's deconstruction of character is consistent with recent feminist theory of gendered identity. His drama suggests that maleness, like femaleness, exists mainly as a performed reality. The protagonist of *The Good Person of Szechwan* affects both qualities, yet these characteristics are by no means intrinsic or natural but simply arbitrary social masks. As Judith Butler writes,

> [G]ender is in no way a stable identity or locus of agency from which various acts proceed; rather, it is an identity tenuously constituted in time—an identity instituted through a *stylized repetition of acts*. Further, gender is instituted through the stylization of the body and, hence, must be understood as the mundane way in which bodily gestures, movements, and enactments of various kinds constitute the illusion of an abiding gendered self. This formulation moves the conception of gender off the ground of a substantial model of identity to one that requires a conception of constituted social temporality.[59]

Shen Te/Shui Ta may be Brecht's most notorious split character, but this character is pathetically empty, even at those moments when he/she seems most full of emotion. Alone on stage in scene 7 Shen Te rehearses to herself and to her unborn son her plans to defend him:

Then I
At least will defend my own and must
Become a tiger. Yes, from the hour
That I've seen this, I will break
With them all and never rest
Until I have saved my son, at least him!

What I have learned in the gutter, my school,
Through brawls and deceit, now
Will serve you, son. To you
I will be good, a tiger and wild beast
To all others if need be. And it
Needs be.

(P. 249)

Moved to rage by the sight of starving children, Shen Te vows to act with
the brutality necessary to feed her own offspring. That is why her preg-
nancy is so ironically self-effacing, for biological realities compel her to
perform the role of the tigress-mother. Her compassion moves her to become a fiercely protective mother, but that identity too, like the cousin Shui
Ta, already exists as a fiction within social discourse. It is a powerful scene,
but, as is true of so many of Brecht's most intense moments, it is undercut
ironically by its own self-conscious theatrics. Shen Te's "natural" instinct
for motherhood is decentered by a process that directs attention to its inevitable economic and social consequences—corruption, greed, selective
starvation, in short, business as usual. And it is by means of this decentering that Brecht defines his protagonist's character: character is not intrinsic
but theatrical, not that which lies within, but that which, like the masks
and costumes worn by actors, is temporarily put on.

Chapter Three

Character Portraits/Portraying
Character: *Krapp's Last Tape,*
Rockaby, Catastrophe

You actually have to *be* these women.
BILLIE WHITELAW

Why are the characters created by postwar
dramatists often so resistant to traditional languages for describing character? A preliminary answer must be that these playwrights do not invariably
associate character with literary pictures of a discrete individual mind. The
attitude is a familiar one. We have seen how, from the polemical "The Actor
and the Übermarionette" to the particular designs for stage environments,
Gordon Craig made the primary grounds of theatrical performance physical and not psychological. And we recall how Brecht insists in his essays as
well as his plays that questions of motive cannot be answered by appeals
to human nature or to a coherent substratum of personal identity. Character, for Brecht, is theatrical: "The human being copies gestures, mimings,
accents. . . . Only the dead can no longer be changed by their fellow-men"
(*Werke* 7, pp. 432–33).

But of course such redefinitions of character are not unique to Brecht
and Craig. As a matter of fact, it is relatively easy to find numerous modern
and postmodern playwrights willing to testify that character is accretive
but not necessarily coherent. Strindberg in his preface to *Miss Julia* (1888)
wrote that his characters were not internally coherent beings but "con-
glomerations of past and present stages of civilization, bits from books and
newspapers, scraps of humanity, rags and tatters of fine clothing, patched
together as is the human soul."[1] Nearly a century later, Sam Shepard defines
an identical concept of character in his note to the actors of *Angel City:*
"The term 'character' could be thought of in a different way when working
on this play. Instead of the idea of a 'whole character' with logical motives

behind his behavior which the actor submerges himself into, he should consider instead a fractured whole with bits and pieces of character flying off the central theme. In other words, more in terms of collage construction or jazz improvisation."[2]

Trying to identify a single motive for so comprehensive a change in literary history can be as complicated a task as defining modernism by way of its many individual artists. But it is not therefore unprofitable to single out for close examination the character studies done by a few representative contemporary dramatists. In the first two chapters I used the work of Craig and Brecht to demonstrate two theoretical standpoints, respectively, figural and political or social, from which one might view some ways character has been represented in modern drama. I want now to broaden the study to include more recent figurations.

In denying that their characters possess a coherent inner life, Shepard and Strindberg set their personae squarely against familiar conventions of character but also apparently everyday experience. "Since the Enlightenment," writes Wayne Booth, "people have increasingly thought of their own essential natures not as something to be built, or built up, through experience with other characters but rather as something—a 'true self'—to be found by probing within."[3] The oppositions between these two views of identity are familiar enough. In the past, they have been framed as debates between art and life, between public and private identities, and between organic and mechanistic models for selfhood. Partly the persistence of the "true self" can be explained as a practical concession; no matter how fictitious in theory one believes the continuous self to be, it is necessary within a variety of existential frames (e.g., juridical, pedagogical, or economic) to believe that the identity who makes a commitment can in some real sense persist to carry it out. Even among social psychologists there seems to be some allowance made for a continuing and characteristic being in some way distinguishable from an otherwise haphazard collection of doings. Erving Goffman comments that

> The individual comes to doings as someone of particular biographical identity even while he appears in the trappings of a particular social role. The manner in which the role is performed will allow for some "expression" of personal identity, of matters that can be attributed to something that is more embracing and enduring than the current role performance and even the role itself, something, in short, that is characteristic not of the role but of the person—his personality, his perduring moral character, his animal nature, and so forth. However,

this license of departure from prescribed role is itself something that varies quite remarkably, depending on the "formality" of the occasion, the laminations that are being sustained, and the dissociation currently fashionable between the figure that is projected and the human engine which animates it. There is a relation between persons and role. But their relationship answers to the interactive system—to the frame—in which the role is performed and the self of the performer is glimpsed. Self, then, is not an entity half-concealed behind events, but a changeable formula for managing oneself during them.[4]

In the question of the subject, less may be at stake than meets the eye. As Goffman's analysis of a recurring "formula" for selfhood clarifies, it may be misleading to posit an absolute tension between views of character that refer, on the one hand, to something like an "epidermally bounded container" (the phrase is Goffman's) for certain affects and information, and, on the other, only to an indeterminate "field" or (more recently) "site" where certain forces express themselves or on which certain qualities can be written by (say) culture, language, or ideology. To state the premise very broadly, Beckett, Bernhard, and Fornes do not write dramas without character but redefine their characters according to more subtle notions of subjectivity. In their work character is written as a social or "dialogical" phenomenon or according to different "archaeologies" of the mind's interior. Individuals are "characterized," respectively, as essential particulars (that is, in terms of a given ontological—but not psychological—reality), or as "relational nuclei" (these can be thought of as psychological dyads), or as aggregations, largely mimetic composites. In each case characters are presented in such a way as to complicate their apparent subjectivity. They seem to possess no stable and predictable inner identity; sometimes they even lack a coherent body image. In these playwrights' dramas character refers less securely to a stable narrative identity and more often than not to a temporary construction or creation or depiction peculiar to time and circumstance.

Portraying Character

Actors who perform Beckett's late dramas often speak about the various difficulties they encounter in trying to fit their acting to their personae. The roles indeed make extraordinary demands. Many of the plays are unusually challenging physically: depending on the particular play, actors may be entombed or enurned, strapped down (or up), blinded or blindfolded, immobilized, or made to pace seemingly endless sets of rectangles. ("Some ballet training desirable," Beckett remarks laconically in his production notes for *Quad*.) As if physical discomfort were not enough, the texts require almost impossible concentration from actors if they are not to lose their way among a maze of subtly varying repetitions and broken syntax.

Memory alone is an inadequate guide to these labyrinthine pathways; even the slightest wandering of attention invites disaster. In the interview cited in the epigraph to this chapter, for example, Billie Whitelaw tells of her experience playing Mouth in *Not I:* "A couple of actor friends of mine, I was furious, they thought I put it all on tape. I told them, 'No it is not on tape, unfortunately. Each night I have to go through this torture, although sometimes I had the feeling I can't go on, I can't go on.' " [5]

But perhaps the most severe restriction Beckett places on his actors is his frequent injunction, "No color." To forbid actors to suit their acting to individual personae goes—or seems to go—against the core of representing character. Time and again Beckett enjoins actors *not* to act—that is, not to approach their roles analytically so as to "understand" (that is, to imagine within a narrative frame) the person they present. Above all actors feel especially pressured (often by Beckett himself) to forgo psychology for more formal modes of portraiture. According to Dame Peggy Ashcroft, who acted in Peter Hall's production of *Happy Days* (1976) and who was accustomed to "work in terms of character" so as to represent accurately the inner life of her role, "Beckett would answer questions like 'Why does she gabble as she does at a certain point?' by saying 'Because it has to go fast there.' " [6] Many actors tell of similar experiences. If the enigmatic texts were themselves not sufficient bars to naturalistic acting, Beckett was himself often at hand during rehearsals, advising if not actually directing actors to eliminate "color" from their playing.

This feature of Beckett's theater is amply documented in interviews and works of criticism, but since it is so crucial to my aims in this study it will be useful at this point to review familiar material. A very extensive summary of actors' experiences with Beckett's late plays can be found in Jonathan Kalb's important recent study, *Beckett in Performance*. In that work Kalb distinguishes between the kinds of actors' representations found respectively in Beckett's early full-length works for the stage (mainly *Godot* and *Endgame*) and the late shorter dramas:

> [T]here is no question here of good and bad acting, but rather of different types of acting, both done well. [Alvin] Epstein's skills were

undoubtedly central to his success with Lucky and Clov; for those roles demand that an actor excel at conventional character research, in order to fill out the human dispositions that Beckett's unconventional milieus leave sketchy. In *Godot, Endgame,* and the other early works, the actor may adopt a specific, eccentric personality, justify all his activities with realistic motivations, and be assured that his character's, and the play's, metaphoric aspects will come through—depending, of course, on the competency of the director. In late plays like *Ohio Impromptu,* however, that same acting technique seems to have the opposite effect of limiting the spectator's access to metaphor, as if these works lose significance in proportion to the extent that actors engage in analysis, and gain significance to the extent that they forgo it.[7]

The characters in Beckett's famous early works, whatever their eccentricities, are for the most part conventionally drawn—they have pasts (however poorly they relate them), personalities, and familiar relationships (for example, Pozzo and Lucky are master and slave), and they exist in a landscape (however barren) they can call their own. A one-leafed tree may parody a host of conventions or beliefs relating to naturalistic sets or seasonal progress, but it still calls to mind a tree; that is, *Godot* and its characters are shaped entirely by traditional mimetic assumptions.[8] Acting contexts for the late plays differ in several ways—these works are more rigorous physically, for example—but the crucial distinction between *Godot* and *Endgame* and works such as *Quad* or *What Where* involves the object of the actors' representations. The later plays not only lack external referents for character, they cannot be performed successfully—and this is the crucial point, according to Kalb—whenever actors try on their own to supply such referents.

The only problem with these excellent observations is the logical implication that character is not therefore an important element of Beckett's dramas: "[I]t is the live actor, the fact of life in the actor, that finally animates Beckett's stage pictures and amplifies the impact of their disturbing, melancholy beauty—even though that animation gains expression only through the most highly calculated sounds and movements. And every bit of psychological characterization, every hint of a complex nonfictional life extending beyond the simple picture, weakens the effect of that sense of pure existence."[9]

It may be that characters in these plays are drawn to a new compositional scheme, one requiring (in Ben Barnes's words) actors "to forfeit the notion of character."[10] At the same time (Billie Whitelaw puts it succinctly) the task for the actor in Beckett's late dramas is the same as it presumably was for Thespis: you have to *be* the character.

Before we go further, then, it is useful to pose the question of character in Beckett as simply as possible: what remains of character when character as we know it (or think we know it) has been eliminated? Conventional notions of character depend normally upon the coincidence of external spectacle with internal experience; as Michael Goldman has argued, modern representations of character invariably depend on the actor's playing a specific subtext that

> is understood to represent the authentic source of the text. The character may not be in touch with the source, but the actor is. In the Stanislavskian system, the character may not be aware of the drives or inhibitions that run beneath the text of a Hedda or a Lopakhin, but the actor makes them available to the audience as a truth in terms of which the text can be located. In the Brechtian system, this privileged truth lies in the actor's commitment to the social interpretation of the character, which gives the *gestus* its effect.[11]

Yet Beckett's texts, according to Goldman, deny the existence of such a privileged subtext; thus his actors must build character without drawing on an imagined extrinsic reality or for that matter on any kind of sustained interpretive analysis of the text at all. Indeed, according to Kalb, success in performing Beckett seems to depend on actors abandoning character in one of two ways: either actors (Whitelaw, or David Warrilow, for example) play the roles intuitively and so "never consciously adopt recognizable personalities" in the first place, or, like Hildegard Schmal, turn to a "colorless" mode of portraiture only after heroically striving and failing to find a sustainable realistic basis for their behavior.[12]

Given this abundance of informed testimony from the actors who perform Beckett's late plays—and perform them apparently in accord with the author's intentions—it is a little surprising to discover that conventional character readings pervade Beckett criticism. Monologue and voice-over, for example, are typically (and anachronously) assumed to be occasional, private revelations in the manner of sentimental asides or Romanticist confessions. One recent critic has proposed that Beckett's (and Pinter's) characters' monologues are elaborate portraits of self-deceiving minds; the aim (as with soliloquies in older dramaturgies) is psychological verisimilitude. For modern audiences the monologue is psychologically more believable than the conventional soliloquy because it capitalizes on the fact that whether or not "people" speak thoughts aloud in private . . . both real and fictional people actually do hide certain feelings not only from others but even from themselves. . . . Thus the story . . . can become a complex mechanism of revelation and concealment which uncovers, for the audience, depths of the speaker's interiority unfathomed by other theatrical conventions.[13]

There is no doubt that Beckett's characters' monologues speak of numerous acts or experiences whose credibility can be verified by testing them against actual experience. Like the reference to Charles's Wain over the new chimney in *I Henry IV*, there are moments in Beckett's literary texts whose referentiality lies beyond all reasonable dispute, and in my discussion of *Rockaby* I take several such moments into account.[14] But to treat W's monologue in *Rockaby* as the same kind of interior mental portrait as, say, the extradramatic confessions of George Barnwell in *The London Merchant* is likely to yield only a partial view of her character. Between appearances and individual inner mental life, where truth lay, Lillo saw only an absolute disjunction; as Barnwell puts it, the gap between being and seeming is "torture insupportable." Beckett, on the other hand, is less likely to trust apparently sentimental confessions (whether intentional or gratuitous) as necessarily truer to selfhood than surfaces. When, for example, in *Play,* M confesses that he loved W1 "with all my heart," one might well wonder whether his apparent confession is any more accurate an expression of selfhood than the sentiments expressed on a greeting card. Where, in this most familiar of romantic clichés, hides the individual?

I think notions of inwardness need to be resisted in giving an account of character in Beckett's playlets and dramaticules. To equate the stage space even metaphorically with human consciousness sidesteps—to name just one important issue—what seems to me to be the crucial relationship between body image and identity. Again it is Beckett's actors who provide the most useful orientation. Pierre Chabert, in an essay entitled "The Body in Beckett's Theater," writes that "in Beckett's theatre the body undergoes metamorphoses. It is *worked*, violated even, much like the raw materials of the painter or sculptor, in the service of a systematic exploration of all possible relationships between the body and movement, the body and space, the body and objects, the body and light and the body and words."[15]

The most accurate thing one can say of character in these plays is that it cannot be approached by actors (nor, presumably, by readers) looking for coherent inner landscapes for consciousness. The acting techniques most commonly evoked depend on music or gesture (when they are not intuitive or deliberately ignorant), but nearly all who act Beckett successfully stress that in any case psychology must be avoided.

A second and increasingly common approach to Beckett's late plays shifts the discussion from persons to poetry. Formalist critics discuss these plays as dramatic poems in prose, arguing for a correspondence of word and image or more elaborately for a grand collaborative genre in which "language art and theater art have finally become one." [16] A variant of this position stresses Beckett's theater as heir (ironically, given its diminutive stature) to Wagner's elaborate *Gesamtkunstwerk:* "For every element in *Footfalls*," writes James Knowlson, "is a part of a total choreography of sound, light, and movement." [17] This sounds like a lofty achievement. But if we persevere to the point of asking how such criticism distinguishes Beckett's art from that of many other avant-garde artists (to have art approach music was the ambition of the symbolists, for example), or from any well-executed stage production, for that matter, we might decide its vague insufficiencies are due in large part to its ignoring important ethical qualities of the specific text. [18]

I do not mean that Beckett's later dramas cannot helpfully be compared to dance or to music or to painting (later in this chapter I read *Krapp's Last Tape* and *Catastrophe* as paintings). But if we take the view that Beckett's greatness lies not in his prose works but in his drama ("his prose fiction," writes Kalb, "is no longer perceivable entirely apart from his drama" [19]), then it is likely that this work would be distinctive not only in its form but also in its epistemology. Reading Beckett (as in reading any major playwright) we discover what drama is capable of. This theater may indeed be "depersonalized"; but Beckett's attempt to avoid depicting conventional "depth" portraits of character leads him to record a "new language for being." [20]

The closer one examines these late works, the more one is struck by their differences from conventional short forms of theater—one-acts, impromptus, monologues. The most obvious feature is their repetitious structure. They tend obviously away from stage realism and toward formalism, toward an abstract patterning that reduces life to geometry or mechanics. By dramatizing repeated monologues or serial variations of a remembered event or story—the shape Beckett gives to works like *Play, Rockaby,* or *Ohio Impromptu*—the playwright is not merely representing aspects of life that conventional authors normally overlook. It is patently ludicrous to claim (as the claim sometimes is made) that a play like *Quad* was written to show how repetitious life can be.

Krapp's Last Tape

In "An Essay of Dramatic Poesy," John Dryden insists that dramatic action need not be mainly physical action, all strength and swordplay; instead, he argues, the noblest part of drama consists of "the painting of the hero's mind."[21] In discussing Beckett's work in the rest of this chapter I want occasionally to push further this implicit connection between theater and painting. To read plays as pictures does not mean that I regard them as exercises in choreography or as plays straining to be something other than plays; likewise, to read Beckett's achievement as a "painting" of the hero's mind does not mean that I regard him as interested primarily in creating plausible images of human psychology. Rather I propose a kind of meditation about Beckett's plays from a painterly viewpoint; describing these dramas as if they were paintings can be a legitimate way to learn more about the human figures in them. For example, one can comment about Beckett's characters as they are defined by highly disciplined uses of color, line, and light. Or one can study the way Beckett tends to create character according to a sense of visual proportions, making the human conform to geometrical or mathematical ratios. Most important perhaps will be the way a pictorial reading of Beckett highlights the differences between Beckett's portraits of character and those painted by more conventional dramatists.

At this point it is useful to clarify the difference between Beckett's characters and the visual expressiveness of stage characters in general. Once more, Strindberg provides a reference model. The informal clutter of people and objects in the opening scene of *Miss Julia* suggests the spontaneous ease with which Strindberg's characters move in the familiar spaces of their environment:

> KRISTIN *is alone. A violin is heard faintly in the distance playing a schottische, and* KRISTIN *hums the tune while she clears up after* JEAN, *washing the plate at the sink, wiping it, and putting it away in a cupboard. Then she takes off her apron, and, bringing out a little mirror from one of the drawers in the table, she props it against the jar of lilac on the table. Then, lighting a tallow candle, she heats a hairpin and curls her fringe with it. Then she goes to the door and stands listen-*

ing. As she comes back to the table, she notices the handkerchief which MISS JULIA *has left. She picks it up and smells it, then she spreads it out reflectively, smoothes it, and folds it in four, and so on.*[22]

In comparison with Kristin, Beckett's characters are radically self-contained. Little if anything connects them with unique social or historical backgrounds, and, as a matter of fact, what few references there are to such contexts are more enigmatic than enlightening. (This is true even of the more conventionally drawn early characters; it does not necessarily enlarge our view of Estragon, for example, to be told that he once threw himself into the Rhône.) It is common to see such relative isolation in terms of Beckett's habitual "lessenings," but I would add that any attempt at environmental ornamentation or specificity would betray these characters' peculiar visual expressivity. Stanton B. Garner, Jr., has shown recently how useful a "visual poetics" can be in assessing Beckett's theater.[23] I would like to extend Garner's argument in order to examine *Krapp's Last Tape* as a character portrait.

The figure Beckett creates in *Krapp's Last Tape* is in many respects at odds with conventional figural representations. In the first place, even though the scene is set in a specific interior ("Krapp's den"), Beckett stages his figure as if in hieratic isolation. He makes no attempt to depict a complete environment on the stage, and the few elements of the set—table, tape recorder, boxes—are clustered tightly around Krapp as if they formed parts of a piece of sculpture. Indeed the emphasis here—as distinct from illusionistic dramaturgy—is expressly sculptural. Krapp dominates ("clears") the surrounding space: he is placed center front, squared to face his audience directly and formally, situated in a pool of "strong white light" that is cut off sharply from the enveloping darkness. Character and environment no longer seem coextensive; walls, doors, and windows, which in naturalistic drama pointed (even if ironically, as in *Endgame*) to a physical reality, have been replaced by a uniform blackness that is to become Beckett's signatory background from now on.

The result is a commutation of pictorial values: within this new space objects lose their familiarity and become expressly iconic. At the same time there is a corresponding intensification of the character's status as figure. Parallels with the characters on Gordon Craig's stage come instantly to mind. Beckett's reorganization of stage space—it is really almost a denial of the recognizable, three-dimensional space that objects inhabit—also calls to mind some useful analogues in art history. A similar stylistic shift away from illusionist modes of representation, for example, and toward a greater degree of abstraction, occurs during the early Christian era when Roman naturalism (or its immediate successors) begins almost imperceptibly to move toward the more highly stylized art of the medieval period. The parallels between Beckett's drama and early medieval art (even though I do not wish to suggest conscious borrowings) are suggestive.[24] In both cases motion becomes arrested; figures are flattened, moved to the foreground, and squared to face the viewer. As a result the figures become separated from their backgrounds or settings which, in turn, become decorative or simply irrelevant. Perhaps most important, light and dark, rather than defining space and shape and dimensional order, begin to function independently as sources of artistic meaning in their own right.

Art historians consider it a mistake to imagine that early Christian art broke consciously with Greco-Roman realism (the notion that Christian artists were not sufficiently talented to attain classical realism is of course naïve). Rather they suggest that there occurred a deliberate "denaturing" and "archaizing" of the older artistic naturalism, so that over the course of the era "things come to look less and less like the Greco-Roman prototypes from which, ultimately, they derive."[25] I see an analogous developmental process in *Krapp's Last Tape* with respect to older naturalistic drama. Whereas Strindberg's "picture" situates the character within a world visible (as in perspective art) through the picture surface, Beckett begins in this play to cancel the effects of environment on character and at the same time highlights the remaining compositional elements that produce the illusion of character. Modifying the conventions associated with pictorially realistic drama (the three-dimensional space that "realistically" has to be there), Beckett isolates character itself as a pictorial object. Character on this stage is self-contained, self-sufficient, drawn not according to nature (as conventional dramaturgy would have it) but *drawn* nevertheless and with a powerfully descriptive vividness. Character is not primarily a likeness but more like a representation of the phenomenon of character itself, especially its provisional status. Because of its compositional complexities, Beckett's character suggests an attempt to alter or to break with the conventions of realistic depictions of characters in illusory space.

At the same time as he increases our sense of character as heraldic, Beckett collapses traditional dramatic structures for the presentation of character by mocking the conventional form of characters' dialogic interaction. Of one person, Beckett makes many; of dialogue, he makes monologic discourse. Bits and pieces of the character identified nominally as

Krapp are spread everywhere, and the existence of a vast storehouse of taped "Krapps," each identifiably different from all others, underscores ironically how their possessor can never collect them all even though he seems to want to. Even the sounds of the voices seem to indicate the existence of different (and now missing) persons: the old Krapp's voice differs to such an extent from the voices heard on tape that they seem weirdly discordant; the effect is similar to a boy's experience of adolescence in that for a period of months he possesses two distinct voices each of which locates almost simultaneously the real person.

These parodic discontinuities threaten to separate Krapp into a series of discontinuous parts. To the extent that it is Krapp whom we hear via the machine, he speaks as an original. Like a bottle in which is discovered a lost manuscript, the tape recorder functions as an authenticating device for a narrative; the machine affirms that character—Krapp's irreducible self—exists somewhere "out there." But insofar as the presence on stage of the "real" Krapp creates the impression that it is another who is speaking, the taped representation becomes a misrepresentation. It is a perfect image of mimetic transgressiveness. The Krapp we see repeatedly denies the relevance of the recorded voice, either consciously ("KRAPP *curses, switches off, winds tape forward, switches on again*") or unconsciously ("Memorable equinox?").[26] To the extent that the voices represent themselves as authorities, they betray one another. In effect, Beckett rearranges the conventional stage treatment of temporal continuity. Whereas character in drama normally appears as a subject repeated over time, Krapp is presented as if in an arrested moment, almost as if he were the subject not of a play but a painting. One can still speak of the play as a powerful character portrait and yet feel as if the drama lacks the temporal structuring on which our sense of character in realist drama depends, namely, the demonstration of a continuing identity that repeats itself through time.

Paradoxically, then, even the words that ought to give spectators the illusion of this character's individuality are themselves tainted. The same "iterability" threatens Old Krapp as well.[27] The integrity of his speech is compromised precisely by the mechanical medium that is supposed to preserve it. Krapp's live discourse sounds as distant from the "real" Krapp as the words he spoke thirty years ago:

> KRAPP: Just been listening to that stupid bastard I took myself for thirty years ago, hard to believe I was ever as bad as that. Thank God that's all done with anyway. (*Pause.*) The eyes she had!
> (*Broods, realizes he is recording silence, switches off, broods.*

Finally.) Everything there, everything, all the— (*Realizes this is not being recorded, switches on.*) Everything there, everything on this old muckball, all the light and dark and famine and feasting of . . . (*hesitates*) . . . the ages! (P. 62)

The central image of *Krapp's Last Tape* consists of an old man becoming one with a tape recorder; Krapp's progressive identification with his recorder (described by Pierre Chabert in his production notes) empties him of substance and makes him appear childish, even infantile.[28] The image of an individual being absorbed by his environment suggests another front on which character in the traditional sense is here under siege. Krapp's empathic relationship with his machine recalls Craig's *Acis and Galatea,* in which the chorus was clothed so as to be absorbed by the set. In Beckett's play, as in Craig's, the recording apparatus and the character are coextensive physically as well as psychologically, and, as the play progresses, Krapp and his machine are seen to form a "common mass."[29]

It is this dissolution or dispersal of character that seems in particular to interest Beckett, as if he were exploring the boundaries between psychic elements that can sensibly be attributed to character and those that exist apart from it. Beckett does not really dramatize the contradictions that may be found within the mind of a single person, for Krapp is a character largely emptied of psychic interiority. Thus to describe Krapp in terms of Aristotelian mimesis is not necessarily inappropriate—Beckett in his notebooks calls him "dreameaten"—but it is partly misleading.[30] Comments from Beckett's production notebooks prove that Krapp retains few of the features of the desiring but thwarted subject of conventional drama. Beckett always insisted that Krapp was "debris," an image that suggests psychic dispersal or decentering rather than internalized conflict.[31] Likewise, Beckett made clear that it is not error or ignorance—and certainly neither hamartia nor hubris—on Krapp's part that dooms him. Old Krapp knows by the end of the play that his dreams were his ruin, but Beckett denies that his character should have (much less could have) chosen more wisely. Krapp cannot be understood as a modernized Oedipus, a man whose tragedy can be ascribed to a choice made in ignorance. During rehearsals for a 1977 production of *Krapp* in Berlin, Beckett described "with a smile the image of an old Krapp who had made the opposite decision: surrounded by an aged wife and many, many children . . . 'Good God!' "[32] On another occasion, Dougald McMillan reports, "Beckett said to me, laughing, 'I thought of writing a play on the opposite situation with Mrs. Krapp, the girl in the punt, nagging away behind him, in which case his failure and his solitude would be exactly the same,' which only goes to show how little importance should be given to the plot seen in isolation."[33]

We need only take this argument one step further to see that Krapp's every defining activity, from the fondling of a banana to the annual recording and replaying of personal memoirs, is grounded ironically in mimesis. His commitment to record and to retrieve the past, for example, discloses a need to create the self by repeating it. The existence of a ledger suggests that Krapp has at his disposal a whole memory bank of historical documentation, and his growing impatience with certain taped materials—the memorable equinox, the vision on the jetty—imply his need to return to a particular "hour of repetition."[34] The desire to record himself at age sixty-nine yields to a deeper desire to master lost time by repeating it. Three separate times Krapp listens to a portion of tape describing an event on a punt; three times, retrieving a memory that is itself already a memory, he enacts a ritual of "absent presence":

> I asked her to look at me and after a few moments—(*Pause.*)—after a few moments she did, but the eyes just slits, because of the glare. I bent over to get them in the shadow and they opened. (*Pause. Low.*) Let me in. (*Pause.*) We drifted in among the flags and stuck. The way they went down, sighing, before the stem! (*Pause.*) I lay down across her with my face in her breasts and my hand on her. We lay there without moving. But under us all moved, and moved us, gently, up and down, and from side to side. (P. 61, also p. 63)

Krapp plays this portion of his tape just before the play ends. Beckett does not specify an affective state for Krapp, only that toward the end of the recording his lips begin to move in accord with the words to which he is listening. That mimetic act perhaps marks the limit of Krapp's self-understanding. There seems no reason to doubt that he is repeating a text he knows by heart, and Krapp's ultimate silence therefore conveys more eloquently than words his recognition of loss.

It is tempting for this reason to see Krapp as a pathetic fool, but Krapp's attempt to retrieve lost love is no mere romantic sentimentalism. In Beckett's view, the fact that Krapp fails in his attempt to recover this particular moment of the past is less important than the pure compulsion to repeat. But Krapp's fantasies of the past expose ironically the fantastic nature of that time. Hence the perfect irony of the tape banks: the ironic contrasts dramatized by Krapp's listening to the taped voices prove that the original scenes themselves are already fatally divided from themselves. Every recording points toward an evanescent "original" that is itself, by virtue of its having been recorded, only a trace of an absent reality. One could say of *Krapp's Last Tape* that it dramatizes a peculiar modern variant of narcissism. The protagonist installs mimesis—here mechanical reproduction—at the center of his existence in order to preserve a stable identity over time, and in so doing Krapp in effect winds up being nobody.[35]

Krapp's Last Tape, then, is a tale of Manichaean asceticism, but it is also an ironic exposé of character defined only by mechanical, mocking repetition.[36] Beckett's play insists that repetition is the primary human reality. Krapp longs for a version of a unity he had known with the woman in the boat, but that unity is itself defined in terms of one that is prior. His words suggest that he searches not for a particular person but a particular relationship. He dreams of finding the source, the "original," or the first time that underwrites repetition. That is why, in what is perhaps the most moving passage in the play, he cries out for a return to origins, to home and childhood:

> Lie propped up in the dark—and wander. Be again in the dingle on
> a Christmas Eve, gathering holly, the red-berried. (*Pause.*) Be again
> on Croghan on a Sunday morning, in the haze, with the bitch, stop
> and listen to the bells. (*Pause.*) And so on. (*Pause.*) Be again, be again.
> (*Pause.*) All that old misery. (P. 63)

What is striking finally about the passion with which Krapp fantasizes his return to origins, however, is that he simultaneously experiences that passion with repulsion: "all that old misery." This is a paradox of which Krapp remains largely ignorant, though from a psychological perspective such ambivalence is perfectly consistent with Krapp's behavior. As with an infant or schizophrenic, Krapp's ambivalence may be characteristic of a particular psychic conflict in which the subject says "yes" and "no" simultaneously.[37] Following Freud, one might say that Krapp embodies a specific conflict of needs in which he strives simultaneously to immerse himself in otherness and also to articulate and differentiate himself in his own person. This is what his annual ritual of origins seems to be saying: we repeat ourselves in order to recover oneness of being (here imaged as an original union with the mother) and we know simultaneously that our desire for oneness is a desire for a fantasy. Beckett dramatizes ambivalence as an aspect first of Krapp's nostalgia for a lost paradise and secondly as his protagonist's way of coping with irretrievable loss. *Krapp's Last Tape* confirms the desire of the adult to return to childhood as the model for originary unity, but the machine insists that any such return is an impossible fantasy. There is no way that Krapp can ever be anything but an other to himself.

Character and Empathy in *Rockaby*

Definitions of character in terms of ironic mimicry are even more pronounced in Beckett's more recent works for theater, for example, in *That Time* and *Footfalls,* but especially in *Rockaby.* In *Rockaby,* as in *Krapp's Last Tape,* conflict develops between alternate versions of the same basic sequence of events. An old woman (W) sits in her rocking chair and rocks on stage, while a taped voice (V) narrates repeatedly certain events from the woman's life. It is clear from the content of the monologue as well as from the interrelation between W and the voice on tape that the voice speaks the woman's own thoughts. Several times, for example, the narrative ceases, but each time it stops W begins it again by requesting, "More." In the unique dramaturgical style that Beckett creates for his numerous theatrical monologists, content and syntax thus give the impression of a tale that has been told and retold countless times. In the fourth act (or movement) of the play, the voice tells of the last days of the woman's mother:

> right down
> into the old rocker
> mother rocker
> where mother rocked
> all the years
> all in black
> best black
> sat and rocked
> rocked
> till her end came
> in the end came
> off her head they said
> gone off her head
> but harmless
> no harm in her
> dead one day
> no
> night
> dead one night

in the rocker
in her best black
head fallen
and the rocker rocking
rocking away
                    (P. 280)

This passage once again shows Beckett's tendency to picture consciousness as a kind of interchange between versions of a divided self. W hears a voice telling stories in much the same way that Krapp listens to himself, and similar motives govern both characters' desires to rehear familiar tales. The voice speaks memories for the old woman in a poignant effort to keep them (and her relationship with her mother) alive. But here too the relationship of tale and teller is ambivalent. Like Krapp, like the speakers of *Play* (and like so many of Bernhard's tortured protagonists), W ceaselessly repeats the past in an effort both to save it and to exorcise it. Even as she takes pleasure in hearing a familiar story, repetition intrudes as a mechanism that does not compensate for loss but only substitutes for it.

But there are differences between W's narrative and the obsessive, mechanistic repetitions that identify Krapp or May in *Footfalls*. Note, for example, how at one point W unexpectedly interrupts her story with an odd retraction:

dead one day
no
night
dead one night

Why, one asks, this peculiar verbal backtracking? The answer tells us much about the way Beckett's verbal decorations can on occasion give the illusion of psychological depth. Whitelaw's performance of this reversal ("authorized," by the way, by Beckett's syntax) turns what could have been stylized pathos into something less harrowing and yet more full of mystery and emotion simply because W insists on telling the truth. During the commentary that precedes this complication in the narrative, Whitelaw listens intently but passively: head down, eyes closed, rocking slowly, as if listening to a favorite recording or speaking a familiar poem to herself. Her attitude combines passivity with satisfaction, even pleasure; she is wholly absorbed by her story, almost as if—like May—she were "not quite there." But the words "dead one day" bring instant change. It is a stunning moment: Whitelaw jerks her head up, eyes fully open, alert, alarmed. "No," the voice corrects itself. "Night. Dead one night." No sooner has this fact been established than Whitelaw again changes her expression. She appears satisfied, even pleased, and settles down to hear the remainder of the story. Her behavior in this brief sequence resembles nothing so much as that of a child listening to a favorite story. Pleasure in such cases depends upon absolute fidelity to the text that the listener knows by heart. Yet the submission to a repeated text does not result in an endless repetitive sequence. In replacing the conventional narrative idiom "one day" with its inverse, "one night," the voice restores our faith in its accuracy *and* in its ability to return to "originality." The memory of the mother can be kept alive only by resisting the corrosive effects of linguistic habit.

Actors do not have to bring to such moments a recognizable personality in order to make them effective dramaturgically as representations of character. Whitelaw plays this sequence without "color"—that is, without seeming to bring to it any psychological motivation—and yet one feels the presence of character so keenly that it is harrowing. It is a moment of intense action, as Dryden might have understood it, and so vividly paints the hero's mind. Despite the abstraction of W from time and space, in other words, Whitelaw acts her in accord with naturalistic motives. She assumes at some level that the grief W feels is real, and that the only way to represent it is to reach it by identifying with it.

It is true that the foregoing analysis leaves many questions of character unanswered. Who is this woman? When and where does this take place? Nevertheless, from a psychoanalytic perspective, what little material exists is rich. In fact Beckett in this work treats familiar psychological materials of Western tragedy. Like *Oedipus Rex* and *Hamlet, Rockaby* is a play about parents and children; and, like both earlier tragedies, *Rockaby* shows that the relationship between parent and child is turbulent and deeply ambivalent.

At the same time Beckett's drama deals with a thirst for imitation so desperate that conventionally realistic characters and characterizations look shallow against the woman in *Rockaby*. The play clearly dramatizes mimesis from a new angle, defining it as an overpowering need on the part of a child to identify with a parent. And if the child happens to be an old woman and the parent long dead, what does that matter? Childhood is not a matter of years; it is rather a relationship with one's parents, in particular a mimetic involvement with the persons who brought us into the world. *Rockaby* implies that the bonds between parent and child lie very deep and involve not only ambivalence and fierce competition but also instinctive identification, a kind of desperate shadowing born out of love and need. W not only narrates the death of her mother. She dresses like her mother and rocks in her mother's chair, and for much of the play she repeats herself in an autistic manner until finally she enacts her mother's death.

The key to this pattern of increasing identification of child and parent goes beyond language to include a concept of body image and mimetic engulfment. It is a theater of representation that is yet not mere representation because it is far too enveloping, far too troubling. In the first place, Beckett has created a character whose body image is connected with that of her absent mother. At the immediate level of appearances the distinctions between W and her mother have been erased. By dressing in "best black" like her mother, W constructs her appearance in the image of a loved one who is otherwise beyond reach. This act can be understood within a psychological frame as a kind of merging with her mother; if the mother's clothes become part of the daughter, she isn't really gone. We confront a paradox of character: here it seems that Beckett's nonrepresentational theater best represents the real syntax of human identity as fusion of self and other. References to the real world are almost nonexistent in *Rockaby*, and yet the primary ground for performance in this respect is not music or poetry but psychic reality. We may adduce one similar case from real life: G. Alan Stoudemire tells of a woman who carefully distributed the clothes of her dead husband among the belongings of her new spouse so as to conflate their two identities.[38] The anecdote corresponds not only with the activities of Beckett's protagonist but with Whitelaw's performance of the part. Whitelaw's own mother died shortly before the play opened, writes Enoch Brater, "and when the actress was going through her mother's possessions, she came upon a jar of cold cream. She suddenly realized that the last hand to touch it was her parent's. She placed the jar on her dressing room table and, before going on stage to perform *Rockaby*, she dipped her finger in the cold cream. She did that for every performance, 'for luck and for memory.'"[39]

Here the love and need that motivate the actor are identified with the definition of character. Whitelaw acts in such a way that her own identifications with her mother become thematic. *Rockaby* is thus a drama about identity as well as about the role identification plays in the formation of the self. In the process of listening to her own (recorded) voice, W increasingly absorbs the qualities of her dead parent so that in dying mother and daughter become a single identity. In French the play is titled *Berceuse*, a word that links in somber fashion the images of cradle, lullaby, and rocking chair. Mother and daughter, age and childhood, sleep and death become fused in a single compelling image.

But Beckett's title contains perhaps an irony even more sinister: it insists that the authority of the parent is so great as to deny the child an original, independent existence. We can see this most clearly in the English "rockaby," which refers to the traditional lullaby that mothers sing to their children; it calls to mind a whole class of songs as well as an idealized image of mother and child. "Rockaby" implies more than a metaphoric compression of cradle and grave, therefore, and the English title complicates character in a way that is as new as it is disquieting. Whatever comfortable images we associate with mothers crooning to their children, most lullabies are conspicuously rhetorical. The lullaby is sung specifically to quiet a child, especially to put it to sleep. We tell ourselves it is an act of love, and I cannot believe it is not. But that common belief can easily obscure another purpose. The lullaby is also an incantatory act, a bit of magic performed by a person skilled in seduction, and part of that skill consists in shifting the infant's attention away from itself and its body to a self-awareness via the body image of the parent. Beckett's title implies that the lullaby stands for a kind of engulfment of child by parent; it constitutes an attempt by the parent to dominate the child. She (or he) stands in for the child and becomes the primary means by which the child interprets itself. Unavoidably this standing in is unacknowledgeable; it may even—and this is the cruelest implication of Beckett's title—be illicit.

Does the mother of *Rockaby,* then, represent a model that the child chooses? Or is the parent a role that the child has no choice but to play? The child is engulfed in the parent; this is perhaps the way life is most like theater. In *Rockaby* (as in *Krapp's Last Tape*) we sense the identification with the mother long before she appears in the text. Beckett specifies that the chair in which W rocks should have "rounded inward curving arms to suggest embrace," and the chair's mechanical rocking (like the punt in *Krapp's Last Tape*) establishes a soothing, rhythmic mood. Beckett's production notes emphasize the mimetic strategy of W's actions. Her mother died

> in her best black
> head fallen
> and the rocker rocking.
>   (P. 280)

So W costumes herself for death; she wears a "black lacy highnecked evening gown. Long sleeves. Jet sequins to glitter when rocking. Incongruous flimsy headdress set askew with extravagant trimming to catch light when rocking" (p. 273). As for W herself, she is to appear "prematurely old. Unkempt grey hair. Huge eyes in white expressionless face. White hands holding ends of armrests" (p. 273).

These details are surprisingly extravagant. They give the somber mise-en-scène an unexpected sensual appeal, but at the same time they suggest an entirely different mood. There is an angle from which *Rockaby* looks like bizarre comedy. It reminds one of *commedia*, with W as Pierrot. The huge, staring eyes, the pallid face and hands, the flamboyant, theatrical costume—such details almost make the woman's pathos ring hollow. In this context W seems less tragic than naïve and moonstruck, the very embodiment of the faithful and foolish Pierrot. One is tempted to agree with the actor Irene Worth, whose understanding of the play Beckett doubted because she could not take the role seriously.[40] As for W's dying words, they are almost a parody of the inner harmony and rhetorical composure one expects of tragic protagonists:

> rock her off
> stop her eyes
> fuck life
> stop her eyes
> rock her off
> rock her off[.]
>   (P. 282)

Obscenities are scarcely remarkable on the contemporary stage, but rarely are they used with such devastating effect. Hearing them, one is caught up in an agony of disbelief; the tragic decorum that normally consoles us at the end of a play is brutally violated. It is a shock that the dying woman's last words sound so little like "last words." Moreover, the final couplet is an echolalic inversion of her own mental state as well as that of her mother: rock her off / off her rocker. High seriousness suddenly becomes obscene humor. In an age in which tragicomic effects have become commonplace, even expected, it is an arresting and sinister moment. If nothing else, it proves that Beckett can convert any experience into burlesque.

The comic dimension of *Rockaby* is invariably discounted (Beckett has said the play is "not a funny piece"),[41] and in stressing its potential for humor I risk being misunderstood. It would not be appropriate to discuss *Rockaby* as essentially comedic. In this play, as in most of Beckett's late works (but in contrast to the early plays), the comedic imagery exists in traces or fragments and cannot produce a distinct aesthetic response. The grotesquerie with which W imitates her mother can be understood as a kind of subjugation to the parent so that in death the daughter can be said to enact a kind of suicide. W exists only as the double of V. In the end the question of identity remains unanswered as both mother and daughter vanish; only a metaphor of theater remains.

This is not the first time Beckett treats the question of selfhood in terms of the parent-child relationship. But nowhere else does he express so graphically the link between the body's spontaneous mimetic predispositions and the necessary ground of individual identity. For W (as for an infant) there is no stable and coherent sense of separateness that differentiates her from her parent. Indeed, like an infant, W's responsiveness to the parent is so great that despite her age she remains susceptible to postural "impregnations" or "transgressions." As W nears death her experience becomes increasingly syncretic:

> dead one night
> in the rocker
> in her best black
> head fallen
> and the rocker rocking
> rocking away
> so in the end
> close of a long day
> went down
> in the end went down
> down the steep stair
> let down the blind and down
> right down
> into the old rocker
> those arms at last
> and rocked
> rocked
> with closed eyes
> closing eyes[.]
>   (Pp. 280–81)

"Those arms at last": the words are heartbreaking, for they reveal the woman's longing for an original symbiosis. There is simply no way of talking about W without taking into account V and the dead mother, not to mention all the other voices that echo throughout the text. "Character" in this case is not individualistic but synchronic as the daughter literally dies the mother's death.

Thus character in *Rockaby* is not a self-sufficient subject but a being who is formed from beginning to end by mimetic interaction. The daughter lives (and dies) in the body and words of the mother, as the mother lives and dies again in the child. Between daughter and mother there exists a constant empathic exchange that in Whitelaw's performance especially becomes choreographic, symphonic. These intercorporeal synchronizations suggest that W has no continuous and coherent sense of separateness that differentiates her from her parent. Both Beckett's text and Whitelaw's performance provide compelling evidence of the way our primordial sociality influences self-development and self-definition. Another way of putting this is to say that in *Rockaby* (as in *Krapp's Last Tape*) there is no clear way to distinguish self from other. Character is not self-expression but imitating, resonating, ghosting.

Identity in *Rockaby* therefore results from a process of mirroring and echoing, and the subject, Beckett suggests, is formed according to the body's spontaneous mimetic predisposition. The play locates within an aged protagonist the instinctive sociality of infantile experience. Repetition-compulsion offers W a way to remember the dead mother as well as a substitution for her or for unretrievable memories, and it also provides her a method of self-definition. Like a child, she constructs herself through the gestures and postures of the adult. (In Freudian terms, one could say that W exhibits the developmental stage called "primary narcissism," in which the child is "especially susceptible to mimetic transfer influences—postural 'impregnations' and 'transgressions' by the other." [42]) Because Beckett's protagonist exists only by virtue of her mirrorings and echoings, furthermore, the image we see is more like a photographic negative than a conventional portrait. One might say that W does not so much remember her mother as act her; as Freud wrote in "Recollection, Repetition, and Working Through" (1914), "We may say that here the patient *remembers* nothing of what is forgotten and repressed, but that he expresses it in *action*. He reproduces it not in his memory but in his behaviour; he *repeats* it, without of course knowing that he is repeating it." [43]

This is a reasonably coherent description of the relationship between W and her mother, especially when one takes into account the Freudian dynamic that links the repetition-compulsion with memory and grief. In "Mourning and Melancholia," for example, Freud comments on the way in which the mourner sometimes blames himself or herself for the loss of the loved one. The dead mother haunts the text of *Rockaby* almost with the force of fate. As W replays in her mind the events of her life, she searches constantly for the peace and sanctity of which the rocking chair—and her mother's arms—are the model. At the end of her life W still lives in symbiotic relationship with her mother. She possesses no stable and coherent sense of separateness that differentiates her from her parent, and she experiences this synchronicity with love as well as with resistance. Billie Whitelaw (in the Buffalo performance) speaks the first request for "more" with vigor, but as the play proceeds her manner grows more timid so that the last "more" sounds less like a distinct word than a primitive moan— "maaa." For the audience, the more W grows as a stage character the more she returns to the impotence of childhood, and her death is an ironic inversion of the tragic protagonist's ultimate self-realization. Beckett's character dies when she discovers total identification with the mother.

Surely, therefore, the merging of daughter with mother is a discouraging sight. The viewer interprets all the woman's acts in terms of a displaced and unappeasable mother-love, and, while that love is indisputably total it is also enigmatic. In the film of the production of *Rockaby* Alan Schneider insists that the play is "not about dying." "It's about accepting death," he tells Whitelaw, and he speaks of her character as an image of "Mother Earth." One wishes perhaps for the consolations of such philosophy, but the view that mother and daughter meet in the peacefulness of death is fondly romantic. In *Rockaby* character takes on a brittleness and an insubstantiality rarely seen on stage. What does it mean, first of all, to say that the daughter literally becomes the mother? In becoming her mother, W is finally able to overcome the mourning occasioned by irretrievable loss. Though she dies, in a way she gets what she wants; Whitelaw imagined her character as driven to die, and, near the end of her working copy of the script, she wrote the comment, "Hurray!"[44]

But what does it mean to say that W wants to die? Because the form of the mother ultimately informs the daughter, W can only be described in negative terms. Possessed by the memory of the mother, the daughter experiences her self in terms of an alienation:

> time she stopped
> let down the blind and stopped
> time she went down
> down the steep stair
> time she went right down

was her own other
own other living soul[.]

                    (P. 281)

To the extent she identifies with the reflected image of the mother, in other words, W radically distorts her own identity. Confronted with an increasingly potent image of the parent, one might ask, with Jacques Lacan, Where is the child? The more the parental presence is felt, the more problematic becomes the status of the child. In this case the woman's cry for "more" is not simply the request of a subject to hear once more her own personal myth. It is the plaintive cry of the impotent and unformed child for something more than it has been given—that is, something else, something in addition, some selfhood not made up of role-playing. *Rockaby* produces character ironically: the representation of self is set against the perfect sign for its denial. Identity is the result of an act of theater so automatic, so deep, so mysterious that it is written in our genes. Beckett is not dramatizing the failure of family relations, simply their failure to be defined except as an untranslatable mystery.

Let me sketch this a bit further. *Rockaby* exhibits a character who constructs herself experientially—a kind of self-fashioning. Yet the character that emerges must be counted as two separate persons, parent and child, who share a single body image. Both claim the unique identity that only one can hold; the daughter cannot develop without competing with the mother for space, for objects, for experience. So far, we are on familiar theatrical ground. Thus, for example, the tragedy of Oedipus is that he should compete with his father while trying to avoid doing so. But traditionally dramatists have focused on the hostile competitions between sons and fathers—on sons who supplant or attack their fathers, or on fathers who consciously or unwittingly destroy their sons. Moreover, there has been in the history of drama and criticism of drama too strong a tendency to focus upon the strong, the self-sufficient, or the rebellious child—Oedipus, Cordelia, Hamlet. There are other important parent-child realities, and it is these that Beckett dramatizes. I confess that *Rockaby* made little sense to me until an evening several years ago when I sat with friends watching homemade videos. Seeing for the first time the image of her own body on screen, one of the women commented in awe that she could no longer doubt that she was her mother's child. She moved so much like her mother, she said, that she was profoundly unnerved. The film provided an expressly theatrical insight into a relatively unfamiliar aspect of her identity: she saw herself repeating, ghostlike, a "text" she did not write and did not know she had been playing out. The sense of helplessness she felt when confronted by her instinctive mimicry suddenly illuminated for me the ghostly traces that surround Whitelaw's performance of *Rockaby*. It is as if the child's body image and that of the parent, as Paul Schilders argues (in a general context), were made of "similar material." [45]

The mother's image in *Rockaby* is both spectral and consoling. Though she does not appear, she haunts the play and her daughter's life with promises that can never be kept. As W turns for companionship to one person after another, she searches continually for "another like herself" of which her mother is the model. One thing the published text by itself does not bring out fully is the extent to which a mother or mothering figures dominate the behavior of the protagonist. Beckett stated during rehearsals that the "rocker is mother's—no richness, no ornateness"; "the woman in no way initiates the rock; the memory initiates the rock"; most important, Beckett stressed, the piece was a "lullaby." [46] Thus the playwright makes explicit the intimate interactions between the protagonist and such gestures and language as might indicate her lack of real autonomy in the felt presence of the parent. And Whitelaw seems to have incorporated W's passivity into her approach to the role. The actor, like the character, is susceptible to a range of mimetic transgressions. Acting Beckett, she said, was like "playing the right music." "Beckett blows the notes; I want them to come out of me." "Once I've heard Beckett say it—just once—I've more or less got in my head the music of what it is he wants. That doesn't necessarily restrict me, but I think 'Right. I know what music they're playing.'" Beckett's "mother rocker," Whitelaw said, was like a harp; her acting, she wrote, was to be "soft, monotonous, no colour, soothing, rhythmic." [47]

Instinctive sociality—the passive response to the will of others—is so deeply inherent in *Rockaby* as to suggest a veritable synchrony of persons and voices. What in conventional theater are moments of self-centered intensity are here redefined as intercorporeal and interpersonal synchronizations. Beckett defines human beings not as self-contained and self-sufficient subjects but as creatures who are formed from birth to death by synchronies of words and acts. The essence of the tragedy in *Rockaby*— and Whitelaw's performance highlights this especially—is that our bodies carry mimetic predispositions without our knowing it. As soon as we are born we become impersonators—of our parents, of those close to us, ultimately of ourselves.

One more aspect of the uncanny reciprocity of character in *Rockaby* is worth considering. I refer to the act of listening—the staging of a "listening self" that has become in recent years almost a hallmark of Beckett's theater. As the life of W draws to a close, she returns to her mother's body image and to the incantatory power of the mother's language, the lullaby. At the end of her life, therefore, we are made to think of the conditions of her earliest listening experience. To have reached this moment (the end of the play) we must accept the version of her life that W tells us. We must accept, like W, that there are important things missing and that apparently trivial incidents appear again and again. Most of all, we must accept the intoxicating tone and rhythm of the actor's voice. Intimate, participatory, communicative, *Rockaby* involves us in a relationship of respectful hearing and understanding. If we wish, we can, like W, shut our eyes, but the sound of the play penetrates our entire body. We cannot help being affected by what we hear.

In this way the representation of character in *Rockaby* opens for us the possibility of an identification with language and narrative. If we assume that Beckett's words represent the mind of the hero in the conventional individualist sense, then the repetitions of *Rockaby* will seem unintelligible, nonsensical, absurd; we will be deaf to what W is saying. But there are many different ways to be one with people and things, and the performance of *Rockaby* binds audience and performer in a continuous aural interchange. Experientially we too become decentered—mimetically involved with the spoken words of another.

There is some evidence to indicate that in infancy we shift from an awareness that is mainly auditory to a consciousness that is vision-oriented. Hannah Arendt asserts that mental activity is so often expressed in terms of sight or vision "that we seldom find any consideration bestowed on it, as though it belonged among things too obvious to be noticed. . . . [But] if one considers how easy it is for sight, unlike the other senses, to shut out the outside world, and if one examines the early notion of the blind bard, whose stories are being listened to, one may wonder why hearing did not develop into the guiding metaphor for thinking." [48]

In the end, despite a relatively high degree of abstraction, Beckett's character takes on a realism that makes one reconsider initial impressions of formalized noncharacterhood. By way of mimesis, *Rockaby* returns protagonist and audience to an origin of sorts, a first demonstration of the power of mimesis to define human character in terms of the magical first phase of being. An audience, like an infant, "hears" with the body as a whole. Hearing in this primitive sense is global, elementary; and mimesis in this sense is not only a matter of philosophy or aesthetics but the inevitable source of our selves.

Catastrophe and the End of Individualism

Beckett's late plays seem by definition "figural"—character is invariably at the center of these works—and yet the subjects he figures differ profoundly from the portraits of character drawn by Strindberg or Ibsen. The figural distortion apparent in Beckett's dramas, the inseparability of body and drapery, the sense of the image's manifold expressivity, and above all the diminishing importance of illusory space derive aesthetically less from inherited stage conventions than from the examples of modernist painters. In this respect, of course, Craig clearly provides the model. Whereas in older illusionist dramaturgy, space was the reality within which character was simply located, Beckett—like Craig, of course, but also like Cézanne, Braque, or Picasso—does not think of his medium as providing a window onto a constructed illusion of the third dimension. Instead he sees it more in terms of a pictorial surface, organized in terms of shape, color, and symbol.

Beckett's work can be understood, therefore, as an important experiment in redefining the grounds for representing character. By unmooring his characters from any identifiable location in represented space, he brings viewers as close as possible to the experience of character—as close as possible, that is, to the experience of *being*, in the philosophical sense of the term. Even in the early plays (*Godot, Endgame*) Beckett tends in this direction, but over the course of his playwriting career he extends this strategy until it becomes possibly the most compelling feature of his theater. What strikes one in contemplating that theater is not its minimalist aesthetics or its potential for allegory but a negative quality, what one might describe as the loss of the obligation on the part of the playwright to place before us an illusion of the familiar space through which our bodies normally move. And it is this illusion that we miss while watching Beckett's plays.

"Absurdity" is entirely the wrong word, therefore, for the condition Beckett depicts. This theater not only alienates the human from familiar signifying ground, but depicts character by emphasizing its isolated, uncompromising figural reality. That is to say, we should think of Beckett's characters not psychologically but figurally. Characters, in turn, are rendered as standardized units or forms, distinguishable only in the most purely functional senses, as are pieces in a puzzle or tokens on a board game.

In terms of the history of art in the modern era, it sounds like a logical step from Ortega y Gasset's "dehumanization" of art to Beckett's spare figures. And yet the impression of such ruthless "dehumanization"—as I hope my discussions of *Krapp's Last Tape* and *Rockaby* have shown—is art of the theater in which character is neither obscured nor abandoned but shines with marvelous lucidity. As Brenda Bynum, who has acted in and directed *Come and Go,* said in an interview:

> It was the first time I had to deal with Beckett's requirements to be exact, which for your average theater person is a red flag: they think, "How can I adjust it, how can I fit *me* into the part to make it a little different?" When I actually brought the women together, I found that there was in fact freedom. I found myself as a director watching these women, seeing a kind of graceful dance which seemed to me to be there. To use another image, they seemed almost like three bells standing in a row that you would lift and ring from moment to moment.[49]

All the late dramas by Beckett reconceptualize character in such strikingly graphic ways. In many of these plays—for example, *Ohio Impromptu, Quad,* or *What Where*—characters' identities are figured rhythmically or mathematically, as if the truths of human selfhood could be represented more accurately by means of geometry or motion than by rhetoric. Certainly the actors who perform in these singular works typically forgo understanding the characters they imitate in favor of purely structural representations.[50] In these works (as occasionally in some experimental dramas of expressionist playwrights) characters become visual compositional elements in their own right. Color and geometry replace narrative or psychology, reducing the representation of consciousness to a purely theoretical component of drama. As if to restrict their individuality further, Beckett does not name characters in these late works; he merely codes them by letter. Also their positions on stage are contrived so as to square them frontally or to emphasize their silhouettes. In consequence many of them become pictorial or architectural elements. P in *Catastrophe,* B in *Nacht und Träume,* and W in *Rockaby* are elevated as if Beckett conceived them as pieces of monumental sculpture: W sits in a rocking chair, her hands grasping the armrests, her feet above the floor; B, the dreamt self, is glimpsed on an "invisible podium about 4 feet above floor level"; and P stands midstage "on a black block 18 inches high."

For this reason it is not farfetched to consider Beckett's last works for theater principally iconographic and plastic. The contours he draws for character have more in common with classical sculpture or medieval portraiture than with the psychology of the ego. To see this we might turn finally to one of the last works Beckett created for the stage, the enigmatic *Catastrophe*.

Beckett wrote *Catastrophe* for performance at the Avignon Festival on July 21, 1982, a festival dedicated to public support for the then-imprisoned Czech playwright Václav Havel. Though Beckett has several times created occasional works, *Catastrophe* seems unusual for its specific political import. The play carries a dedication to Havel, and it features an obviously stereotyped Hollywood film director who coldly, sometimes cynically, orders his assistant to adjust the pose of a submissive and obviously suffering human figure (P, the protagonist). "Terrific," shouts the Director, when at last P has been bent to his will. "He'll have them on their feet. I can hear it from here" (p. 301). At that moment P suddenly acts on his own: he *"raises his head, fixes the audience. The applause falters, dies. Long pause. Fade-out of light on face"* (p. 301).

P's disobedience is often interpreted allegorically, and, for a play by Beckett, surprisingly optimistically. For Rosemary Pountney, for example, the play points expressly to Havel: "P's silent gaze is more eloquent than language and the final comment is Havel's. D's carefully prepared political statement has been silently challenged—the performance has gone beyond the director's control. For him, it is a catastrophe."[51]

Comments such as these are problematic for several reasons, not least because they substitute a triumphant humanism for Beckett's habitual skepticism. But read in this way the text also seems (again, in comparison with Beckett's other texts) alarmingly simplistic if not downright lame. As a political satire it comes close to trivializing its subject; Chaplin's Little Dictator or Brecht's gangsters satirize tyranny more persuasively. I do not mean to say we ought to take Beckett seriously only when he is being pessimistic. Given the play's dedication and the circumstances of its production, to claim *Catastrophe* is other than politically motivated seems unwarranted special pleading. Yet allegorical readings of *Catastrophe* are possible only if one does not take actual productions of the play into account, and under these circumstances a very different referential system seems to develop. Take, for example, the "storm of applause" that follows P's staged torture. That enthusiasm for being witness to suffering is undercut ironically by P's sudden defiance—he raises his head and fixes the audience in a silent stare. But that reversal is itself undercut by an irony more perfect and considerably less heroic—that is, by the sound of the real applause that inevitably completes Beckett's play. I have never seen a performance of *Catastrophe* that did not conclude with a storm of applause that, predictably, soon faltered and died. As so often is the case in Beckett's theater, the staged moment is embarrassingly close to reality. One suspects that Beckett, having created an image of heroic defiance, felt compelled immediately to debunk it. Why would he have so scrupulously recorded the sounds of an audience's applause if he had not wished to comment on it?

Stated another way, Beckett has less interest in political particulars than in the aesthetics of suffering. Like René Magritte's painting that both is and is not a pipe, the art here seems to be concerned primarily with its own regrettable limitations. Audiences watch P with an eye trained to appreciate staged catastrophe (Beckett might have said "tragedy" as well) every bit as keen as the director's. This is the point so often overlooked, not least by writers trained habitually to scan literature for transcendent humanist values. In trying to read into *Catastrophe* the myth of heroic individual resistance to tyranny, we ignore Beckett's long-standing conviction that art is helpless to deal with actual politics. Perhaps here (as elsewhere) Beckett "structures his play so that it actually teaches the viewer how to view it";[52] in my experience, the longer one looks at *Catastrophe* the more paradoxical its allegory becomes, the more unclear exactly what moral if any is to be drawn.

Another problem with the allegorical approach to *Catastrophe* is that it privileges the message over the medium. Beckett's late plays are more like paintings than traditional plays. By way of contrast (but in keeping with Beckett's late style in theater), *Catastrophe* dramatizes primarily a physical condition—no more, but surely no less. Let me explain this in greater detail: David Warrilow makes several very interesting distinctions between the characters in *Catastrophe* solely on the basis of his experience in acting them. According to Warrilow,

> *Catastrophe* is such a realistic play if one is doing the Director, which I did in Paris this time. . . . *Catastrophe* is like a classical structure, and there's real psychology in the playing of it. . . . I far preferred to play the Protagonist in *Catastrophe;* that's a much more interesting role to do, much more interesting. For one thing because it's sculptural, and there's an infinite amount of delicate muscular work to be done. It's also very interesting to deal with the problem of not feeling

like a victim. He can look whatever way he looks to the audience, but not to be involved in self-pity while standing on that block is a very interesting task.[53]

Warrilow's distinctions are useful because they highlight a difference between acting that expresses the inner life of a character and acting a Beckett character whose mental life "passes show." P lacks a subtext, nor can one be invented for him. Put another way, the task of the actor here is to represent character without seeming psychologically to "support" it. Twice the Assistant notes that P is shivering, but representing that act must convey nothing more than the physiological reality that under certain conditions (cold, fear, occasionally disease) muscles twitch spasmodically. P is denied an inner life, much as he is denied the usual signs representing character on the Western stage—words and facial expression. All we see of the person is the drapery. Beckett's protagonist is an empty representation, a classical statue lacking the customary individuating marks, a contemporary *Dying Gaul* somehow lacking its sufferer's identity. Stagecraft here is expressly visual: character is reduced to a piece of architecture, a dimensional composition not of emotion or language but purely of line and light.

And the politics, then, of *Catastrophe?* The play leaves us with a slightly more complicated image of political repression than is commonly imagined. Beckett evokes the conventions of allegorical representation only to frame them skeptically. The image offers us a harrowing definition of character in modern drama. Uniformly ashen, P stands on a plinth almost independent of any defining space. The Director's various commands to remove P's clothing or to adjust his limbs recall the sculptor's art, as does the care his creator takes to imagine how P will be viewed by spectators. All this is grotesque, mechanical, and yet (as Warrilow intuits) figurally realistic. It is as if the suffering protagonist has been clinically denatured. Risking a generalization, I would argue for the historic importance of Beckett's figuration and for what it augurs in terms of changing Western views of the self as it is represented on stage. I would say that in terms of its place in modern representations of character, Beckett's anonymous victim as the subject of artistic representation is analogous to the (then) revolutionary individualized statues carved in the late twelfth century on the portals of Chartres Cathedral. With this exception: the figures on the portals of Chartres heralded the beginning of an era of tremendous possibility for representing individuals and individual experience as supremely meaningful realities. In terms of the history of art, the appearance of the figures on

Chartres Cathedral signaled the beginning of "an era of artistic concern with the realization of personality and individuality." [54] It is not so with *Catastrophe,* on the other hand, for Beckett's art rigorously subordinates the individual personality to a nostalgic ideal. Beckett gives us character in purely graphic terms. Ethos is occluded, but the vision of pathos remains.

Chapter Four

Mental Life in Thomas Bernhard's Comic Types

Answer M D's and Mrs. Dingley's letter, Pdfr,
d'ye hear? No, says Pdfr, I won't yet, I'm busy:
you're a saucy rogue. Who talks?
JONATHAN SWIFT, *Journal to Stella*

What time is it
No don't tell me what time it is. . . .

It is good that you are there
and that you are listening to me
We are a conspiracy
THOMAS BERNHARD, *Ein Fest für Boris*

Of character in the works of Thomas Bern-
hard one might say what Claude Rawson said once of character in Swift's
satires, that discussing it led only to "deserts of circularity."[1] Certainly
the figures in Bernhard's plays are as stupidly and savagely hostile as
any of Swift's cannibals, clergy, or politicians, and, like Swift's characters, they profess with heartfelt conviction the most appalling opinions.
Sadists, megalomaniacs, pedophiles, Nazis-in-exile—no mask, no manner
of hatred, no gross violation of culture or common decency is too outré
for Bernhard to dramatize; as a matter of fact, his characters' irrational
viciousness seems to be the main source of their popular appeal. No human
nor any human institution escapes Bernhard's scorn; his plays, like Swift's
works, are wildly implausible satires of folly and madness.

Nothing in Bernhard's work or life, so far as I am aware, links his art
directly to Swift's; in fact, Bernhard's explicit denials that his art means
anything or has any practical consequences differ radically from Swift's
express interest in righting social wrongs. But there is much room for in-

structive comparisons between the two writers, whether in their running and bitterly polemical feuds with their respective countries and compatriots or in their wholesale misanthropy or, finally, in their preference for literature that is both funny and mad. And there are legitimate correspondences of literary form: for example, the apparent instability of Swift's "I" has long been a question central to Swift studies, and in analogous fashion the plays of Bernhard highlight problems with character similar to those that I have been pursuing in this study. Chief among these is the question of the speaker's responsibility for apparently personal or self-expressive statements. Who talks? Is it the speaker or the discourse? That is to say, are characters' words supposed to express the original thoughts of discrete individuals or are they more on the nature of borrowings (quotations, echoes, repetitions, imitations) whose use defines character ironically, as it were, from without?

Bernhard's stance toward his own work is instructive here. Even though Bernhard's personal investments in his characters' utterances are everywhere apparent—many plays, for example, include characters whose diatribes against Austria and Austrians resemble Bernhard's own—more often than not those authorial commitments are impossible to specify very precisely. In an early novel, for example (*Der Italiener),* we encounter a narrator who says, "In my work, if I see the signs of a story developing anywhere, or if somewhere in the distance between the mountains of prose I spot even the hint of a story beginning to appear, I shoot it. It is the same with sentences: I have the urge to take entire sentences and annihilate them before they can *possibly* take shape." [2] Which is (as Bernhard surely knew) almost precisely what Nazis liked to say of "culture": "When I hear the word 'culture,' I reach for my Browning." [3] A character speaking an author speaking a Nazi propagandist: how does one come to terms with such intimidating abysses of personation? How does one distinguish the voice of the author from those of his represented personae?

Most of the problems one encounters reading Bernhard's plays have to do in some way with interpreting the stance of the speaker toward his or her words, problems therefore in some sense with character, for the actors in Bernhard's plays (unlike Beckett's actors) are not discouraged from inventing psychological subtexts for their various speeches. On the one hand, Bernhard has insisted repeatedly that he writes nonnaturalistic theater; on the other hand, as we have seen in the work of Beckett, to abandon naturalistic or novelistic portraiture as a means of *representing* character under no circumstances means abandoning character. Even in Beckett's most expressly formal works, where actors cannot imitate specific personalities, character indelibly stains the work. *Quad,* for example, has apparently been stripped of agency, and yet agency clearly remains as the central problem. To reiterate for the sake of emphasis, ruling out psychological modes of portraiture does not automatically erase an audience's sense of individual psychology, let alone their sense of character; as Gordon Craig long ago discovered, simply to place a living actor on stage is to create a powerful illusion of character. "We need to confront the fact," says Charles Lyons, "that the image of character in space and time constitutes an irreducible aesthetic unit." [4]

Because his plays demand what Stephen Dowden calls "a special declamatory performance," Bernhard has frequently been described as a philosophical playwright. [5] His plays often have been compared to music or to geometry, but hardly ever to nature. In America especially it has become customary to see Bernhard's characters as puppets or abstractions or, more recently, as "pithed" souls for whom language is the sole source of being. Gitta Honegger (among others) finds in Bernhard compelling evidence for lost subjectivity:

> The idea of language as a mechanism that sets us in motion and keeps us alive, that provides the cues and patterns for our actions, the notion of the loss of the subject, although accepted in theoretical discourse is very hard to introduce to the American theater with its deeply engrained belief in psychological motivation as the basis for a character throughline which must be unbroken and free of contradictions. [6]

It has been clear from the beginning of this study that the study of character in drama cannot be separated from modern discourse such as Honegger alludes to about the nature of the self and personal identity. Much modern criticism of literature has documented the dwindling emphasis (if not the vanishing) of the individual, the authentic subject, the coherent character. In the case of Bernhard, for example, Dowden writes that "the weight of the self always turns out to be inconsequential." [7] I would argue, in contrast, that Bernhard's plays are a good deal more hospitable to character than is normally supposed. This is a proposition that will have to be tested over the course of the chapter; in the main, I will follow two related lines of thought. I want to discuss Bernhard's characters in ways that describe as fully as possible their mental landscapes, and I want also to see what remains to be said of character when the usual stage criteria for identifying ethos, namely, the illusions of autonomy and authenticity, have been discarded.

Until recently nearly every person to write on Bernhard's dramas has stressed a direct relationship between his austere style and his flat characters. For most readers, Bernhard's extreme formalism all but eliminates individual personalities and egos. Thus Martin Esslin:

> [There] is no genuine dialogue in Bernhard because his chief characters are entirely enclosed in separate inner worlds. There are no love scenes or love interests in any of Bernhard's works—narrative or dramatic— because monologue does not allow genuine interaction between human beings. Any interaction that takes place is thus purely mechanical, as that between puppets. Bernhard's earliest dramatic efforts were written for marionettes. He regards and deliberately designs his characters as basically no different from puppets—simply because he is convinced that people in real life are, with very few exceptions, barely conscious, let alone able to act otherwise than as merely propelled by mechanical instincts and reflexes; that, in fact, living human beings, in the mass, are no better than marionettes." [8]

Or Nicholas Eisner:

> The main point to note about the nihilism of Bernhard's plays—as of his prose—is that it is derived essentially from a highly repetitive style of language, which does not allow the development of plot, character, and genuine dialogue. . . . Bernhard's figures are merely "verkörperte Funktionen," (personified functions) used to illustrate the concept which generates them. [9]

Or Denis Calandra, who writes that Bernhard and his "chief exponent," Claus Peymann, "share a concern with the purely linguistic features of their dramas, to the neglect of conventional plot and rounded character." [10] Even Stephen Dowden, who cites individuality as one of Bernhard's principal themes, rules out any concern on Bernhard's part with his characters' affective psychologies: "[P]sychology is beside the point in Bernhard's hyperconscious world because what he aims to capture in his fiction—for the imagination alone can capture it—is the spirit of the conscious intellect as it vies with death for supremacy." [11] Bernhard's figures, says Dowden, are not psychological but allegorical. Not only do they "lack psychological depth," but "[t]hey exist more as personified ideas than as plausibly imagined people." [12] "Bernhard operates," he continues, "under the assumption that we cannot fathom the true interior of a human being. . . . The self is unique and so cannot be described in conventional language. It is a hidden process, ephemeral and unfathomable as a whole." [13] Such assumptions about "flat" and "round" characters, in particular the notion that subjectivity belongs to the latter but not to the former, are hypotheses about character that I want to question by examining some of Bernhard's plays.

A Tragedy of Humors

Bernhard seems to have needed no apprenticeship in playwriting; his first play (*A Party for Boris, Ein Fest für Boris*, 1968) provides the model for nearly all that follow. In this and other works, characters seem to lack internal structuring; rather than existing as discrete individuals, they seem bound together into relational units in which emotional intimacy is assumed but rarely dramatized. To an audience these relationships give the appearance of being mechanical or possibly theatrical because the people involved so clearly do and say things they have said and done before. In such an atmosphere even the most intensely personal statements can sound like humorous caricatures of selfhood; "A person," says the protagonist in *A Party for Boris* (named, ironically, Der Gute, "the good one"), "is a person who is in hate with another person."

Bons mots like these are typical of Bernhard's mad satires; one can hear the burst of laughter as the sentence is spoken. At the same time the remark is not only a farcical inversion; there is a real sense in which The Good Woman here exposes the truth of her own situation. The relationship she has with Johanna, her servant, consists of verbal abuse—it is an almost ritualistic tirade—directed by the employer at her employee. Both women hate each other, and yet both in some fundamental way also seemingly need each other. Why otherwise continue this painful relationship? One feels, in other words, that circumstances have conspired to draw together with diabolically humorous symmetry two people who cannot stand one another.

The President's Wife and Mrs. Frolick (*The President*), Vera and Clara (*Eve of Retirement*), or Bruscon and The Innkeeper (*Histrionics*) provide variations on this infernal comedy of odd couples. The relationship is invariably politicized, normally by class or status, creating a situation in which one member is empowered to speak and another expected more or less submissively to listen. Typically the scene takes the form of a rambling disquisition on the current sorry state of the world, Austria in particular; also typically the speaker maliciously degrades the listener, criticizing him or her for lacking education, sense, taste, imagination, social background, even for choosing the wrong village to be born in. Against these charges the listener is compelled because of his or her station to keep silent.

Yet silence on Bernhard's stage functions as powerfully as speech, and in many cases the longer the monologist talks, the more his or her words become ironically self-expressive—expressing, by indirection, the psychic reality they intended to avoid in the first place. Against the background of the listener's continuing silence, the speaker's words become a desperate attempt to fill a bottomless existential void. It is a dramaturgy of surprising power. Bernhard's characters have little new to say to each other; on the contrary, we get the clear impression that what is being said and done has been said and done many times before. Yet the repetitiousness is not banal or uniformly comedic; indeed, at times it can be unexpectedly moving to watch Bernhard's eccentric pairs circle repeatedly round one another, locked forever in a mutually destructive and mutually supportive pas de deux. Ultimately, rather than seeing individual characters progress toward intellectual or emotional insight, we become aware of their profoundly empty spiritual state—in Kundera's marvelous phrase, of their "unbearable lightness of being."

The inner landscape of such terrible lunacy has never been more acutely explored than on Bernhard's stage. Bernhard depicts character, in part, by means of a play of mutual echoes and deep-seated if mysterious psychological collusions. The significant psychological unit for Bernhard is less an individual than a dyad. Here is a small portion of The Good Woman's harangue to Johanna; throughout much of the scene, while talking, she has been aimlessly trying on hats and gloves:

> *tries on a green glove*
> But if you travel to England
> and do not understand the English language
> or to Russia and understand no Russian
> It is good
> that I put a stop to it
> put a stop to it
> *wholly soft*
> put a stop to it
> *admiring the green glove*
> It wasn't as if I had been surprised by the accident.
> it wasn't so.
> *takes the green glove off again*
> To be dead
> to plunge down a light shaft
> to be dead like my husband

In truth I have not dreamed about him for weeks
not for years
When you clean your shoes
do you not then think about me[.] [14]

How can it possibly be said that the speaker of such discourse lacks psychological depth? The mention of dreams alone, quite apart from any psychological portraiture an actor may wish to give to the part, produces clear evidence of this character's narrative extensiveness. One senses not only that The Good Woman *has* a mind, one also imagines her mind following its own inner pathways. Various cues or signs, for example the sudden recurrence of dreams about the dead husband, allow us to imagine several different possibilities. Certainly The Good Woman's words have none of the self-conscious analysis typical of earlier forms of stage realism. Taken at a different level, however, the speech makes perfect sense as an instance in which verbal repetition signifies the mind's—*a* mind's—unwillingness or inability to let go of a particular subject.

Or consider the moment briefly from an actor's point of view: why does The Good Woman not dream of her dead husband? It is a provocative remark, to say the least brutally frank. How is it to be spoken? With regret? relief? Or perhaps she is lying and if so, to whom? It should be evident that no one of these possible representations, whether denial or regret or some other mental strategy, by itself accounts for the inner workings of her mind. But it should be evident also that Bernhard's actor, in sharp contrast to Beckett's, cannot in such circumstances rely on sculptural portraiture or stylized speech. The moment insists that the actor construe behavior (speech) in firm relation to *some* mental strategy and so allows for a model of mind to be staged.

That Bernhard intends any single specific psychological profile to be staged in this or most other instances is unlikely; the psychological depth here apparent is more illusory than clinically certifiable. But the illusion of depth is present nevertheless, and crucial; it identifies the deepest motive power of the play, the instinctive conjunction of one person to another. To be joined is, for better or worse in Bernhard's world, the primary condition of character.

Over the course of the play Bernhard provides considerable evidence that The Good Woman's acts are symptomatic of a buried mental life. First, like many of Bernhard's protagonists, her psyche has been scarred by the intrusion of terror into everyday life.[15] Next, The Good Woman mentions the dead man only three times, each time briefly. Upon scrutiny, none of the references is random. As in the above instance, her narrative accounts of the dead husband are triggered involuntarily by an accidental association—a double-edged phrase, the color black, the circumstances of remembering her first year with Johanna. We know too that part of Johanna's obligation to her employer is never to speak of the husband—though if we believe The Good Woman, she has a morbid obsession about the subject. Both women are therefore bound together in part by means of the single obscure trauma; barely manifest, the accident is nevertheless crucially important. One might say that it becomes a subtext that secretly directs their daily lives:

> You always wanted to hear something in connection with the accident
> in connection with that evening
> whenever you asked me something
> whenever you ask me about my nightdress
> about my necklace
> whenever you ask me if I want to go out or downstairs
> you only ask
> how the accident was[.]

(P. 25)

Bernhard's play interweaves trauma, memory, and speech: yet of the key event, the accident, we know relatively little except that it occurs before the play begins in so-called diegetic space, that is, within a narrated or "virtual" past. To plunge down a light shaft! It is an outrageous way to die. Among the multitude of shocks literary flesh is heir to, it is one of the more novel. Apart from Stephen Dowling Bots, whose death by falling down a well was immortalized hilariously by Mark Twain, I cannot think of a similar literary misfortune. It is not that such things do not happen naturally in real life, but rather that this is assuredly not a "natural" way for characters in imaginative literature to die. Stabbings, poisonings, shootings, illnesses, suicides of one sort or another—these are the kinds of dyings one expects on stage. But characters in literature do not fall down light shafts, and the lack of conventional literary support makes almost impossible interpretive demands. Are we to laugh? are we to sympathize? (It is worth mentioning in passing that students almost always misread this passage. They assume that the accident involves motor vehicles, and that "to plunge down a light shaft" represents a near-death experience. Presumably their awareness of literary convention is insufficiently broad to help them guess that convention itself is here being exposed.)

Our response to the event is made even more difficult by the attitude of The Good Woman. She is not melancholy, but neither is she bitter or reflective. Indeed, she seems suspiciously unaffected by it at all. She seems deficient in the marks—the affects, the insights—by which we customarily recognize individual literary mentality.

But if we look more carefully at the implicit relation between trauma and its remembered recurrence, we may discover that many of The Good Woman's acts point to a bizarre individuation. She writes letters but never mails them, tries on costumes with no intention ever of buying one; legless herself, she sends her servant on daily excursions to purchase stockings and shoes, dreams of travel and "walking the pavement" (p. 37), and marries (there is some evidence she views it as an act of expiation) a legless cripple from a nearby asylum. This bundle of acts does not define a "self," perhaps, but if we cannot derive from them a clinically coherent psychology we cannot also imagine them without simultaneously imagining behind them a center of human energy or will.

It would be incorrect to say that Bernhard is interested primarily in detailing the inner life of The Good Woman; in a way, her obsessive behavior forestalls full insight into her unconscious. In a very real sense, she has within her that which "passes show." In another sense, however, it is precisely such an unconsciousness, and how the landscape of that unconsciousness haunts the play and its action, that determines character in this play. Consider, for example, how we are introduced to the new husband, Boris, of the play's title:

A cripple I said
a cripple who like me
has no legs any more
in the house
marry
Boris[.]
        (P. 25)

Bernhard plays upon what he knows will be viewers' predilections to seek psychologically plausible motives for characters' words and acts. Only the slightest hint is necessary to establish for modern audiences the illusion of a hidden psychological agenda. We intuit this directly by way of numerous hints or allusions. At times, for instance, it seems almost as if Boris, the new husband, is indistinguishable rhetorically from the anonymous first husband. Having got used to hearing The Good Woman refer to the dead man as "my husband," it comes as a mild shock to discover in the following passage that the referent has shifted:

is my husband sleeping
I said, is my husband sleeping
is Boris sleeping[.]

(P. 48)

To the degree that we allow for such overlapping, one might suspect that The Good Woman has chosen a husband who mimes in life the condition of her first husband, dead ten years. A number of physical congruencies suggest several levels on which the two men symbolically might be linked. Boris is crippled, immobile, and sleeps incessantly. Much, too, is made of the fact that he sleeps in her first husband's bed; The Good Woman says that

Boris has a long bed
in which he can stretch out
that is the least he can ask of me
that I give him a bed in which he can stretch out
to BORIS
right
you can stretch out in your bed
BORIS *nods*
Tell your friends
that you can stretch out
when you like
Only he never stretches himself out
Never
I know that he never stretches out
but if he wants to stretch out
he can stretch out
He has the bed of my first husband
He was one ninety
to BORIS
Say that you can stretch out in your bed
when you like
BORIS *nods*[.]

(Pp. 81–82)

Moreover, the action takes place on Boris's birthday, an anniversary that is specially significant to The Good Woman. "How I look forward to this party," says The Good Woman; "the whole year I look forward to the party on Boris's birthday" (p. 94). Boris receives a great variety of presents from his friends at the asylum, including a drum, a rattle, a hat, telescope, a stuffed raven, a bottle of mead, and—from The Good Woman—officer's boots and long underwear. Of course these latter presents are superbly useless.

The relationship with Boris, in short, despite its contradictory nature and in contrast to that with the first husband, is amply documented, richly suggestive, emotionally turbulent. That it is satire adds complexity to the representation but hardly renders it psychologically empty. At one point The Good Woman reminds Johanna of how she chose her husband:

> What is the point
> of talking to him
> when he has no understanding
> when he has that foul smell
> But I have him
> I have sought him out myself
> *to* JOHANNA
> We went to the asylum and sought him out ourselves
> And I married him
> him
> him
> Say that we sought him out ourselves
> you forced me
> He feels nothing
> he is nothing and he feels nothing
> He knows nothing[.]
>
> (P. 50)

The apparent contradictions themselves are significant. By assuming and then denying responsibility for choosing Boris, The Good Woman can in effect act independently to produce events while yet maintaining an illusion of her own passivity. In a sense, The Good Woman marries Boris to kill the memory of her husband and so gain power over it. By electing a stand-in or double for the dead husband she can both have the husband (that is, cause him to return) and at the same time will him to die by dominating his replacement. Only by selecting a hopeless cripple could she exercise so completely her desire for revenge; like the little boy Freud describes in *Beyond the Pleasure Principle*, The Good Woman plays with Boris as if he were an inanimate object. Acting on whim, she orders his hair parted and forbids him to finish an apple he has been eating:

THE GOOD WOMAN
  Why has he no part
  I told you to give him a part
  Why has he no part
BORIS
  I don't want a part
THE GOOD WOMAN *to* BORIS
  I want you to have a part
  to JOHANNA
  Give him a part in the middle
BORIS
  I don't want a part
THE GOOD WOMAN
  a part in the middle
BORIS *makes a point of taking an apple from his pocket and biting into it*
THE GOOD WOMAN *shocked*
  He has an apple an apple
JOHANNA *takes the apple away and hides it*
THE GOOD WOMAN
  Make certain
  that he gets no apples
  I can't stand to hear it when he bites into an apple
  to BORIS
  Does your food taste good Boris
BORIS *nods*[.]

(Pp. 59–60)

It is probably a mistake to try to make too clinical a descriptive frame for The Good Woman's acts. As a matter of fact, the drama achieves much of its force by satirizing concepts such as emotional unity and voluntary agency. But in calling attention to Bernhard's characters' "mental life" I mean to suggest the survival of something like the psychology of character within a dramaturgy apparently inhospitable to it. In what follows I want to try specifically to reestablish psychology and psychic experience as relevant components of Bernhard's dramatis personae.

Layered Characters

At the time of his death Bernhard had become one of Europe's most controversial and widely admired playwrights, yet his works remain largely unknown to English-speaking audiences, especially Americans. Few of his plays have been translated, and productions are almost nonexistent, even though in academic journals his works receive considerable attention. Much of his commercial unpopularity seems a case of mistaken genres. Bernhard is an expressly comic writer, but the laughter that sounds throughout his plays is derisory, cruel, grisly. That does not make the plays any less funny—comedy is not often fair—but it disturbs audiences who think that the comic spirit is civilized and genial. Exposure to bourgeois comedy (and overexposure to Shakespeare's festive comedy) predisposes English and American audiences to interpret satire as misanthropy or outright nihilism. In addition, topical satire such as the following harangue, spoken by the protagonist, Bruscon, in *Histrionics* (*Der Theatermacher*, 1985), proves extremely difficult to transfer outside Austria:

> A thoroughly stupid country
> populated
> by people who are thoroughly stupid
> It doesn't matter who we talk to
> it turns out
> that it's a fool
> it doesn't matter who we listen to
> it turns out that
> it's an illiterate
> they're socialists
> they claim
> and are only national socialists
> they're Catholic
> they claim
> and are only national socialists
> they say they're human
> and are only idiots
> *looking round*
> Austria

Osterreich
L'Autriche
It seems to me
as if we're touring
in a cesspool
in the pus-filled boil of Europe
beckoning to the LANDLORD
whispering in his ear
Why does everything stink round here
What a horrible return
my dear sir
in a normal tone again
At every street corner
there's something to turn your stomach
Where there was once a wood
now there's a gravel pit
where there was once a meadow
there's a cement works
where there was once a human being
there's a nazi
And always on top of everything else
this electrically charged atmosphere of the Lower Alps
in which a sensitive person
is in constant fear
of an apoplectic fit
This tour is proof positive
This country
is not worth the paper
its travel brochures are printed on[.] [16]

The self-characterization in this tirade has as much to do with Bernhard as with Bruscon, nominally the speaker. Indeed, part of learning to appreciate Bernhard seems to involve learning to read speeches and personae such as these in terms of the "family relations" between them and characters and speeches in other plays, as well as between them and Bernhard himself. (As is sometimes said of literary villains, such are the characters we love to hate. At the premiere of *Der Theatermacher,* it is said that "the audience broke into gleeful laughter as the protagonist went into the anticipated tirade about the present-day Nazification of Austria." [17])

Doubtless "character" in the conventional sense is inadequate to describe

Bruscon. For one thing, he cannot stably be described as round or flat, individual or type. Like most of Bernhard's protagonists, Bruscon is in some ways a figure out of humors comedy. But his humor is subtly modern. He is a megalomaniac—he says so himself—and in fact he displays the requisite symptoms of megalomania, clinically described as a delusional disorder marked by infantile feelings of personal grandeur and omnipotence. Despite their repetitiousness, his speeches clearly depict a mind fixed upon some goal and proceeding logically toward that goal by means of numerous contradictions and conflicting emotions. As was true of the speeches of The Good Woman, Bruscon's monologues constitute an open invitation to actors to invent for themselves plausible narrative subtexts for representing character.[18]

But Bernhard freely compromises even predictably humorous moments of character representation. Consider the play's ending, a comedic explosion of cries and confusion caused by the offstage burning of the local parsonage:

> BRUSCON *staring at the ceiling through which it has already*
> *begun to rain while loud cries are heard in the hall*
> The parsonage is on fire
> the parsonage is on fire
> on fire
> the parsonage is on fire
> *the whole audience rushes out*
> BRUSCON *and* SARAH *peer through the curtain until the hall*
> *is empty*
> BRUSCON *after a pause*
> The hall is empty
> an empty hall
> perfectly empty
> *rain drips on them all*
> SARAH *embracing her father, kissing him on the forehead, very*
> *tenderly*
> My dear father
> *brings him an armchair into which he collapses*
> BRUSCON *after a pause in which the thunder and rain have*
> *reached the highest pitch of ferocity*
> I might have known that it would come to this[.][19]

The way one responds to this scene will doubtless depend on the way the actor plays Sarah's overall relationship with her father, but surely Bernhard's rare affective specification, "very tenderly," indicates the moment is one of exquisite personal sorrow. As he paints this scene, however, Bernhard cannot help but mock his own efforts. The catastrophe seems to echo an older theatrical moment, specifically the burning of the orphanage and the grim pietà of Ibsen's *Ghosts*.[20] It is a little like the realizations so popular on the Victorian stage, those climactic moments when the stage picture suddenly composed itself according to a familiar work of pictorial art. As for its effect on the apparent representation of heartfelt emotion, Bernhard implies that even grief might reveal nothing more of character than any other artificially constructed response.

If the foregoing comparison with Ibsen can suggest some of the power of Bernhard's modes of figuration, it can suggest as well one of the misconceptions involving his work, namely, its seeming derivativeness. As Amity Shlaes writes in a review of Bernhard and contemporary German literature, "The problem with all these plays is that they feel derivative. Bernhard studied Artaud and Beckett, and his plays are often "German" reworkings of postwar existentialist theater. . . . [F]or those not born on the Danube or Rhine, Bernhard too often remains too much the German student of the great originals. Why see *Force of Habit* when one can see *Endgame?*"[21]

Parallels with the works of Samuel Beckett are indeed numerous. Bernhard's characters, like Beckett's, must cope with an uncooperative and imperfect world. Trains are always late, hats always fall off, and appointments are never kept. Bernhard shares also with Beckett an apparent fascination with wounds, disease, or physical impairment, for the majority of both men's plays feature characters who are crippled or partly immobilized. And Bernhard, like Beckett, values aesthetic technique often at the expense of subject matter. Beckett more than once asserted the primacy of form over content, and Bernhard's notorious criticisms of art and artists paradoxically confer on aesthetics a kind of legitimacy. (Of theater, he once wrote: "The curtain goes up, and a pile of shit is lying there, and more and more flies come in, and then the curtain falls again."[22]) Nobody could protest so much and mean it. The list of comparisons with Beckett is so long, in fact, that it is easy to see in Bernhard an Alpine Beckett.[23]

But there are difficulties with this view. One of the most striking involves the different use each playwright makes of stage objects. For Beckett, a prop—and there are not many in his works for theater—often involves several levels of significance. It can be a symbol, an extension of the human figure, an opportunity for stage business, even an aesthetic luxury. One thinks of the tree in *Godot*, of Winnie's umbrella or Krapp's tape recorder, of the dazzling sequins on W's black dress in *Rockaby*. In contrast, the props in Bernhard's works are shallow, and they seem somehow drained of the heightened semiotic capacity we expect of stage objects. Yet paradoxically they are at the same time more aggressive. One example: during the first act of *The President,* The First Lady talks to her dead dog's empty basket. The basket is a natural object, and her grief for her pet seems real. Yet Bernhard's unrelenting scrutiny of the object—some twenty times during the course of the scene The First Lady stares at the basket or refers to it directly—makes it hard to say whether the object is being parodied or honored. In such a context the basket is reduced phenomenologically to a neutral "basketness": like a word endlessly repeated, it becomes sheer presence, drained of any referential capacity whatsoever.

Another crucial difference concerns the respective attitudes Beckett and Bernhard take toward another aspect of the dramatic script, stage directions. Beckett's stage directions are perhaps the most explicit in theater history; most of his later plays and especially the plays he wrote for television are created with an extraordinary sense of their detailed pictorial realization. But Bernhard's texts include almost no information about production mechanics—lighting, blocking, pacing, and so on. It is not as if Bernhard were uninterested in figural aspects of character; his texts contain numerous objective instructions to actors to perform specific acts—actors are told to look in the mirror or to stare at a dog basket, to puff on a cigar or to shoot a pistol—but they rarely give information regarding individual affects. (The notation "very tenderly" in *Histrionics* is a remarkable exception.) His plays are a reaction not only against what commonly passes for character determinants in playtexts—the elaborate narrative specification of states of consciousness or affect such as is widespread in much modernist drama, for example, in Ibsen or Kaiser or O'Neill—but also against the modernist fondness for figural abstraction.

It is all the more surprising, then, that in performance Bernhard's plays are not formal abstractions but remarkably naturalistic; Bernhard Minetti (who is Bernhard's favorite actor) has said that Bernhard's monologues are especially challenging for actors who must themselves determine the numerous movements of characters' minds. Actors must choose "which spoken words are merely private reflection, which are less controlled emotional outbursts, and finally, which are uttered for the sole purpose of evoking responses from others on stage."[24] This variation creates the impression of a ceaseless self-awareness; in contrast to Beckett's actors, who are normally enjoined to speak neutrally and with "no color," Bernhard's actors are free (even encouraged) to color their representations with "character."

Perhaps the best example of inappropriately drawn parallels between

Bernhard and Beckett concerns the formal doubling or patterning so typical of their stages. It is here, of course, that Beckett's theater seems definitionally antinarrative; nearly all of the late works replace plot (mythos) with verbal or visual design. In Bernhard's drama also repetition forms an important aesthetic element. In all of the plays, for example, banal catchphrases are distributed among several characters and repeated insistently (and often unconsciously). Such repetitions give rise to the peculiar impression that certain thoughts are "in the air," part of a Zeitgeist, possibly, or at the least an identifying structural feature, like a rhyme in poetry or a song's refrain. In *Force of Habit*, for example, the phrase "tomorrow Augsburg" (*Morgen Augsburg*) and its variants ("tomorrow in Augsburg," "tomorrow we will be in Augsburg") occurs (so it seems) on every other page. Spoken repeatedly by four of the five characters, it surely carries, as Martin Esslin writes, "a multitude of associations and overtones in a number of different contexts."[25] Esslin calls such visible recurrence a structural element analogous to music more than to drama.

This being the case, however, it is ironic that one might equally plausibly call such echolalia a sign of genuine subjectivity. The formal (almost ritual) display of mirrorings and echoes in Beckett seems at times to approach an autonomous aesthetic system, independent of the individual. Because of the naturalistic subtext from which they originate, however, Bernhard's figures' repetitions suggest a palpable attempt to show the eerie theatricality on which human character ultimately rests. When words spread so infectiously from one individual to others, the separate characters from which they normally issue become alarmingly similar; a new identity is created, what one might call the mimetic subject.

The mimetic existence binds one character to another in various ways in various plays; at its most innocent it takes the form of a congenial assent of one person to another, as when The Niece repeats "in Nuremberg" in response to her grandfather's promise to tour "in Nuremberg" in the fall. We all perform such repetitions dozens of times daily, and here mimesis simply indicates an empathic attentiveness to what the other person is saying. In other circumstances, however, such automatic repetition of another's words seems to break down the apparent integrity of character. When, in *The President*, The First Lady defers repeatedly in her opinions to her friend The Chaplain ("the chaplain says . . .") and The Chaplain, in turn, obtains *his* opinions on manners and morals from the great European authors (Goethe, Voltaire, Proust, among others), individuality in the conventional sense of self against world becomes gravely threatened.

Does this mean that character has been forfeited in favor of formal or philosophical objectives? Not at all. Suppose character is not something essential, unchanging, or intrinsic, but a state of existence more like that imagined by social psychologists or like the social or dialogic self described by Mikhail Bakhtin or the dramatistic self Kenneth Burke invents to account for our verbal exchanges with others.[26] Selfhood is not to be understood exclusively as the expression of an original or private voice; rather it is something one acquires naturally by way of affiliation with others. Character, then, is acquired almost as a form of contagion, and subjectivity spreads as a system of ethics and values from person to person and from generation to generation. It is a curiously Platonic insight: one "catches" character by way of mimesis, by falling, that is, into imitative modes of being. Originality and individuality, of course, have significantly less value in this world, for everybody, it turns out, is a clone of everyone else.

A world peopled by characters cut from the same pattern is by definition humorous, yet in Bernhard's hands the follies of typically humorous characters are transmuted into an appalling bizarreness. It is one thing to parrot a chaplain who parrots Voltaire; it is quite another, however, to push psychological collectivity to its logical and (inevitably) political limits. One example: In *Eve of Retirement* (*Vor dem Ruhestand*, 1979) two contemporary Nazis, a sister and brother, secretly celebrate Himmler's birthday. The celebration is an annual ritual and involves, among other things, wearing clothes from the Nazi era and committing incest. At one point during the party the pair turn to a photo album and begin to reminisce about their life during the National Socialist regime. It is a scene of unparalleled sardonicism: idyllic country views and family snapshots from their childhood are nestled alongside photographs of corpses and concentration camps. At one point Vera, the sister, turns to her brother, Rudolph, and says, after a nostalgic pause, "Oh Rudolf that we have to hide / and look at this so secretly."[27]

Theater history has never known such a brother and sister, and yet Bernhard seems not to have considered his characters fantastic or even extraordinary. (Indeed the play was written during a time when the problem of ex-Nazis establishing themselves in high government positions was real.) But the most striking feature of the play is its comic underlayment. Despite its credible horror the foregoing scene is uncomfortably risible. Vera and Rudolph seem less individuals than one-dimensional caricatures, mindless generic Germans of the sort one sees in propagandistic cartoons from the Second World War or in more recent films such as Zero Mostel's and Gene Wilder's *The Producers*. And the play's conclusion is downright farcical.

Rudolph, impossibly drunk, waves his pistol wildly about the room, then collapses of a heart attack. As he lies groaning, Vera tries desperately to revive him with kisses and at the same time starts to remove his SS uniform. Meanwhile Beethoven's Fifth Symphony plays loudly in the background. The play ends with the summoning of a physician, apparently (and of course ironically) Jewish: as the curtain falls we hear Vera speaking on the phone, "Doctor Fromm, please."

The behavior of these characters is as mechanically predictable as that of any of the protagonists of Jonson or Molière. But to call Vera and Rudolph humorous parodies of past or present Nazis seems dangerously inept. Nothing in the play proves that unrepentant and vicious anti-Semitism is any less a reality now than in 1940. Also wide of the mark, however, is the description of *Eve of Retirement* as "a humorless mix of Strindberg and Beckett . . . as repulsive as Fassbinder's, though more upscale."[28] The objections of Robert Skloot (who wrote the preceding comment) to Bernhard's Holocaust drama cannot be waived arbitrarily. He regards the lack of a humane voice in the play as a damning ethical mistake on Bernhard's part, and I have taught the play unsuccessfully often enough to half-believe him. Told to read *Eve of Retirement* as comedy, students are aghast; told to read it as politics, they miss the humor and so (in my opinion) miss the point. In this humors comedy, buffoons have the power to play out exaggerated, violent fantasies. Of the characters who endow *Eve of Retirement* with the horrors of the National Socialist era, Bernhard has written that such people "are in me, just as they are in everyone else."[29] If his plays are any guide, these remarks must be interpreted as more than a metaphoric expression of innate human depravity. Bernhard suggests here for drama a heterogeneous model for selfhood, one whose component parts are by no means complete and exclusive. Other people are part of us as we, in turn, are part of them. It is a model for character that is multiple, relativistic, open, and, as Bernhard dramatizes it, psychologically plausible.

The issue of character arises also in a work like *Der Präsident* (*The President*, 1975). Like *Histrionics*, *The President* presents characters who seem at first almost featureless. No assembly of traits can describe them, and indeed there seems little to describe: they lack determinate pasts, consistent opinions, coherent affects. The play begins just after a group of anarchists have bungled an attempt to assassinate the president of an unspecified European country. Instead of shooting The President, the assassins kill a nearby colonel and The First Lady's beloved pet dog, who apparently dies of fright. The play ends several days later with the anarchists' second, and successful, strike. In the meantime, with crushing finality, The President waits for death.

The President can be read as a *pièce à thèse*, a cheerless lecture on mortality and the relative irrelevance of literary form. Since all plots end in death, Bernhard seems to be saying, why pretend that one is different from any other? By conventional standards the play seems monochromatic: its plot is emphatically static, and its characters are powerless to act in their own interests. The President's situation is of dramatic interest only as an exemplar of "the blight man was born for." Like the child in Hopkins's poem, The President is psychically oriented toward death, even though he cannot bear to acknowledge it. Thus he spends his remaining time in a frantic effort to deny what he knows to be true.

Even though the play dramatizes a moral as succinct as that of any medieval allegory, it cannot be said that Bernhard creates characters mainly to illustrate philosophical principles or to conform to abstract formal patterns. (One might for a start point to its mordant political realism. No one aware of the ghastly ironies of contemporary international events can think Bernhard dwells entirely in fancy.) Next, the play draws odd emotive power from its haunting images of individuals. Even though their words do not directly express the inwardness that in conventional drama passes for psychological realism, one responds empathically to the bleakness of their situation and the extremity of their suffering. These people are mutilated so far beyond recognition that, like the grisaille figures in Picasso's *Guernica*, their pathos is convincingly real.

It is the latter dimension of Bernhard's characters that has thus far gone unrecognized. If they do not fit familiar norms for the depiction of mentality, neither do they conform to our notions for "flat" characters in literature. Consider the following speech in which the representation of character seems largely subordinated to formal matters; The President speaks to his lover, an actress:

> And what does the director plan for you
> a leading role or a supporting role
> You can renounce the lead role my child
> you play it with me
> you play your supporting roles in the theater
> *kisses her on the cheek*
> with me you play the lead role
> *suddenly pathetic, raises the glass*

You are the greatest actress
that I know
and so you play the lead role with me
you play the greatest role that any actress
in any of our theaters has played
Duse
You Duse
Duse
throws his glass in her face
You Duse
The actress raises her glass even higher and throws it in his face
My Duse
my Duse you[.]
Curtain[30]

Like so much of Bernhard's theater, the scene defies easy classification or explanation. It takes place in a "flat" or neutral space, and on the page seems largely empty of subjective interiority. On the one hand, it is a satiric portrait of a comic type (again, a megalomaniac); on the other hand, even though the scene takes place on the edge of slapstick—the head of state is revealed to be nothing but a drunken lecher—the speech cannot be played for laughs. The President's monologue differs qualitatively from a speech by, say, Volpone or Harpagon, mainly because its mode of expression and its peculiar mechanisms suggest a state of mind that is paralytic rather than intent upon action. Its attraction for an audience is therefore more mesmeric than comedic. The speech manifests fear, a sinister hysteria that means nothing in itself because it is only an unreasonable deferral or displacement of emotion. The "I" expressed by the monologue is again infantile, and, incidentally, pathologically accurate. At the same time the repetitive, patterned style adds a pathetic counterpoint to the childish outbursts:

You can renounce the lead role my child
you play it with me . . .
with me you play the lead role . . .
and so you play the lead role with me[.]

From the point of view of an actor the speech is as complex psychologically as any of Ibsen's characters' revelatory declamations. The President represents his needs symbolically; his words suggest, for example, the protective devices that schizoid individuals use to avoid the dangers of emotional involvement. Early in the scene he speaks of his wife's infidelity with a bizarre objectivity:

she lies in her bed
she thinks about her butcher
about the butcher on the one hand
about the chaplain on the other
in the night they both run through her head
and they won't reconcile themselves in her head
but neither can she go mad
in this stage
And if she is ever with me
she is still with the butcher
or with the chaplain
This explains her increasing nervousness
This also causes her to torture
the servants[.]

(P. 130)

The speech first of all structures individual identity as a schizophrenic attempt to reconcile disparate (or other) components of the self: The President's wife's nervousness and cruelty can both be attributed to her awareness of the sway competing authorities hold over her. And The President's monologue carries out his own unapprehended willing. The President claims to be indifferent to his wife's behavior, but the peculiar references to her in his monologue suggest otherwise. There seems to be a causal relationship between his rambling, bitter narrative and an unexpressed wish to deny that his wife means anything to him. His ramblings make perfect sense, for example, if they are understood as coming from the mind of a man who dreads meaningful emotional connections. In one instance during The President's monologue, for example, he begins to link himself with his wife in a sympathetic, caring way; his language, however, almost immediately becomes abusive and repetitious:

a hair's difference my child
and I would not now be in Estoril
The assassination is the reason
that I am here
You have suffered a shock
said my wife

go to Estoril
she said
And she said it only
so that I would go away
so that she could go to the mountains herself
with her butcher
or she might go with the chaplain to the mountains
With the butcher
or with the chaplain
it is all the same to me with whom she goes to the mountains
the main thing is that I am with you in Estoril my child
   drinks
two thousand police all to look after
my person
And you my child
my little actress
with the diplomatic passport
and with the official protection of the president
the day after tomorrow we'll travel to Sintra
on official business
and enjoy ourselves
like that waiter in Sintra last year
didn't I read him a lecture
a lecture
first in French
which he didn't understand
then in English
which he didn't understand either
finally in Portuguese
In the night we never sleep together
my wife and I
not for twenty years
when she lies in her bed
she thinks about her butcher
about the butcher on the one hand
about the chaplain on the other[.]

                (Pp. 128–30)

    The foregoing speech hints at a psychic reality that determines the course of the fragmented, repetitive, hostile verbal surface. The memory of Sintra, for instance, although introduced apparently at random, masks a subtle attempt on the part of The President to recover through memory a situation in which he could dominate events and persons absolutely. His pleasure in remembering the incident at table seems therefore the product of a blunted psychic need. By repeating the story he reconstitutes the power he held over a waiter who knew neither French nor English and could not respond therefore to verbal abuse. Of course this part of The President's speech can be interpreted conventionally—evidence, perhaps, of a sadistic streak that can never be understood—but given his imperiled situation his words suggest an instinctive psychological strategy. This portion of his monologue is clearly motivated and, from one perspective, perfectly coherent. In context—a nostalgic recollection that contrasts markedly with the bitter commentary on his wife's sexual infidelity—the story of the waiter at Sintra seems to be a delaying tactic, an attempt to kill the memory of his wife.

Bernhard here opens a void beneath The President's humor, thereby giving the effect of genuine interiority. When The President strikes his various poses or discards one personality in favor of another, he defines character as a problem in itself. Indeed, much of the melancholy power of this scene derives from our sense of a character struggling to win a stable sense of self. The President is not talking gibberish; his speech is a performance, a complex tangle of contradictions, assertions, and denials the sum of which testifies to a severely damaged and tormented psyche struggling to articulate itself. His consciousness, to the extent that it can be inferred from his discourse, attracts psychological interpretation. The repetitions, the sudden outbursts, the bitterness, the nostalgic lapses—these are not merely formal elements of a "musical" drama, they are distinctive marks of character. In *The President*, Bernhard dramatizes character effects appropriate for our own age—"the age of the schizoid," as it has been called.[31] For example, the apparent digressions contained in his speech can be interpreted as attacks on "linking," the purpose of which is to deny meaningful relationships.[32] Significantly, the apparent digression via the waiter at Sintra ironically leads The President back to his subject:

In the night we never sleep together
my wife and I
not for twenty years[.]

Digressive topics in The President's speech almost always mark the return of the repressed. The more we observe the peculiar repetitions of The President's monologue, the clearer it becomes that they are closely tied to his obsession with his wife's infidelity. He may not understand fully what moves him to speak, and, indeed, at times his words take on a life weirdly remote from their speaker. To the extent that he is in the grip of his repetition compulsion, he is constituted exclusively by it. But if his own interiority is not always available for The President himself to explain consciously, his repetitions are for us the signs of a pathetic subjectivity. The mental journey the President takes during the course of his monologue has about it the same sinister quality of the Italian walk Freud describes in his essay on "The Uncanny" in which time after time he arrived at the same red-light district from which he was trying to escape. Freud likens his experience of apparently unintended repetition to the helplessness one sometimes feels in dreams, and a similar anxiety pervades The President's speech as, like Freud, he returns by devious paths to the very place he intends to leave. The recognizable landmark in The President's speech is his obsession with the butcher and the chaplain. It is the sign of a repetition compulsion that appears so often and so clearly out of context that it marks his real concern.

The President's speech is as unintentionally revealing of character, therefore, as any of Browning's dramatic monologues, and it is possible to read it for similar kinds of insights into the speaker's mental life. There is a single crucial exception, however. Browning's characters' monologues are invariably gratuitous; their utterances, as Robert Langbaum once observed, remain largely unmotivated.[33] Hence the peculiar formal expressiveness of the dramatic monologue: lacking exterior motive for speech, characters' speech then approaches the condition of lyric poetry. The poem becomes (in Langbaum's description) "the occasion for a total outpouring of soul, the expression of the speaker's whole life until that moment."[34] Bernhard's characters too feel compelled to burst into speech, but for entirely different reasons. The President cannot help but produce himself by speaking, but in another sense (a sense that distinguishes his monologue from, say, that of Browning's Bishop), he loses his command over words to such an extent that he is possessed by them.

The President, therefore, is in some sense an effect or product of discourse. But to say this does not foreclose discussion of The President as a character. Human presence dominates this scene, though it is no longer centralized as it was, say, in Renaissance or nineteenth-century realist drama. Certainly it would be wrong to invest The President with the kind of autonomous expressive power one finds in Shakespeare's or Ibsen's protagonists. But this may well be for Bernhard the crucial issue, to define figures for the self in terms of a revolutionary and expressly negative dramatic language. Characters on stage are not ipso facto deprived of mentality—Forster's illusion of "roundness"—because they lack existence apart from the discourse that animates them. In the foregoing speech, for example, the mental life of The President is individuated, coherent, and to a great extent knowable. Bernhard's figuration of character is archaeological; like Freud's model of Rome as a psychical entity, The President is a site for cumulative layerings or doublings.

To read The President's speech in this way permits the speaker a measure of psychological credibility or wholeness without at the same time reducing him to conventional grammars for character. The President's repetitions are consistent with an internalized struggle, for his monologue reproduces the familiar double structure of a compulsion. Like anyone driven by compulsion, he both controls it and is controlled by it. On the one hand, this makes him a puppet whose repetitions are entirely out of his hands; on the other hand, however, there are moments when, during his infantile outbursts, one senses a self struggling through repetition to assert control. For The President, in other words, repetitive language dramatizes a complex psychological duality involving surrender and control.

Seen in this way, character is a critical issue for Bernhard, and his stage functions as a forum for contemporary definitions of identity that stress the self's multiplicity. Beneath their torrent of posturings, accusations, repetitions, evasions, and silences, Bernhard's characters struggle to articulate their tortured experience. To substantiate this claim fully will require the rest of the chapter, and perhaps the best way to begin will be to discuss in greater detail the kinds of mimetic involvement with others—repeating, imitating, mirroring, echoing, quoting—that distinguish Bernhard's characters.

Repetition, Self-Fashioning, and the Force of Habit

One of the most remarkable features of all Bernhard's dramas is the extent to which they are infused with linguistic repetitions: all characters repeat the same stories, situations, catchphrases, and allusions. In *The President*, for example, the phrase "ambition, hate, nothing else" is spoken eleven times. Such repetitions at first seem common literary devices. Like the refrain of a ballad or the phrase from Vinteuil's sonata in *Swann's Way*, their significance depends on their being repeated so often as to become a motif or signpost rather than an expression that distinguishes one individual from another. As this bitter phrase echoes throughout Bernhard's play, its significance becomes increasingly ironic until it finally indicates little about its speaker. Like the women's "talking of Michelangelo" in Eliot's poem, the repetition eventually highlights the discrepancy between an original and its subsequent abuse through thoughtless duplication. By the time we hear for the eleventh time, "ambition, hate, nothing else," it has become a prefabricated linguistic response, in effect a kind of comic malapropism. Bernhard coldly mocks the characters whose failures he exposes. Entrapment within language depicts character, but negatively; as in conventional humors comedy, it signifies the absence of thought, the loss of individuality.

Repetition of this kind can also serve formal ends. It can become a unifying structural element as in music, adding intensity or significance, synthesizing or centering the work. Of a similarly repeated phrase in *Die Macht der Gewohnheit* (*Force of Habit*), for example, Martin Esslin remarks that "the sentence 'tomorrow in Augsburg' (referring to the circus's next stop on its tour) occurs on almost every page. Simple as it is, it carries a multitude of associations and overtones in a number of different contexts."[35] Esslin classifies repetitions of this sort as autonomous, technical features of the work of art, unlike the repetitive conversations of other contemporary dramatists (notably Harold Pinter) "who are mainly concerned to show that real speech in real situations *is* largely repetitious." Esslin writes that, "In Bernhard's case, there is no pretence to naturalism. His dramatic language . . . is strictly rhythmical."[36]

Bernhard is a trained musician, and he often borrows from music structural elements for his plays. But the musical or rhythmical analogy, while accurate, does not fully account for the wide-ranging effects of Bernhard's imitative patterns. As we saw in the foregoing analysis of a portion of The President's monologue, repetitions tend in spite of their definitional formalism to cluster around character and to stamp language with individual desire. Whatever their logic as formal elements of a composition, in other words, the repetitions tell an enigmatic story. The President's repetitious language can be read narratively as the symptom of a drive mechanism that holds constant sway over his life and through which he tries to articulate himself. One can track, for example, traces of The President by means of the texts he articulates. Or one can (using late Freudian theory) describe a psychic economy that governs The President's various defensive strategies. When The President returns again and again to "the butcher or the chaplain" he deals with highly negative feelings. He can be said to discover repetition (as Freud theorized in discussing the now-famous *fort/da* game in *Beyond the Pleasure Principle*) as a tactic that transforms passive suffering into a game of control. His compulsion to repeat combines infantile pleasure with a perverse, sterile, and cruel mode of mimesis.

The President cannot see into his repetition, of course, but his monologue clearly tells his story—the story of one who cannot see. Obsessed with his wife's sexuality, he complains incessantly about her lovers, her dead dog, her charities and intellectual pursuits, and even her manner of chewing. And the scene culminates in a pathetic moment of insight and denial:

> The wife of the president of the Republic
> is a whore
> a whore
> *after a pause*
> A whore who now only
> stares into an empty dog basket
> stares into it you understand
> stares
> stares into it
> into the empty dog basket
> *both empty their glasses*
> It is a play my child
> in which alternately
> the most impossible people and arrangements occur
> and possibly
> it is already the revolution[.]
>
> (Pp. 137–38)

The world is a drama staged by actors who inevitably betray the roles they find themselves obliged to play. Bernhard identifies the self's inherent theatricality and pursues that concept to its macabre extreme. His experimental dramaturgy represents inner experience by linking it with external caricatures—a definition of the ego in terms of a set of mechanistic and mimetic responses. Character can be identified as a primary subject of Bernhard's concern, in other words, even though his characters rarely use words or acts to explain what they are doing and why. Consider evidence from another play, the introductory scene of *Force of Habit*:

> *A piano left*
> *Four music stands in front*

Chest, table with radio, armchair, mirror, pictures
The "Trout Quintet" on the floor
CARIBALDI *looking for something under the chest*
JUGGLER *enters*
   What are you doing there
   The Quintet is lying on the floor
   Mr Caribaldi
   Tomorrow Augsburg
   right
CARIBALDI
   Tomorrow Augsburg
JUGGLER
   The lovely Quintet
   lifts the Quintet up
   By the way I have
   received the letter from France
   puts the Quintet on one of the music stands
   Imagine
   a guaranteed sum
   Experience proves however
   that an offer
   should not
   be accepted immediately
   That is what experience proves
   straightens the Quintet on the music stand
   In Bordeaux above all
   the white wine
   What are you looking for then
   Mr Caribaldi
   takes the cello leaning against the music stands
   wipes it with his right sleeve and leans it back
   against the music stands
   Covered with dust
   everything covered with dust
   Because we play in such a dusty place
   It's windy here
   and dusty
CARIBALDI
   Tomorrow Augsburg

JUGGLER
   Tomorrow Augsburg
   Why are we playing here
   I ask myself
   Why should I ask
   That is your business
   Mr Caribaldi
CARIBALDI
   Tomorrow Augsburg
JUGGLER
   Tomorrow Augsburg
   naturally
   The cello
   let stand open
   for only a few moments
   blows dust from the cello
   Carelessness
   Mr Caribaldi
   takes the cello
   The Maggini
   right
   No
   the Salo
   the so called
   Ferrara cello
   leans the cello against the music stands again and
   takes a step back, contemplating it
   an instrumental
   expenditure
   But naturally it should
   not only
   be played
   in concrete arenas
   North of the Alps
   the Salo
   south of the Alps
   the Maggini
   or
   afternoons before five o'clock

the Maggini
and after five o'clock in the afternoon
the Ferrara cello
the Salo
blows dust off the cello
A dying occupation
suddenly to CARIBALDI
What are you looking for then[.] [37]

The scene (like so much of Bernhard's theater) at first glance seems barren of motive and strictly formal, as if we are being told nothing essential
about The Juggler and Caribaldi. But in fact the text generates a character-
centered aesthetic. The Juggler's incessant speech seems almost surreal in
contrast to Caribaldi's relative wordlessness. Why does Caribaldi not respond when The Juggler asks what he is doing on the floor? Why does The
Juggler not repeat his question but instead change the subject, not once
but twice? Why does he perform a sequence of highly specific acts during
his speech—straightening sheets of paper, perfunctory dusting? Why does
he devote so much attention to the two cellos? And what motivates him to
visit Caribaldi in the first place?

Such practical questions cannot be brushed aside as irrelevant specu-
lations; they are the salient grounds of the dramatic encounter. Actors
performing the scene need to know the answers to such questions, and
audiences or readers too may profitably institute similar inquiries. It is not
true, in other words, that everything we need to know to read this play
is contained within it. The need to read The Juggler's monologue for its
implicit narrativity is proved first by Caribaldi's relative silence and next
by the sequence of linguistic repetitions. Despite its stylization the scene
remains rooted in personal neuroses and family relationships. Motives that
we would call psychological give this encounter (and most of *Force of
Habit*) its extraordinary blending of abstraction and verisimilitude.

The Juggler several times begins to speak by repeating Caribaldi's phrase,
"Tomorrow Augsburg"; this suggests, by extension, that his speech is both
mimetic and inauthentic, that it is conditioned by response to exterior authority. By establishing echolalia as a point of reference, Bernhard mocks
the convention that words are the distinct property of the person who
speaks them. The Juggler's speeches and actions are usually triggered by
an interpenetration of his discourse by Caribaldi's, or—more important—
by his perception of Caribaldi's mood or needs. As the scene develops, The

Juggler's individuality is gradually revealed to be a function of Caribaldi's. (And vice versa: as I show later, Caribaldi cannot act in character, as he is here in character, unless there is someone present whom he can dominate; his behavior, too, is the product of emotional need.)

Under these circumstances, it is impossible to displace character as a legitimate object of inquiry. Awareness of individual psychologies or distinct movements of mind beyond (or beneath) language is certainly central to our experience of the play. Those inner realities are necessarily experienced imperfectly, fleetingly. Likewise their relation to language is problematic; no character's rhetoric is conventionally self-dramatizing or self-expressive. Still, the scene seems to depend on our awareness of language as somehow expressive of character. It is character's shadow, or its sign, and it presupposes the existence of a subject in much the same way that symptoms of a disease presuppose the existence of a host. When, for example, Caribaldi and The Juggler repeatedly speak the phrase, "Tomorrow Augsburg," their words are rhetorical and expressly ethical. At the very least the scene presents individuals who receive language and respond to it with a waxlike impressionability. Even from the very first moments of the play, when The Juggler says "Tomorrow Augsburg" in hope of setting his own rhetoric in accord with that of his employer, one senses the formal linguistic ties that convey to us the play of mimetic correspondences on which character depends for its production.

The continuity of language from speaker to speaker indicates how easily and naturally men and women fall into familiar, repetitive configurations. *Force of Habit* shows a reality that has lately become a sociological commonplace, that human relationships at any level are weirdly choreographed. The play contains sequences of mechanistic actions that are both predictable and comedic, and, as is true of many of Bernhard's plays, its structure resembles conventional humors comedy. The story develops as follows: Caribaldi, a ringmaster of a small troupe of traveling circus performers, is also an amateur cellist. Each day for more than twenty years he and the other four members of his circus have tried to play Schubert's "Trout Quintet." Yet not once have they been able to complete the piece without error; always someone makes a mistake. Bernhard's thesis is ingenious if not exactly novel: perfection, as everyone knows, belongs to another world. (One might note in passing that earlier generations might simply have praised Bernhard for being "true to life"; it is hard to imagine anyone who could not supply his or her own examples of the kind of aspirations and frustrations that Bernhard's formalist art represents.)

In any case, Caribaldi's desire to perform the quintet successfully eventually becomes an obsession, and, when the play begins, he tries to assemble his musicians for yet another rehearsal. Among the players, in addition to Caribaldi and The Juggler, are a Clown, a Lion Tamer (Caribaldi's nephew), and a tightrope dancer (Caribaldi's Granddaughter). Almost as soon as the performance begins, things go wrong. Caribaldi loses the resin for his bow, and The Juggler whines constantly that his artistic talents are unappreciated. The Clown keeps losing his hat, and each time the hat falls he loses his place in the score; and each time the hat falls the dancer giggles and loses *her* place too. Worst of all is The Lion Tamer. He is drunk, and his left arm is bandaged like a club because one of his big cats recently bit it. All he can do with his wounded hand is to pound the piano. Predictably, this rehearsal, like every other rehearsal for the past two decades, never proceeds beyond the first few notes. Screaming in frustration and fury, Caribaldi finally banishes his sorry collection of "art destroyers." Alone on stage, near despair, he putters about the wagon, slowly restoring to order a mess of instruments, music stands, and scattered sheets of music. He turns on the radio, and suddenly the stage is filled with the "Trout Quintet": five measures of music, then silence. These last seconds of the play are moving almost beyond belief: Schubert's music never seems so incomparably beautiful.

Caribaldi is a perfectionist in a fallen world. Driven by his humor, he is surrounded by other humorous types. He and the rest of the characters in *Force of Habit* are puppets, and each of them is basically an archetypal clown whose contours are easily recognizable from several comic traditions—*commedia,* medieval farce, Renaissance humors comedy, Plautine theater. But these formal referents establish the frame for an elaborate subtext. The introductory scene between Caribaldi and The Juggler, for example, is a comic routine involving the relationship between a worker and his boss. The Juggler enters the stage intending to ask Caribaldi to raise his salary, and he brings with him for bargaining power a letter containing a contract offer from a carnival in Bordeaux. In outline the scene has the features of a cartoon, and, in fact, one could easily supply an appropriate caption: The Employee Asks for a Raise.

The key to the encounter, however, is that it is not an original confrontation between The Juggler and Caribaldi but an imitation or duplication of a scene that has been played out numerous times before. Created first and foremost as a fall guy, The Juggler is likeable but dimwitted. He knows when he enters that "the letter from France" is a fiction, and, what is more remarkable, he knows that all his past attempts to fool his employer with contract offers from France have failed. Caribaldi says as much toward the end of the scene when he accuses The Juggler of trying to dupe him with an old trick. So Caribaldi too knows that the letter from France is an illusion. This foreknowledge is not literally part of the text, but it constitutes nevertheless a vital element of the working relationship established between the two men; competent actors would surely have to consider it as part of their representation. Because spectators understand this relationship implicitly, its repetitive quality is the essence of the joke; it is funny because we discern it has all happened before. The Juggler must know, therefore, that Caribaldi will recognize his strategy. How then does he request a raise? Incredibly, like an animal that has been taught only a single trick, he produces the fictitious contract offer from France. This is force of habit with a vengeance.

One can see clearly underlying the scene Bernhard's humors approach to theater. Dramatic action results not from antagonism between two discrete individuals but from the programmatic harmony of interdependent subjects who carry out a prefigured behavioral pattern. J. Henri Fabré once described the "abysmal stupidity" of a group of moth caterpillars who took seven days to discover that their food supply had been shifted nine inches. In the meantime the insects circled wearyingly round and round the empty track that had once contained their supply of nourishment. Like Fabré's caterpillars, Bernhard's Juggler clings to familiar behavior because he lacks the rudimentary sense of opportunism that would enable him to abandon or alter it. He enters Caribaldi's room, one imagines, after having rehearsed a scenario such as the following: greet Caribaldi, confirm tomorrow's booking, introduce the letter into the conversation, and so on. But habit betrays him. He is surprised to discover Caribaldi on the floor—bosses do not normally crawl on their bellies—and that novelty renders his prearranged script useless. Before he can begin to play his part, The Juggler must first acknowledge Caribaldi's location, and he never recovers from that reversal of expectations. He pins his hopes on a direct encounter with his employer, but how can he ask for a raise when his boss is lying on the floor? Withdrawing immediately to a defensive position—"What are you doing there?"—he cannot at the same time break free of habit. So he clings desperately to a repetitive text that subjects him to increasing confusion and humiliation. In the artificial way he introduces the subject of his raise we see his lack of imagination: "By the way [*übrigens*] I have received the letter from France." But Caribaldi's silence compels The Juggler to abandon the subject, and the lame repetition ("That is what experience proves") signifies that the question of the raise is dead. Only at the end of the long first scene is the matter reintroduced, this time by Caribaldi as a way of cruelly humiliating The Juggler:

> And your letter from the manager of Sarrasani
> is one of hundreds of forged letters
> that in the whole ten or twelve years
> you have been with me
> you have held under my nose
> Show me the offer
> Show me the offer
> *plucks the strings briefly a few times and holds the bow steady, as if to play.* THE JUGGLER *takes one, then another step back*[.]
>
> (P. 54)

Bernhard's text suggests that humans cannot achieve spontaneous behavior or original thought. But this is not to say that he displaces or downgrades character as an element of the dramatic text. The director of an American production of *Force of Habit* told me that Caribaldi as a character is more difficult to perform than Shakespeare's Lear, mainly because he requires an actor to display a range of subjecthood that stretches mimesis to its limits. Not only must the actor speak with his body and by way of Bernhard's text, he must over the course of rehearsals become skilled enough with the cello to be able to "speak" as well through the instrument.

To permit actors so great a range of expressive power surely militates against the nihilism that is often attributed to Bernhard's artifice and abstract patternings. In fact, one may well describe art such as this as "postmodernist humanism." If, for example, The Juggler's unthinking repetitions make him into a humorous type, they also constitute part of his unique "character-armor"[38]—a personality borne of suffering, pathetically manifest as a mechanism of displacement, deferral, and denial.

Let me sketch this more elaborately: in repeating the fiction of his "contract offer from France," The Juggler stands no chance of fooling Caribaldi, but that repetition—even though it does not win what he requests—enables him to avoid facing his own extinction. It is as if he repeats the very strategy he knows will fail precisely because he can predict its failure. The abundance of references to France suggests that The Juggler to some extent believes in his own fiction, and that *he,* not Caribaldi, is the person for whom the story is told. As The Juggler develops his rambling monologue, he returns again and again, obliquely or directly, to the subject of France. "France" thus appears at the center of his particular narrative fantasy of self-definition. In truth, hardly anything The Juggler says or does lacks a French connection; images of France weave in and out of his speech as though his life there were a living presence to him:

> In Bordeaux above all
> the white wine
>> (P. 10)

> They are expecting me
> in Bordeaux
> a five year contract
> Mr Caribaldi
> My plate number by the way
> is decidedly a French number
>> (P. 13)

> and the possibility
> to work together with my sister
> CARIBALDI *lets the resin fall*
> THE JUGGLER *picks it up*
> Above all else
> in France
> Mr Caribaldi
> the greatest impossibility
> a blessing
>> (Pp. 23–24)

> extra clothing allowance
> and the French fresh air[.]
>> (P. 24)

Interspersed among The Juggler's repetitious conversation with Caribaldi are repetitions of a particular sort—memories, anecdotes, confessions that seem to indicate that in an indirect (and perhaps unconscious or automatic) way The Juggler is once again telling his own story. As with The President's speech to The Actress, character here develops as a weird and yet deeply moving narrative of loss. The Juggler cannot speak directly for himself, but his repetitious and disintegrating discourse conveys eloquently his interior solitude and his emotional distress. The speech is a broken-down autobiography: The Juggler recollects a memory from his childhood when he played the violin, storing extra pieces of resin in "emerald green boxes." He describes his mother with pride: "French was the mother tongue / of my mother" (p. 15); "That exceptional woman / my mother / by the way in Nantes / left the Church" (p. 15). He alludes briefly to his father—"As you know / my father was from Gelsenkirchen / an unlucky man" (p. 26)—and to his sister, from whom he has long been separated. He often mentions cellist Pablo Casals, who apparently has inspired him since childhood. And he repeatedly speaks of himself as an "artist," even though he makes his living juggling plates and training poodles. In his opinion such juggling is "art" and he himself is "admittedly a genius" (p. 34). Even when he performs in the most humiliating conditions, playing out his act as the tent is pulled down, The Juggler imagines that "the concentration of the audience / is centered on me" (p. 26).

That this last sequence of self-references exposes his unthinking folly cannot completely subvert our sense that there is a "being" under this text. Knowing so much about his background, we have difficulty dismissing The Juggler as a comic effect of discourse. He is as vain as any Restoration fop. But is this simply a satiric exposure of folly? In my view the repetitions that run throughout The Juggler's monologue—while they are not, properly speaking, a coherent narrative—reveal an impulse toward a narrativity that could, ideally, organize the disorder of his life. Repetition in this respect is not a sign of the Juggler's lack of ideal sociability but the symptom of a subject desperately struggling to consolidate itself. The problem is that The Juggler cannot find a way to act that does not lead him to repeat himself, and so repetition both affirms and denies his authenticity. If he attempts to create a life apart from habit, he cannot act except according to a pattern that guarantees his failure. If, on the other hand, The Juggler attempts to use the principle of repetition to sustain or to define himself, he is similarly humiliated to discover that exact repetition is impossible. Even his habits of dress betray him. The Juggler prides himself on maintaining an impeccable appearance. He always carries a handkerchief and a shoecloth, but toward the end of scene 2 he is discovered to have placed these items in the wrong pockets:

[CARIBALDI] A polished, gleaming mirror
   you love that
   your shoes glistening
   THE JUGGLER and CARIBALDI and the GRANDDAUGHTER look
   at THE JUGGLER's highly polished shoes
   You have

as I know
a shoecloth always
in your pants pocket
in your right pants pocket
in the right a shoe cloth
in the left a handkerchief
shoe cloth
handkerchief
shoe cloth
handkerchief
ordering THE JUGGLER
Yes show
show
orders THE JUGGLER *with motions of the cello bow to turn his
pockets inside out*
Turn
your pants pockets out
Turn them out
THE JUGGLER *turns his pants pockets inside out, but the shoe cloth
comes into view out of the left and out of the right the handkerchief,
not the other way round*
You see
you have the handkerchief
not in the left pants pocket
but in the right
in the left you have the shoe cloth
Even you err
Mr. Juggler
Put it all back again[.]

(Pp. 93–94)

Of course this is the theme of *Force of Habit*, that the world leaves little room for perfection or original creativity. But my point is that Bernhard's Juggler, despite his manifest humor, ought not to be seen as an experiment in dramatic formalism but as an attempt to characterize the deserts of selfhood.

Caribaldi too is a "flat" character, and in some ways his mechanistic behavior is a metaphor for broad social or aesthetic matters. It is possible, for example, to see Bernhard's protagonist at the center of a treatise on power and subjection, perfection and human fallibility, art and the artist, and discipline and freedom. But the ringmaster, like The Juggler, possesses a haunting inner landscape. In his interactions with others he is often brutal and insensitive, as, for example, when he compels his granddaughter to perform an exhausting series of calisthenics:

CARIBALDI *keeping time with the cello bow*
Onetwo
onetwo
onetwo
onetwo
onetwo
onetwo
onetwo
onetwo
onetwo
onetwo
onetwo
onetwo
onetwo
onetwo
onetwo
onetwo
Now stop
GRANDDAUGHTER *stops, exhausted;* CARIBALDI *orders:*
Peel the apples
Polish the shoes
Boil the milk
Brush the clothes
And get to rehearsal on time
do you understand
You can go[.]

(Pp. 50–51)

Caribaldi's behavior is not particularly funny, although clearly the scene resurrects older forms of comic theater—the master-slave relationship of New Comedy is one parallel, *commedia* violence another. But there is an important distinction between Caribaldi's compulsive behavior and that of his theatrical antecedents. The blur of commands—onetwoonetwoonetwo—is sadistic but also compulsive, almost as if it were an incantation or a conjuring ritual. The outburst—it is not really speech—cannot easily be played without conferring on Caribaldi a distinct interiority that drives him to act as he does. Like The Juggler in the first scene, Caribaldi here is "not his own." The effect is to remind us of the extent to which the self can be corroded by orders of mimesis, namely, drive mechanisms or transferences. We know, for example, that Caribaldi imagines resemblances between his granddaughter and his own daughter, her mother. Repeatedly he refers to the young dancer as "my child," and it seems as if he uses that patronizing idiom more than idiomatically. On one occasion at least he seems unconsciously to be superimposing the image of the mother on the girl, as in dream:

> Tomorrow Augsburg
> do you sleep well
> in the night
> I don't sleep
> I don't dream
> Show your legs
> GRANDDAUGHTER *shows her legs*
> Your capital
> Your mother
> had the most beautiful legs
> You must practice
> in the strictest way
> Practice
> Wake up
> Get up
> Practice
> Practice
> Practice[.]

> (Pp. 74–75)

The Granddaughter seems to provoke two kinds of responses from Caribaldi, both of which involve repetition as the basis for the production of character. First of all, his language creates a humorous monomaniac. But Caribaldi's brutal treatment of the girl often manifests itself as part of a network of habitual associations. In the foregoing scene, for example, it is the memory of the mother's beauty that provokes him to demand incessant practice on the part of The Granddaughter. Breaking off from his memory, he becomes a machine suddenly animated by hidden springs. His sudden reversion to habit (one order of repetition) is motivated, in other words, by another kind of repetition, the likeness of daughter to granddaughter. Caribaldi cannot deal consistently (or lovingly) with his granddaughter because he is unable to separate her from her mother. But that woman died some years ago, the result of a grisly accident on the high wire. Built into Bernhard's drama once again is the pathos of family tragedy, and even though the behavior demonstrated here is essentially humorous, its source is once again a *particular* mental life. Forces that are clearly psychological operate to produce an image of the subject that seems devoid of the marks of individual character precisely because it is compulsively characteristic.

In *Force of Habit* Bernhard poses some challenging questions about the interior structure of subjecthood. Working within the familiar conventions of humors characters, Bernhard isolates psychological realities on which mechanistic (hence characterless, in the sense of lacking individuating control) behavior can be founded. Some of the examples are innovative and ultimately mysterious, as in the case of The Juggler; others are almost textbook case histories. For example, a likely explanation for Caribaldi's tendency to confuse his daughter and granddaughter is given earlier in the scene by The Lion Tamer. He tells The Clown about the way Caribaldi's daughter died:

His daughter
you should have seen her
a beauty
she was completely mangled
Before that her father
made her practice
the drill How does one bow
fourteen times
just as he makes
his granddaughter
perform the same drill
fourteen times
She made a mistake
do you understand
The collarbone
driven into the temple
indicates this
   THE CLOWN *imitates him*
Into the temple

JUGGLER
A third class funeral
the father so loved the daughter
she was buried in such haste[39]
that a year later
not a single person knew
where
he looked for her in vain
in the cemetery
Since then he never returns
to Osnabrück
Osnabrück no more
CLOWN
No more Osnabrück
LION TAMER
Like a dog
his own daughter
the dirt just thrown over her
do you understand[.]
(Pp. 62–63)

The Lion Tamer despises Caribaldi because he fails to show expected re-
morse. He cannot understand why the father seems so little affected by the
daughter's death, and so he condemns Caribaldi as an unfeeling brute. But
could Caribaldi's apparent indifference and his hostility toward his granddaughter indicate paradoxically an unmanageable excess of grief? There
is some reason to think so. For example, there is considerable overlap between Bernhard's character's behavior and the descriptions of pathological
mourning to be found in psychoanalytic literature. I am not trying to prove
that psychoanalysis uncovers the secret of Bernhard's art. But it is striking
to see how closely the behavior described in actual clinical studies corresponds with Bernhard's bizarre stage fictions, and while that correspondence is probably neither Bernhard's ambition nor his greatest success, it is
surely not irrelevant. This does not make *Force of Habit* a work of naturalistic psychology, but it does suggest how "painting the hero's mind" might
be an important part of Bernhard's drama.

To see more clearly how Bernhard's drama might illustrate how individuality or society unfold themselves in literary forms, we might turn
for a moment toward recent psychoanalytic literature. In that literature,
as on Bernhard's stage, we can see a concern with a variety of affective

disorders of the self that defy those represented by classic neuroses or conventional dramaturgies. For example, Julien Bigras, in an essay entitled "French Psychoanalysis," tells of a former patient, a young girl "who had been sent to me on the advice of her school-teacher because she had shown absolutely no reaction after her mother had been killed in a car accident." Bigras writes that

[t]he girl had also been involved in the crash but has suffered only a very slight brain concussion.

Her teacher could not understand why the girl's conduct at school had not changed in any way whatsoever; she behaved as though absolutely nothing unusual had occurred. I too was at a loss to understand the phenomenon. I therefore accepted her as a patient. I had already dealt with several cases of traumatic neuroses and thus knew that spontaneous sketches, dreams, and fantasies of the patient should reveal violent scenes linked to the accident in which her mother had been killed. This was not the case; the girl would say, "I don't have dreams. No, I'm not afraid. Everything is fine, I assure you."

There was nothing left but to hope that, as a last resort, the spontaneous sketches done by the girl would clear up the mystery. But here also I drew a blank: a cozy little house, a road, a tree; in short, the ingredients of the typical child's drawing. True, a little star or two were in the first drawing, but who would have paid any attention to them? And since it was around Christmas, who would see anything unusual in stars at the tips of the branches of a Christmas tree? Yet in subsequent drawings the stars reappeared again and again scattered among blue flowers or atop a mountain and even at times next to a dazzling yellow sun. Six months went by and still I saw nothing significant in this fact.

Then one day I had a kind of illumination. "Tell me," I said, "when the accident happened I'll bet you saw stars."

She had indeed seen stars at the moment of impact. She immediately burst into tears and told me that she saw stars every night. She was afraid to fall asleep and see them appear again. In addition, from that day forward, she became sad both in my presence and at school. Only at that point was she able to comprehend that before it was neither possible nor permissible for her to mourn her mother's death.

As I listened to "On Death-Work" [a lecture which prompted Bigras to remember his experience with this patient] it was my turn to become aware of something: the subtle and cunning ways in which the death drive works. Suddenly this notion became tangible and vital. It was the "work of death" which, without my young patient or myself being aware of it, had held constant and silent sway over the life of a child and continued to exert its influence upon the cure process she was going through with me. Surely it is striking to see how awesomely the death drive worked its way into the very cure, even concealing itself beneath the things children are so fond of, like wonderful scenes depicting nature or Christmas.[40]

Caribaldi's repetitious behavior, like that of the little girl who added stars to all her drawings, accords with the existence of an unseen drive or instinct. From this perspective, it looks less like "humorous" cruelty or artistic formalism and more like the frenzied activity often associated with actual narcissistic personality disorders. Certainly Caribaldi's behavior with respect to his daughter is more complex and more pathetic than The Lion Tamer imagines. The acts immediately following her death—the swift burial, the period of denial, and then the desperate search for the grave and the subsequent taboo that he attaches to Osnabrück—are consonant with the compulsive actions one finds in case studies of pathological mourning or in accounts of so-called narcissistic disorders or schizoid fractures of the self. The central experience in the lives of such people, writes Ernest Wolf, is "the experience of unbearable emptiness that comes with loneliness . . . a loneliness that almost immediately elicits some relieving action to restitute the crumbling self." This activity commonly is frenzied, according to Wolf; it is "often tinged with the excitements of sexuality or of aggression, is used to create a sense of aliveness, to banish the dreaded nothingness that comes with the loss of self."[41]

Bernhard's work extends character, then, in two directions simultaneously. In the texts I have chosen to discuss, individuality tends to be represented as dependent both on interior as well as on exterior repetitions. In the latter case Bernhard's characters are almost neoclassical—the image not of an individual but a species or type. They show us what people habitually do (or are), and as characters they can be imaged theatrically as masks or humors. The force of habit requires that we behave like automata. At the same time, however, Bernhard's characters own a discrete core of individuality, and this in turn makes it hard to efface Romantic (or individualist) impressions of subjectivity from the text. Caribaldi's humorous mask does not rule out his possessing a hidden self. On the contrary, his mask is clearly the sign of his inner distress. His behavior is like the tip of an iceberg—a misleading distortion, a clinical symptom with limited reference to the actual malaise. There is more than enough material in the text to prove that Caribaldi attempts to control the mother, whom he cannot reach, by controlling her daughter. His desire to turn his granddaughter into a marionette indicates that he has a control instinct and is using her as a child might use a toy. The comic humor in this case represents the individual's response to pain. Caribaldi invents a game whose express purpose is to effect the illusion of control. Thus Caribaldi's humor is not imposed on him from without, nor does it indicate a complete lack of subjectivity. Insofar as it results in predictable or characteristic behavior, it is an aggressive mode of self-production. The passive and annihilating situation imposed on him by death can be transformed into an aggressive reaction. Not only can Caribaldi control the trauma of losing the mother by dominating the granddaughter, he can even enact on the missing mother a kind of revenge: onetwoonetwoonetwo, daughter away, daughter dead.

To be sure, Caribaldi's humorous behavior in this scene is a defensive strategy only. Of the trigger mechanism we know almost nothing except that it is an event that is neither possible nor permissible for him to accept. From The Lion Tamer's point of view, Caribaldi is inhuman, a megalomaniac. From another perspective, one can see that his life is a profoundly moving horror. His aberrant behavior hints at disordering forces that exist at the foundation of character and yet conceal themselves beneath the masks of egoism, motion, and tyranny—ironically, those very forms of behavior that most suggest the power of individual will.

"The most remarkable peculiarity of melancholia," writes Freud, "and one most in need of explanation, is the tendency it displays to turn into mania accompanied by a completely opposite symptomology."[42] Caribaldi is a textbook melancholic; common sense tells us that his humor imitates something real. Caribaldi's megalomania, his insane quest for perfection, his absurdly repetitive schedule, all are instinctive strategies that have no other aim than their own ceaseless accomplishment. The aim of such repetition (as Freud postulated) is not to obtain pleasure but to ward off death. Ironically, only the force of habit sustains the illusion of life. The perception is both fearful and funny: funny, like the coyote in the children's cartoon, who falls only when he looks down and his legs stop churning; fearful, as when Caribaldi responds to The Clown's monotonous bowing of his instrument by saying that

if he stops
he's dead

with his bow
in death
laid out[.]
    (P. 103)

The final irony is that all the characters in *Force of Habit* owe their identities to habit itself. On Bernhard's stage, however, habit does not constitute a mask that must be dropped if the wearer is to recover his or her "self." Against textual or centerless grammars for character Berhnard sets distinct signs of innerness, and the resulting gaps or inconsistencies give his characters their unsettling reality. Caribaldi, like the majority of Bernhard's characters, exists because of a grammar of identity sufficiently sophisticated to redefine literary flatness with both psychology and sociology. Likewise, Bernhard's experimental stylistics and conscious deformation of genre create a new topography on stage for self-experience and self-definition. He writes humors comedy as if authorized in turn by Plato and Freud—a theater in which character is a function of mimesis and where images of the self and its representations create a remarkably chilling hilarity.

Chapter Five

The Characters of Maria Irene Fornes: Public and Private Identities

Contemporary women playwrights have been among the most innovative experimenters with dramatic conventions, and it is their strategies for representing character that will be my concern in this chapter. Jonathan Culler proposes in *Structuralist Poetics* that in literature the conscious, independent subject by now has been "deprived of its role as a source of meaning." [1] As a generalization about the direction of modern literary history, Culler is surely right. Yet discontinuous subjects are not exclusively the invention of modern authors; they exist elsewhere in literature, sometimes in surprising places. The heroes of Aristophanic comedy, for example, rarely seem shackled by the limits of a coherent identity. [2] Another particularly vivid collection of "selfless" souls occurs in Homeric epic poetry. Homeric Greek lacks a term for what we might call the "self"; as a consequence, Homer's words for people are invariably material, designating, for example, generic realities such as age or social status: "young man, old man, maiden, married woman, and so on." [3] What is perhaps surprising, however, given Homer's relative lack of words that express what we would call individual psychology, is his interest in portraying mental activity. Homer activates his characters by means of forces exterior to the mind (dreams or gods, for example, occasionally drugs) or by representing mental activity as if it were mainly somatic experience ("hearts" suffer, for example, while "limbs" fight). Or he will structure the self as dialogic rather than private or psychological: in Book 19 of the *Iliad*, for example, Achilles' thoughts before battle are rendered in the form of a dialogue between him and his horse, Xanthos. Bennett Simon writes that

> [t]his portrayal of inner states by dialogue is powerful poetry. At the same time it indicates a kind of spilling over of the boundaries of the

self, and this aspect has attracted the interest of several classical scholars. Hermann Fränkel in particular has formulated a characterization of Homeric man that captures the essence of this phenomenon. He views Homeric man not as an "I," an ego, a closed and private entity, but rather as an "open force field," having no structural bounds that would help separate it and insulate it from the effects of forces all around it. Lacking structure as it does, it cannot be represented by any coherent, articulated concept of the self; instead we have a collection of parts, *thumos, kradie, phrenes, noos,* as well as limbs, strength (*menos*), courage, and the like, which seem to infuse the various parts. Their sum represents the ego or whole mind, including the man "himself" and his character.[4]

Simon adds that Homer's representations of mind "are closer to fantasies about the mind than to theories," but that such fantasies nevertheless "constitute data for interpersonal, or field, theories of human mental life."[5] Such models for character are especially appropriate, according to Simon, for societies that value "a self that is amenable to the influences of others."[6]

So far as I know there is no case to be made for Homer's influence on contemporary drama. But if we take the view that not all good criticism is necessarily contextual criticism, it may be useful to cast about literature for conceptual systems, whatever their historical status, that are adequate to the task of defining characters who seem to disappear when their identifying functions are appropriated by various external systems that act in their name. I want to try to develop some connections between mimetic models for selfhood outlined broadly by Simon and the "collective subjects" typical of recent feminist drama.

In much contemporary feminist drama character is itself at issue, and "characters" in the traditional sense are superseded by figures who exist as collections of parts with no inherent stability.[7] Some playwrights treat this kind of psychic disintegration as a symptom of individual schizophrenia or widespread social malaise or more specifically as evidence of women's cultural alienation from themselves—witness the fractured protagonists of Marguerite Duras or Caryl Churchill. Pam Gems's *Piaf* is a case in point. There seems little cause to doubt that Gems wrote *Piaf* (1978) as a character study, the object being partly to undermine the popular but seriously distorted romantic version of the singer's life. Yet it proves difficult to understand this presumably truer "Piaf" either in sociohistorical or psychoanalytic terms. As for the philosophical problem raised by Gems's drama—the question of whether Piaf's singing (and by extension all art) is an expression of "self," or whether the artist is better understood simply as a medium for art's expression—that question is never resolved, even though unofficially it is central to the play. To the extent that Gems dramatizes the "real" person instead of the legend, one is tempted to see Piaf's personal misfortunes as the motive force for her art. But that sentimental image of the artist gives way to a prospect much less consoling, much tougher intellectually to accept. Piaf's songs appear at random throughout the play, and while that spontaneity gives the singer a kind of romantic charm it also makes the connection between art and the artist much more problematic. The songs appear almost accidentally, as if they issued not from within the artist but from without. By the end of the play we may well agree with the opinion of a physician who treats the person and her art as he might treat a patient and a disease, that is, as separable and discontinuous realities: "You may, Madame, be a vicious and foul-mouthed slut . . . but I salute the artistry."[8]

One wishes for a more coherent link between the public and private elements of character, but Gems's episodic dramaturgy (like Brecht's) allows for no such conventional portraiture. Doubtless the absence of represented psychological narrative in *Piaf* prompted American reviewers almost en masse to condemn the play and its protagonist as superficial. But in retrospect that judgment itself seems superficial. If we think for a moment of Gems's Piaf not as one of Ibsen's oversized and over-psychologized women—which is what most of those who reviewed the American production in 1981 seemed to want—but as a fragmented portrait drawn more along the lines of pop art, the play makes more sense. Gems assembles a collection of biographical details into an arrangement that makes character seem something inaccessible, half-finished, or damaged. Gems's play features a character whose multiplicity contradicts the singleness or solidity of the conventional—and often male—protagonist. In other words, the drama emphasizes the distance between the art and the artist as a corrective to more sentimentalized notions. As for the implicit question of the source of art, that is defined as an accidental product that reveals little if anything of a subjective interiority; Piaf as Gems defines her is little more than a song machine.

Character in *Piaf* appears, then, merely a surface effect, as if it were an accident of time and place. It is in this sense that the character Piaf does not seem to cohere as an individual in her own right, and in fact much of the criticism of the performance reflects this apparent psychological discontinuity. One reviewer complains that the play "unfolds through sketchy vignettes." Another suggests that Gems cure Piaf's "superficiality" by concentrating more on the singer's "affairs with several young men, any of which might have been shaped into a play with focus and emotional content."[9]

But having male spectators complain that Gems's play ought to be more conventional underscores Gems's success as an expressly feminist playwright: *Piaf* makes clear the extent to which the identity of a woman involves specific hierarchies of power and control. The quest for the "real" Piaf is quickly abandoned in order to expose the various ways her core identity is incommunicable. We are never sure who we are looking at because Piaf is always represented in pieces, so to speak; no matter what angle we see her from, she is "not quite there." As for the ways in which Piaf might be conventionally represented—family, friendships, lovers—these are absent or uncomfortably repetitious. Even her singing is largely impersonal, a text that moves through her but over which she has little control. Piaf is so little herself a source of being or identity that she becomes simply a commodity available for consumption. Ultimately the play comments on the way the subject or self (especially the female self) is written from the outside.

In dramatizing the life of Piaf, Gems both reproduces her subject's passivity ("Ladies and gentlemen, I give you . . . your own . . . Piaf") and makes that passivity the basis of a feminist dramaturgy. The figure of the artist through whom external voices speak—it is, of course, Plato's famous model for artistic "creativity"—is modified to foreground the position of woman as passive medium written or spoken for by others. Gems's work, for all its fidelity to the details of the life of the real Piaf, does not represent an autonomous and (in the traditional dramatic sense) fully conscious subject. Nor should it. Indeed, that is Gems's point: there is no such person present.

To return to Culler's notion of the loss of the continuous self, one could say that missing persons such as Gems's Piaf are a common feature of contemporary theater. But a number of feminist dramatists view the collapse of the modern individual from a different perspective. Far from lamenting the loss (or the suppression) of the stable and enduring subject, they view the self in the first place not as fixed or coherent but rather as diverse, shifting, metamorphic. The fragmentation of individual and private identity is not to be mourned, in short, but is taken to be a necessary condition for the development of a healthy, full self.

Brechtian Dramaturgy, Feminist Politics

The similarities between this model for character and Brechtian theater are striking, and in fact there are parallels—almost congruencies—between Brecht's theories of representation and some feminist dramaturgies.[10] The connections between Brechtian theory and recent women's theater and theory are apparent at several points. At its most general the alignment takes the form of a mutual rejection of "Aristotelian" drama.[11] Another interesting similarity would be their mutual interest in collaborative theater and in the text as an unauthorized (and therefore communal) entity rather than a finished, private product;[12] still another might be their desire to replace linear plots with fragmented or episodic patterns. But for our purposes the most interesting comparison lies in their provocative insistence on the psychological consequences of mimesis. Mimetic response to others is at once the source of Brecht's anti-Aristotelian drama as well as the basis for a distinctly feminine (and also anti-Aristotelian) aesthetic.[13] Maria Irene Fornes's theater, like Brecht's, combines play with a heavy (though not unappetizing) dose of reality therapy. "Like Brecht's," writes W. B. Worthen, "Fornes' theater generates the 'fun,' the infectious sophistication of a popular art. . . [by] [j]uggling the dialectic between 'theater for pleasure' and 'theater for instruction.'"[14] Brecht and Fornes both deconstruct the apparatus of naturalistic theater. But while Brecht's object in unmasking theater—a course he pursued generally throughout his career but especially, as we have seen, in the Lehrstücke—was to unmask ideology, Fornes's broader view of mimesis gradually lessens her commitment to educational theater and involves her more deeply in existential psychology where specific political agendas are subsumed by enactments, engulfments, dissolutions of self, and acts of mimetic individuation.

Fornes experiments with transformational possibilities for character over the whole course of her career. In the early work *A Vietnamese Wedding* (first enacted February 1967), members of the audience are invited to participate in the performance by acting out some of the parts. The work is partly narrative, partly ritual, partly mimetic enactment—the mix in fact makes this "piece" (Fornes's word for the work) a sort of latter-day *Lehrstücke*. In the work there are two kinds of roles: four "presenters" played by professional actors and ten members of the wedding party, who are played by volunteers from the audience. The presenters (Florence, Remy, Aileen, and Irene) invite the spectators to help them make the presentation: "We're going to present *A Vietnamese Wedding*, and we're going to ask a few of you to help us. What you have to do is very simple. It doesn't require any acting ability, and we will tell you what to do as we go along." [15]

Volunteers play bride and groom and their parents, an elder, two youths, and a matchmaker, whose job, according to Vietnamese custom, is to approve the marriage from an "objective" standpoint. The volunteers first seat themselves in a semicircle while the presenters briefly explain Vietnamese tradition to the rest of the audience. Then they lead the volunteers through an enactment of a Vietnamese wedding, interspersing the imitated action with explanatory commentary. The presence of the betel nut and areca leaves, for example, is explained as symbolic references to ancient myth. After the ceremony is completed (the performance takes less than half an hour), Florence, Remy, Aileen, and Irene blow on whistles and join the audience (both participants and spectators) in a processional march from the theater.

Like many works of avant-garde theater in the sixties, *A Vietnamese Wedding* confronts spectators with their own separateness and attempts to subsume them along with the performers into a common experience. In order to unite actors and audience in mind, many experimental performances simply merged them bodily, but Fornes attempts to do more than restructure the conventional playing space. She declares that her play is not a "play" at all: "*A Vietnamese Wedding* is not a play. Rehearsals should serve the sole purpose of getting the readers acquainted with the text and the actions of the piece. The four people conducting the piece are hosts to the members of the audience who will enact the wedding, and their behavior should be casual, gracious, and unobtrusive" (*WR*, p. 8).

A Vietnamese Wedding was performed originally as part of "Angry Arts Week," a series of events the purpose of which was to protest the involvement of American forces in Vietnam. But it contrasts sharply with then-contemporary forms of political protest in that the politics of Fornes's play cannot be separated from her dramaturgy. Politics here are not rhetorical but an aspect of mimetic involvement. That is, the play does not inveigh against American policy but subverts that policy by way of empathic involvement of spectators and actors with Vietnamese roles. As the stage directions indicate, mimetic fusion with an other and interpersonal engulfment are essential to the performance. Political enlightenment then occurs as a consequence of empathic attachments or enactments, not rhetorical conversion.

I do not mean to suggest that a less experimental dramaturgy could not accomplish similar ends. Conventional drama often enlarges spectators' sympathies for alien classes or categories of people; this empathic stretching of the limits of one's self is perhaps the most convincing ethical argument that can be made on behalf of theater.[16] But there are crucial differences between the structures of mimetic involvement in Fornes's play and conventional performances. Her play does not move spectators by means of a childlike attachment to a powerful hero.[17] Rather *A Vietnamese Wedding* so situates the audience that the conventional engulfments and enactments of theater become self-conscious and thematic. We are moved not by characters playing out a sequence of acts but by the simple appeal to hearken sympathetically to distinctly feminine voices. The absence of conflict (the essence of conventional dramaturgy) is noteworthy, as is the lack of actors who perform the acts of distinct, autonomous individuals. Emphasis is placed less on oppositional relationships between self and other than on such values as connectedness, kinship, cooperation, and sharing.

Does the piece reflect specific gender hierarchies? Certainly women command most attention during the performance, since the only important roles Fornes writes are for the four female presenters. However, this should not be seen simply as an exclusive attempt to substitute women for men in represented positions of power. Rather Fornes seems in a curious way to use culturally coded "feminine" qualities (such as passivity, relative invisibility, a willingness to listen) to dissolve the tensions that normally exist between actors and audience during conventional dramatic performance.[18] She specifies that the presenters' behavior be "casual, gracious, and unobtrusive." Narration too is an important element of the performance; as in Brechtian theater, narrativity frames the dramatized elements of the performance and lends it the air of fantasy or romance, and, in conjunction with the taped music, creates its own kind of detached, dreamlike rhythmicity:

FLORENCE: The gifts are placed on the ancestral altar by the groom's party.
IRENE *instructs the party to place the trays on the altar (floor mat).*
Then SHE *instructs the* GROOM *and his* FATHER *to stand to the left of the altar, and* THE REST *to the right.*
REMY: The candles are lit.
IRENE *lights the candles with the help of some of the* GROOM'S FAMILY. *The music stops.*
AILEEN: The bridegroom gives the bride jewels—an engagement ring, a necklace and a bracelet.

If the GROOM *doesn't act of his own accord,* IRENE *will tell him what to do. The same applies to any of the following directions.*
  FLORENCE: The father of the groom gives the bride, her father, and
    her mother a certain amount of money.
HE *does it.* (P. 15)

The four presenters help the audience to achieve full affective and gestural participation in the ceremony. Their actions redefine character within theatrical performance. Identification—allowing another person to stand in for one's self—here is framed clearly as an ethical act. The drama moves from conventional modes of representation through a kind of Brechtian distancing of actor and role to an explicit enactment of power, identity, and politics as these are embodied in mimesis.

Fornes's criticism of American foreign policy thus is embodied in part as a criticism of conventional—and "masculine"—forms of theater.[19] (One recalls Norman Mailer's novel, *Why Are We in Vietnam?*—an indictment of international politics by way of an indictment of the "manly" sport of hunting.) Such distinctions between "masculine" and "feminine" aesthetics resemble the conceptual differences that some empirical psychologists suggest may distinguish male and female perspectives on moral problems. Carol Gilligan identifies, for example, two distinct "voices"—one male, one female—that describe the ethics of self and other. One ethics (the "masculine") is "competitive" and tends to promote "values of separation, individuation, autonomy, and a strong affirmation of ego-logical boundaries . . . [but] the second emphasizes connectedness and interdependence, and a strong affirmation of kinship and solidarity."[20]

Whether or not we believe in the existence of a distinct feminine aesthetic, we can sense that Fornes's play cultivates new territory for mimesis in theater. The use of "hosts" rather than actors who are in character redefines the relations between spectators and performers. The intent is not to challenge the audience with the actors' ontological separateness (as was common in then-contemporary experimental performances). The relationship between actors and spectators is cooperative and interactional from the very beginning. The presenters work with the audience as directors might work with their casts. According to this model for mimetic interactions, the director works with an actor from within a matrix of instinctual and nurturing impulses, as a parent might work with a toddler. The object, as with Brecht's *Lehrstücke,* is a developmental process that is both affective and intellectual; the result is the enlargement (or rebirth) of character and identity. Like actors in the early stages of rehearsals, the four spectator-actors are permitted to carry their scripts onstage. Here the text functions as a transitional object; it permits the beginning actors to carry their identities with them as they test the reality of the play environment. Hence their encounter with the text is not at all like that of traditional spectators who encounter authority and power. In effect, the hosts appeal to the child within the individual spectator, saying, in effect, "Come play in front of me and I'll make sure you don't get seriously hurt."[21]

Mimetic involvement seems to be an important source of character for Fornes, as indeed it was for Brecht, although in certain respects her view of mimesis seems more comprehensive than Brecht's. On the one hand, mimesis (which can connote conscious repetition, representation, or assimilation) is connected with personal growth, adaptation, and positive change; it is the very basis of character. On the other hand, mimesis (which can alternately be translated as mimicry or passive repetition) also involves unconscious acceptance of authority; politically and psychologically, therefore, it is potentially deleterious, a weapon for continuing ideological and cultural oppression of women. Fornes is well aware that mimetic involvements can result in the self-effacement of character. Perhaps her best-known work, *Fefu and Her Friends,* dramatizes the disastrous consequences of men's inscribing their own agenda on women. Men never appear onstage in this drama, and yet, like the absent males in Lorca's tragedy *The House of Bernarda Alba,* they are always psychically present and powerfully determine the women characters' thoughts and lives. To the extent that women in *Fefu* cannot avoid seeing themselves within men's frames for them, they remain, like the displaced subjects described by Lacan, alienated from themselves. The results as Fornes depicts them are mental as well as somatic paralysis. Julia cannot help but understand "human" to mean the male gender, while "woman" is "not a human being" but "a mystery," "another species," "undefined," "unpredictable . . . therefore wicked and gentle and evil and good which is evil."[22] The women at one point envy men their freedom, their strength, their very habits of mind; the play ends when Julia, whose physical paralysis condenses emblematically all the women's subjection to male authority, dies suddenly (but appropriately in an iconographic sense) when Fefu shoots a rabbit. Identity in *Fefu* rests squarely on illicit mimesis; to the extent that women in the play are removed from their femaleness, they are socially undervalued and, more important, themselves believe they are who men tell them to be. As one writer describes it, "most of the characters in *Fefu* have difficulty accepting the body as a possible site for the inscription of their subjectivity because their bodies have already been (in)scripted for them with the male codes of their culture."[23]

So frequent are the claims made recently for such preemptive "inscriptions" of identity that one suspects that Hume (later Wittgenstein and Lacan) may well be right: to be a self is to be written by others. Taken to the extreme, of course, this gives an expressly ironic twist to the notion of character in that it excludes not only spontaneity but also originality, the private space (ethos) that differentiates one individual from another. It also codifies a tendency that has been developing in the understanding of character since the eighteenth century, a tendency (as I noted in my Introduction) to collapse distinctions between theater and life by positioning mimesis at the core of both. As in theater, so in life: a character, a person's body and mind, constitute sites on which are written alien languages. A succinct account of this contamination is provided by Gitta Honegger; she writes of Thomas Bernhard, but her comments might be extended to such modern playwrights as Handke, Fornes, and Churchill: "[t]he theater, then, which is based on the quoting, reciting, and impersonating of a text is to Bernhard more than a metaphor for human existence; it is the perfect sign for its mechanism."[24]

One naturally wonders why authors who seem in some ways instinctively averse to theater choose to make it. Again, Brecht's experience provides one answer. To the extent that the inner workings of theater can themselves be dramatized, they can be exposed and so made into something else and something subversive. Some years ago Roland Barthes wrote that "what Brechtian dramaturgy postulates is that today at least, the responsibility of a dramatic art is not so much to express reality as to signify it. . . . Brecht's moral role is to infiltrate a question into what seems self-evident."[25]

If we look at recent criticism of Fornes's works, however, we find that while much of it centers on questions of form and character first addressed by Brecht, we need to sharpen distinctions between old and new models for character to see what changes (if any) have taken place. Take the following recent description of Mae, the central character of *Mud* (1983):

> Mae, a woman with little education, seeks a way out of this imprisonment by learning how to read and write. . . . She lives with two men: Lloyd, who is essentially "good-hearted" but who functions only at an animal-like level, and Henry, who initially possesses a scant amount of the "knowledge" Mae covets so earnestly but who becomes paralyzed, inarticulate, and helpless after he suffers a fall. When Mae decides that

she has had enough of Lloyd and Henry, she announces her intention to leave them both, and Lloyd kills her with his rifle; the play ends with the two men sobbing near Mae's body, which is outstretched on the kitchen table.[26]

To be sure, the foregoing account is simply a plot summary and therefore conforms to the conventions of literary plot summaries; these are mainly narratorial, and they tend to distill any and all works to similar sequences of basic acts.[27] These are familiar problems connected with any plot summary, as Douglas Robinson has observed: "if we think of literature in these terms," Robinson says, "as something to be boiled down to a plot summary or a couple of tidy themes, the truth in a nutshell, literary texts are going to seem like pretty perverse things."[28] I do not want to minimize the extent to which the "intuitive Platonism" described by Robinson can distort a text. But the existence of represented actions naturally presupposes the existence of agents to perform them, and we are likely therefore to wonder—and I do not think this is our own outmoded belief in old-fashioned individualism intruding—why these acts are being done.[29] One correctly supposes that human agency alone can account for the series of acts identified in the foregoing account of *Mud:* seeks, lives, possesses, covets, decides, announces, kills. (P. F. Strawson makes a similar point when he argues that the identifiability of persons can be deduced on the basis of "person-predicates," that is, mentalistic and physicalistic predicates "which involve doing something, which clearly imply intention or a state of mind or at least consciousness in general."[30])

If there is human agency in *Mud,* there also seems to be human change. At the beginning of the play Mae dwells in linguistic squalor ("Fuck you, Mae / Fuck you, Lloyd"), but her dying words sound suspiciously conventional. They are not inarticulate; in fact, they are nearly as grand as Racine's Phaedra's: "Like the starfish, I live in the dark and my eyes see only a faint light. It is faint and yet it consumes me. I long for it. I thirst for it. I would die for it. Lloyd, I am dying."[31] Of this speech, Deborah Geis writes that it is "infused with a voice that clearly comes from her own associative and poetic powers and thus moves *beyond* the mechanical prose of the biology textbook. This linguistic recourse allows Mae the power of self-demonstration, the ability to articulate her bodied subjectivity."[32] If this means, as it seems to, that as Mae dies she "tells us who she is," then nothing meaningful distinguishes Mae from the unified and autonomous characters of conventional theater. At such moments the differences between Ibsen's theater and the avant-garde (not to mention between New and new New Criticism) seem to be semantic rather than substantial. Character in Geis's discourse still refers to that component of an agent which is personally vital, inward, and essential.

My point is not that nothing like the events described above happens in *Mud;* clearly, Fornes's play dramatizes agents who speak certain words and perform certain acts. The point is that there is some question about the motives of the agents who perform these various acts—their sources, their intelligibility—and that Fornes is much more concerned with dramatizing the frames within which character shows itself than with depicting nascent self-determination. Her dramaturgy deliberately thwarts attempts to read the "truth" of a character because she thinks such truths (rather, the belief in them) naïve.

If we look closely at some of the episodes in *Mud* that seem particularly expressive of character, we find that character varies according to some unorthodox determinants. For example, character can be complicated (but not necessarily wholly determined) by material realities ranging from age, health, and gender to social class, education, and economics. A signal example is scene 10, in which Lloyd returns from a medical clinic (he suffers from prostate problems) with a doctor's prescription; in this scene Lloyd's italicized words, according to Fornes, "represent a stuttering" (p. 30):

LLOYD: They gave me *this.*
HENRY: (*Reads what's on the paper while still in Lloyd's hand. He returns to his papers.*) That's the prescription for your medicine.
LLOYD: They said I should buy *this.* (*Pause.*) They said I should *buy* it.
HENRY: Did you?
LLOYD: No.
HENRY: Why not?
LLOYD: I went to the *clinic.*
HENRY (*without looking at him*): I'm glad you did.
LLOYD: It took a *while.* I thought they *kept* me a long time. I went *early* and just came back.
HENRY: How do you feel?
LLOYD: I don't feel *better.*—I feel *worse.* (P. 30)

Significantly, this is the only time in the entire play when Lloyd stutters (it is also the only scene he shares exclusively with Henry); his language in this scene is revealing, therefore, precisely because it is uncharacteristic.

Whereas in every other scene his words are vulgar, belligerent, or sullenly defensive, here he seems simply pathetic, almost comically so. It is not that he seems unable only to pronounce certain words or combinations of letters; the variety of words over which he stumbles proves that the cause is emotional, not physical. One way to read Lloyd's stuttering would be to analyze it for its psychological underpinnings, to see in it a sign (or a symptom) of his emotional inability to cope with the immediate situation. For example, Lloyd may feel unnerved by Henry's relatively greater social status and education. Then, too, Henry is older (men of different generations commonly find conversation awkward), and there are abundant reasons for Oedipal jealousies: Henry has supplanted the younger man's place in Mae's bed.

But the encounter seems to indicate as well an ideological imbalance. Lloyd is compelled to play the role of a beggar pleading for a handout, and as a result there are powerful ideological constraints operating on him. One might say he is torn between his masculine desire to defend himself, his home, and Mae from Henry and his intuitive sense of his own impotence. Because he lacks money, he cannot buy what he needs to make himself whole. "Tongue-tied" in this scene is a trope that makes visible one of the effects of a capitalistic system of medical care; in a very real sense to have money is to be able to buy being. Circumstances here write Lloyd's behavior. Character is culture: to the extent that material realities (Lloyd's class, his education, his illness, his gender) conspire to prevent him from "speaking for himself," he stutters. Geis reads a similar stumbling passage in *The Conduct of Life* as evidence the speaker needs "to affirm her place in an environment where . . . she is marginalized."[33]

This is one of the many points where Fornes's work contributes to modern revisions of the individual humanist subject. But I would argue that Fornes also attempts more than to depict the material or cultural realities from which character issues. While Fornes might agree with Lacan, for example, that there is no subject outside discourse (or even with Marx that capitalism alienates Lloyd from himself), she would not in my opinion so readily assent to Lacan's melancholy conclusion that subjects and subjectivity are forever divided. For Lacan, the subject remakes itself (and thereby loses itself) in encounters with the other, but for Fornes the isolated character does not exist psychologically in the first place.

That one's sense of self is fortunately dependent on mimetic interactions with others offers an attractive alternative to Lacan. That is the reason, for example, that *A Vietnamese Wedding* is conceived as a play that is not a play, peopled by characters who are not identified as characters. Bypassing the static and essentially isolated egos of conventional theater, Fornes introduces her audience and actor-characters into a network of communicative and collaborative relationships. Her work is informed throughout by evidence that humans are constructions or creations rather than essential givens; Brecht (and even Gordon Craig) made many of the same assumptions about theater.[34]

Mimetic interactions in *A Vietnamese Wedding* remind us that theatrical representation is always a matter of ethics. In subsequent plays Fornes likewise proves that character is anchored in society rather than free-floating. It is important to remember, nevertheless, that in attempting to assess the mental life of Fornes's characters we must recognize that health in the individual is impossible without health in the society. This is partly (as Bonnie Marranca has shown) a new concept for character: "Fornes's work goes to the core of character. Instead of the usual situation in which a character uses dialogue or action to explain what he or she is doing and why, her characters exist in the world by their very act of trying to understand it."[35] At the same time this view of the individual and individuality does not lack literary precedents—as in the Homeric poems, for example, where "virtually every kind of mental activity, including the most trivial and ordinary, can be ascribed to an outside source."[36]

In *Tango Palace* (1965; first performance November 1963 under the title, "There! You Died"), actors demonstrate how familiar assumptions about individual identity are exposed as mere assumptions in the face of mimetic predispositions. In that work the script is literally shredded in full view of the audience, as one of the characters repeatedly tosses onto the stage a number of cards on which are written the speeches for his part. Several of Fornes's stage directions emphasize the interrelatedness of ethos and mimesis: "Each time ISIDORE feels HE has said something important, HE takes a card from his pocket or from a drawer and flips it across the room in any direction. (The word "card" in the script indicates when a card should be flipped.) This action is automatic" (*WR*, p. 129).

A striking image of character materializes here as Fornes renders dramatic speech concrete and palpable. At first glance Isidore's ironic self-awareness might seem little different from that achieved by some of Beckett's protagonists. ("What is there to keep me here?" asks Clov. "The dialogue," replies Hamm laconically.) But in *Tango Palace* the characters' obligations to the script are much less demoralizing than ever in Beckett.[37] Isidore's indebtedness to a script reveals the modes of being that are normally unapparent in theater and in life: "I know all my cards by heart. (*Card*) I can recite them in chronological order and I don't leave one word out. (*Card*) What's more I never say a thing which is not an exact quotation from one of my cards. (*Card*) That's why I never hesitate. (*Card*) Why I'm never short of an answer. (*Card*) Or a question. (*Card*) Or a remark, if a remark is more appropriate" (*WR*, p. 134).

Each speech of Isidore apparently repeats what is written for him on his cards, and at the end of the performance the stage is cluttered with the signs of the actors' work, the production of the script. The play (in Susan Sontag's description) depicts "the comedy and the pathos of instruction."[38] But it allows us also to perceive the limits that are invariably laid down for the formation of character. Isidore's scrupulous adherence to a script he did not write is a source both of his folly and his self: "I talk like a wise parrot. Study hard, learn your cards, and one day, you too will be able to talk like a parrot" (*WR*, p. 135). The play moves forward by moving back to its original form, a visible script waiting for agents to speak it:

> *The stage darkens. The door opens. The sound of harps is heard out-side. There is a blue sky.* ISIDORE *appears among the clouds dressed as an angel.* HE *carries a stack of cards.* HE *beckons* LEOPOLD *to follow him.* LEOPOLD *picks up a few cards, then the sword, then a few more cards.* ISIDORE *shakes his head, and shows* LEOPOLD *the cards* HE *carries.* LEOPOLD *walks through the door slowly, but with determina-tion.* HE *is ready for the next stage of their battle.* (*WR*, p. 162)

The particular appropriateness of having the actors produce their script as they speak (reproduce) it is that in so doing they make visible the ethics of mimesis. At the end of the play Leonard "kills" Isidore, but in this play the death of one of the central characters proves nothing. Why does the struggle between Leopold and Isidore continue beyond the end of the play? It is difficult to know for sure, but perhaps the answer lies in Fornes's definition of character as relational, contextual, forever open. Or perhaps Isidore is so little himself a source of his own being that it is impossible to kill him. He is less a character than an echo, and, like an echo, he cannot be destroyed or suppressed. Unlike characters in the conventional dramatic sense, his identity does not depend on his emitting apparently original speech. *Tango Palace* is a play in which the representation of character is subordinated to the production of character: the self is destabilized, set in motion, decentered, and displaced onto a field of echolalic play.

Plays like *A Vietnamese Wedding* and *Tango Palace* show clearly the dramaturgical materials they inherit. Just as many of Richard Estes's super-realist paintings are storehouses of earlier styles and techniques of painting, Fornes's plays conspicuously display theater history and theatrical convention. Yet despite its emphasis on the mechanics of theater—the "enunciators" of stage meaning—Fornes's theater is normally representational. Her actors do not simply convey ironic awareness of their characters *as* characters. With rare exceptions, they do not split off from their roles.[39] But neither do they endow their characters with a subtext in order to give the illusion of psychological realism. As Bonnie Marranca writes, Fornes's principal accomplishment is to create a realistic theater that "lift[s] the burden of psychology, declamation, morality, and sentimentality from the concept of character."[40] Fornes's characters with their quotations and repetitions indicate the extent to which her theater creates a new language for the definition of identity. Her characters sometimes prove disturbing because they possess no inner core that they can project into the public sphere, only an indeterminate and ongoing openness. Character on this stage is therefore never consistently predictable or controllable. For this reason Fornes's characters—like her scripts, which she considers works in progress—are rarely "completed." The provisional nature of her characters restores their status as experimental constructions. On first encounter her people seem mechanical, sinister, and unrealistic, but that is simply a consequence of their abstraction from conventional theatrical frames. Perhaps a comparison with photographic art will make Fornes's people seem less abstracted and more like life. A photograph seems natural to us in part because it so clearly redefines reality on a miniaturized plane: it is what it seems to be, a representation.[41] But we can be shocked if somehow we are made to notice the difference between a photograph and the actuality it represents—as superrealist paintings, for example, seem preternatural in contrast to the "natural" photographs they imitate.

Repetition and Originality in *The Danube*

More recently Fornes has extended her relational model for character so as to combine mimesis and institutionalized authority. Plays such as *Fefu and Her Friends* and *Mud* suggest the powers as well as the dangers of mimetic engulfment. But perhaps her most explicit definition of character as public or transactional occurs in *The Danube*. First performed in 1982 under the title *You Can Swim in the Danube—But the Water Is Too Cold,* the play demonstrates graphically how myriad are the selves that constitute us. If, as Derek Parfit has suggested, we are more like nations than isolated units, then we betray individuals by framing them with a discourse different from that reserved for depicting the life of a group.[42] The language Fornes uses in *The Danube* implicates character with politics, private tensions with public concerns. In this way the play manifests the diverse multiplicity that we actually are. In it Fornes creates a significantly new type of character, new both in relation to conventional drama and in terms of her ideological investment in the human subject as individuated but structurally open.

That Fornes invents a new model for character can be seen in *The Danube* in a variety of ways. Perhaps the most striking feature of the play is its tripled speech. The majority of the scenes, for example, begin with sequences of sentences heard three times, first as taped speech (marked in the text by double solidi) and then as live discourse. At the beginning of the drama, for example, a taped voice is heard speaking first in English, then in Hungarian, in the following manner:

PAUL: / / Good afternoon Mr. Sandor. / / I believe we met at the
    Smith's last night.
MR. SANDOR: / / Yes, I remember. Your name is Paul Green.[43]

After the taped voices are heard, the actors themselves speak the lines. This duality of texts combines visible individuals on stage with some of the properties of radio drama—disembodied, dislocated voices coming out of the dark. The effect resembles that of Beckett's late plays, not only because the taped voices compete ironically with live speech but also because the doubling of voices calls to mind corresponding divisions or doublings of identity.

Contrasting the actors' live voices with their electronic counterparts in two languages may seem to suggest that Fornes is commenting satirically on her characters' lack of autonomy. But her stage directions indicate otherwise; they are unusually specific as to the manner in which the repetitions are to be played:

In order to maintain a flow of life on stage through the recorded speeches it is recommended that the actors do not appear to be aware of the recorded voices. This can be achieved as follows:

1) The style of speaking of the recorded voices should be in the style of speaking of recorded language lessons. But the style of speaking of the actors should be naturalistic.

2) The actors should hear and assimilate a line when it is delivered to them, but they should not respond or react to it till it is time for them

*to reply. If they should react to it immediately but not speak, it would
be apparent that the recording is impeding their speaking and that their
behavior is not autonomous. (P. 42)*

The language tapes are not intended to create an absurd picture, therefore, and if the echolalia develops into parody (as, say, in Ionesco's *The
Bald Soprano*) it becomes pointless. Fornes seems not to intend the banal
talk to expose the emptiness of modern life. The language tapes instead
are to be understood as part of the mise-en-scène, and they contain within
themselves a key to the structure of the play: a mixture of live and imitated actions. Moreover, the language tapes must interact with the actors'
speeches in a specific way; above all the relationship must not appear
mechanistic or comedic, as if the characters were absurdist clowns. Fornes
specifies that the characters' behavior must appear autonomous and that
the actors' speech should appear naturalistic. This means that here (as in
other instances) she imagines her characters to be real persons.[44]

This play of echoes corresponds exactly to the resonances created by the
mixed styles of the set, and, like the other elements of the mise-en-scène,
it carries emotional as well as thematic significance. The stage is a simple
platform, but behind it are placed various painted backdrops done, Fornes
specifies, "in a style resembling postcards" (p. 43). And gestural echoes
complement the repetitions of language and set styles: in scenes 12, 13, and
14 live actors are doubled with their puppet counterparts. To interpret all
these relationships as parodies of originals is slightly misleading. The language tapes are not the source of the actors' representations, just as the
Hungarian language is not a source for English and vice versa. Each of the
three texts is to be understood as merely a version of the others, and each
is apprehended as itself only by way of its differences from its partners,
which in turn have original status only in the context of their relationship
with their alternates.

The result is a constellation of speeches and speakers with no definable
center or originary source. The Hungarian not only contradicts the English
tape, it distances it, and the tapes, in turn, are contradicted and distanced
by the actors' imitations. The repetitions multiply to such an extent that
they undermine conventional oppositions between text and translation,
original and copy, self and other. Once echolalia has been established in the
play it spreads like a contagion. The effect on the production of character is
both novel and disquieting; one could say that in this play egos are defined
as echoes. As soon as the live performance is revealed to repeat in part the
words heard on the language tape, the actors' words acquire the status of

a memory—something imperfectly quoted, something heard before. This is the reason that the actors must not seem aware of the recorded voices, that they speak prerecorded texts unconscious that they are doing so. The taped speeches resemble material forgotten or repressed but repeated compulsively in behavior. In a way, the actors reproduce themselves, without of course knowing that they are doing so. In much the same way the painted backdrops ("in a style resembling postcards") and the puppet stage turn out to be ghostly repetitions or preternatural anticipations of events that do not show their faces. Whether it be in the postcard art, the language lessons, or the puppet theater that reenacts the previous scene or forecasts one to come, the overall emphasis is on familiar surfaces. Everything in *The Danube* turns out already to have been heard and seen.

Given such dramaturgy, it is impossible to speak of character in *The Danube* as originary. Neither can character be located in a private center of will. All that exists is a haunting tissue of relationships involving repetition, substitution, resemblance. Especially haunting is the doubling of parts that Fornes builds into her script. As with the repetitions of language, Fornes's stage directions are explicit: "*It is suggested that Mr. Kovacs, the Waiter, the Doctor and the Barber be played by the same actor*" (p. 43). Doubling actors' roles is sometimes an economic necessity, but in this case the playwright turns a feature of "poor theater" into a component of her art. As with some of the plays of Caryl Churchill (who also specifies doubling for some of her roles), the cumulative reappearances of the same body in different costumes and contexts makes character itself an issue.

These enforced negations of the insular character mark its disappearance, and in much the same way the distorted chronology of events hollows out history. "The play starts in 1938," writes Fornes; "[h]owever, it soon departs from chronological realism" (*Plays*, p. 43). The events that occur in *The Danube* occupy no identifiable historical space and follow no clear chronology. Everything in this work is artificial, quintessentially theatrical, and therefore already at one remove from reality. By beginning most scenes with language tapes that forecast the coming dialogue, Fornes illuminates the relationship of conventional actors to the script they pretend not to know. But the various repetitions also induce a growing anxiety. Because everything that happens seems already to have happened before, the mood grows queerly nostalgic. Even the most banal conversations come to us as echoes, as if the words are being spoken at some great distance:

A neighborhood cafe in Budapest. MR. SANDOR *sits at a table. He wears a brown suit, a white shirt and a black tie and shoes. On the*

*table is a shot glass containing spirits and a newspaper which he has
folded to a manageable size.* PAUL *approaches him. He wears a tweed
jacket and hat, a wool plaid shirt and wool tie and trousers.*

ON TAPE: *"Unit One. Basic sentences. Paul Green meets Mr. Sandor
and his daughter Eve." Also include dialogue in English and
Hungarian up to "Are you Hungarian?"*

PAUL: / / Good afternoon Mr. Sandor. / / I believe we met at the
Smith's last night.

MR. SANDOR: / / Yes, I remember. Your name is Paul Green.

PAUL: / / Yes.

MR. SANDOR: (*Standing and shaking* PAUL's *hand.*) / / Please, take a
seat. (*They sit.*)

PAUL: / / Thank you.

MR. SANDOR: / / Are you Hungarian?

PAUL: Oh no. I'm from the U.S. (P. 44)

In this crossover of representations the traditional outlines of character
vanish. No one in *The Danube* speaks for him- or herself; rather characters share language the source of which is presented as external to the
individual. Ego, self, identity are mere reproductions dependent on the
mechanisms of repetition and imitation. Fornes depicts human experience
as cut off from spontaneous, original thought or expression; as soon as Paul
and Mr. Sandor speak, they establish themselves as imitators—shadows
of others, shadows even of themselves. *The Danube* is a chilling play, not
only because it never names the horror of nuclear war (if that is what the
play is "about")[45] but because the replays and repetitions enact a life that
looks dead because it is never more than a memory, a trace, or a dream.

Thus *The Danube* submerges all speakers in currents of repetition. We
cannot locate, for example, the origin of Paul's chauvinism; all we have are
the metaphors and phrases he has inherited. Paul as character is merely a
vehicle for the transmission of speech, as he speaks rapidly and apparently
without thought a series of banal and increasingly contradictory observations:

(THE WAITER *and* EVE *freeze. The music stops.*)

PAUL: (*Speaking rapidly.*) I came from a country where we hear out
suggestions. We invented the suggestion box. The best suggestion
may come from the least expected place. We value ideas. We don't
hesitate to put ideas to practice. We consider ideas that are given to
us. We don't hold back our suggesting of ideas for fear of appearing

foolish. We are not afraid to appear foolish, as good ideas disguise themselves in foolishness. We are not afraid to appear foolish. We are the foolish race. (P. 51)

Paul's words issue forth in a steady stream, yet it cannot be said that his monologue belongs to him. Paul's speech manifests itself as a repetition not only because of the rapid-fire delivery but because the silence and frozen actors that attend him indicate the extent to which his words and body are framed or "cited" by the medium in which he exists. The tableau focuses attention on the split between body and words as Paul's discourse, far from being an extension of his inner self, comes from somewhere beyond it.

Similar effects can be found throughout *The Danube*, not only in language but in gesture. Bodies in this play are staged or quoted just as much as words, and, like words, they prove just as difficult to assign to an individual. Fornes transforms characters into marionettes, grotesque deformations, or ghostly shells whose incompleteness exposes with breathtaking pathos the dying of the West. Her dramaturgy is highly artificial and self-conscious (one critic calls it "deconstructive") but also simply educational. The taped speeches, for example, are in contemporary theater familiar deconstructive strategies, but here they are also simple imitations of real loss:

Fornes was walking past a thrift shop on West 4th Street, saw some 78 records in a bin, liked the way they looked even before she knew what they were . . . so she bought one for a dollar. Turns out it was a language record, the simplest sentences, first in Hungarian, then in English. "There was such tenderness in those little scenes," she recalls—introducing people, ordering in restaurants, discussing the weather—"that when the Theater for the New City asked me to do an antinuclear piece, I thought of how sorrowful it would be to lose the simplest pleasures of our own era." [46]

The Danube, no matter how much it might resist the conventions of realistic theater, still imitates an absent reality. Fornes therefore shares with all but one of the authors of this study—the exception, of course, is Gordon Craig—the presupposition that there exists a superior reality that is both accessible intellectually and expressible through the medium of theater. ("The presumption of the reality of the world and people," writes Earl Miner, "is an obviously necessary premise of mimesis." [47]) In this respect *The Danube* may well offer a new language for realist representation of character precisely because of its radically stylized dramaturgy. [48] "The formal intricacy of *The Danube*," writes Worthen, "opens a dissonance between speech and language, between the bodies of the performers and the gestures of their enactment, between life and the codes with which we conduct it." [49] This formalism, argues Worthen, bleeds personalities from the personae:

> Onstage, *The Danube* suspends the identification between language and speech. The performance dramatizes the problematic of "social being," the dialectical encounter between the individual subject and the codes of his or her realization. . . . To be known in *The Danube* is necessarily to "talk like a machine," say only what the "machines" of language and behavior permit one to say. [50]

My objection to such a description is that it makes Fornes's characters seem like a collection of soulless bipeds. I would stress a more positive response to *The Danube*'s dramatis personae. The focus of Fornes's experimental dramaturgy is not after all the process of losing identity—"talking like a machine"—but the process of taking on identity in the first place. There is no nostalgia here (as there is, for example, in Peter Handke's *Kaspar*) for prelinguistic being or for a self somehow untarnished by culture; on the contrary, we have the author's word that she wrote out of sorrow that the "simplest pleasures" of sharing culture and discourse might be lost. Neither are Paul's and The Waiter's monologues (unlike Kaspar's) sardonic portraits of hollow men. Behind The Waiter's division of people into classes of "us" and "them" one senses a desperate but oblique striving for self-definition by way of absorption into a larger group. The Waiter's obsessive concern with the difference between Europeans and Americans can be read as a displacement of his own anxiety, an attempt to achieve a fragile sense of individuality within a social context. Such a blurring of the boundaries of character implies a redefinition of the individual in terms of the collective or society. The play moves away from the autonomous characters of conventional drama toward a model for character more open and unstructured. It is an expressly public notion of identity: we are who we are only by way of our mimetic engulfments with others.

Bruce Wilshire (citing Henri Gouhier on the theater's "essence") offers an inspired description of such acts of characterization:

> Gouhier points out that it is just because the everyday self is permanently installed at what it feels to be "the center" of the world experienced by it that it is oblivious to its most characteristic and habitual modes of action. These are really mimetic. One is already an other for others who has been formed by others, so he cannot be that center

which is in itself and for itself as he feels himself to be. . . . One exists on a periphery of mimetic fusion with others which remains unilluminated for him for two reasons, first, because this periphery is so constant and contrastless that it remains unnoticed—only when we observe another culture are its lines of mimetic fusion clearly evident—and, second, because the distinctiveness of the person's bodily position and bodily point of view convinces one of one's distinctiveness as a self.[51]

It is these normally "unilluminated" fusions that constitute character for Fornes. Worthen argues of *The Danube* that the affective disjunctions and linguistic dead-ends can be explained by reference to external constraints (the various political and linguistic codes that demarcate the bounds of character), but I would add two important qualifications: first, this method of "characterization by contamination" does not seem to be something her personae regret, and, second, it seems actually to be presented as normal by the playwright. It is the way one discovers selfhood. In discussing Fornes's characters, therefore (as we saw in *Tango Palace* and *A Vietnamese Wedding* but also in *Mud*), it is essential to remember that they are individuals in a group and of a group. Even when they are isolated (as, for example, in scene 9—"*a sanatorium*") the characters engage with others. In that scene Paul is seated alone at his desk, but he writes to Eve: Dearest Eve. How are you? Have you missed me? and so on.

Soliloquies in *The Danube* do not represent private points of view so much as choric discourse. Worthen sees them as "unscripted," lacking context, and incomprehensible—failed attempts at "self-expression."[52] But another possibility for these trancelike monologues is that they originate from no single person but from a composite identity. (A useful dramaturgical comparison might be made between these monologues and some of the speeches in No drama, a dramatic form in which individuality as it is commonly understood has little relevance.) They are distinctly expressive, in other words, but not recognizably *self*-expressive. This portrayal of inner states as a collection of echoes or common voices indicates that Fornes is at least as interested in the components of the self that result from mimetic interactions as she is in the elements of discourse that distinguish one individual from another. At the same time such portraiture indicates a breakdown of conventional boundaries between public and private selves. Her characters cannot insulate themselves from others; when they speak they reveal only a continuous interaction with a larger social whole.

There is little room for idiosyncrasies in Fornes's model for character, nor for original speech. Nor is there a place for autonomous gesture, as if bodies themselves were interchangeable. And why indeed should not body language be learned and shared as is speech? We present our bodies, like our discourse, on the basis of our experience of others. "Mimetically learned body-images may compete," writes Wilshire, "or alternate to some degree, given various circumstances. [Paul] Schilders also contends that persons sometimes take only parts of the experienced bodies of others and incorporate them into their body-images."[53] ("They may also," he adds, "incorporate animals."[54] This method of character building, too, is perfectly normal, indeed desirable; idiomatic expressions suggest that one can learn to be brave as a lion or quiet as a mouse.) In scenes 13 and 14, puppet actors stand in for the actors playing Paul, Eve, and Mr. Sandor; by doubling their images, they diminish the physical autonomy of the characters they represent. The puppets are a visual embodiment of the blurring of personal boundaries so apparent in the dialogic repetitions. Fornes describes scene 13 as identical in every respect to the previous scene, save for the replacement of live actors by puppets:

> *There is a theatre curtain placed on the downstage posts. A puppet stand is placed on stage. On the floor of the puppet stage down right is a blanket. To the left of the blanket and facing it is a chair. To the right of the chair is a breakaway table. On the up left corner is a chair.* PAUL, EVE, *and* MR. SANDOR *operate puppets whose appearance is identical to theirs. The following scene, which is the same as scene 12, is performed by the puppets.*
>
> PAUL: Eve, I'm leaving. I can't take this any longer. You take care of the place or burn it if you want. I don't care what you do.
>
> EVE: Why don't you take me with you? (*He sits.*)
>
> PAUL: If you go, we'll never get anywhere. It is you who has polluted me. I am clean of body and mind.
>
> EVE: That's not so. I have not polluted you.
>
> PAUL: It is you who have caused all the trouble.
>
> EVE: You are losing your brain, Paul. You are talking like a machine. You are saying what the machines say.
>
> PAUL: It must be true if machines say it. (*She screams and hits him repeatedly.*) I am sorry, Eve. I don't know what made me say that. (*He hits the table with his fist. It breaks apart. He cries.*) I didn't mean any of it. I don't have a mind. And I don't have a soul.
>
> MR. SANDOR: (*Startled as if awakened from a nightmare. He remains so through the following scene.*) What happened!

EVE: Paul got angry, father, and he smashed the table. (EVE *has a coughing attack*.)

MR. SANDOR: Is she ill!

PAUL: Why do you ask that?

MR. SANDOR: She's coughing!

PAUL: She always coughs.

MR. SANDOR: What's wrong with that!

PAUL: Nothing. She coughs, I throw up, and you have diarrhea.

MR. SANDOR: Let's call a doctor! (Pp. 61–62)

The doubling between live actors and puppets is itself doubled in the ensuing scenes 14 and 15. Scene 14 is performed by the puppets:

ON TAPE: *"Unit Thirteen. Basic sentences. Paul and Eve pack their suitcase." The scene is performed without a language tape.*

PAUL: Eve.

EVE: Yes.

PAUL: Let's go.

EVE: Yes.

(PAUL *gets a suitcase and puts it on the table. They each get the items of clothing indicated in the script from the drawers and put them in the suitcase.*)

EVE: Stockings. Five pairs of underpants.

PAUL: Eight pairs of socks.

EVE: Five shirts. Three blouses.

PAUL: Trousers.

EVE: Shorts. Six pairs of shorts. A skirt. A dress.

PAUL: Handkerchiefs. Seven handkerchiefs.

EVE: Everything is here.

PAUL: Let's go.

(MR. SANDOR *enters.*)

MR. SANDOR: What's this?

EVE: Please, father, come with us.

MR. SANDOR: Don't go. (EVE *embraces* MR. SANDOR.)

EVE: Good bye, father. (*Walking to* PAUL.) Good bye.

(*Lights fade. There is music. As the scenery is changed, smoke goes up from the stage floor. The puppet stage is removed.*) (Pp. 62–63)

Scene 15, the last scene of the play, duplicates the action of scene 14 up to the point at which Paul says, "Let's go." At that point the scene varies from its double in the following manner:

PAUL: Let's go.

EVE: (*Taking a revolver from the suitcase.*) What's this?

PAUL: (*Reaching for the gun.*) A gun. (*First she resists. Then she releases it. He puts it in his pocket.* MR. SANDOR *enters.*)

MR. SANDOR: What's this?

PAUL: (*Taking the suitcase.*) Good bye.

EVE: (*Embracing* MR. SANDOR.) Good bye, father.

MR. SANDOR: Don't go.

EVE: Please come with us.

MR. SANDOR: I live and work here. My family lives here.

EVE: Please, father, come with us.

MR. SANDOR: It doesn't matter, Eve. There's no place to go.

EVE: Good bye. (EVE *walks downstage and speaks front.*) My Danube, you are my wisdom. My river that comes to me, to my city, my Budapest . . . I say good bye. As I die, my last thought is of you, my sick friend. Here is your end. Here is my hand. I don't know myself apart from you. I don't know you apart from myself. This is the hour. We die at last, my Danube. Good bye. (*She joins* PAUL. *They start to exit right.*)

MR. SANDOR: Eve!

(*There is a brilliant white flash of light. Black out.*) (Pp. 63–64)

Similarity and difference mix so indissolubly that *The Danube* is a play not only informed by doubling but informed about it. The aesthetic elegance of *The Danube*—the language tapes, the stylized speech, the puppet enactments, the postcard set—remind one at times of high modernism. One thinks of Eliot's *The Waste Land,* of Meyerhold's ironic exploitation of theater, of the painter James Ensor's macabre *commedia,* of the tendency of modernist artists to make brilliant art out of the darkest shadows of the individual psyche.

For all its familiar trappings, however, *The Danube* lacks the consolations we have come to expect of modernist art. If we compare the dissolutions of individual character in *The Danube* with Prufrock's schizophrenia or even with the sundered protagonists of Beckett's late plays, for example, we see that Fornes lacks these writers' ironic, detached playfulness. There runs especially throughout Beckett's elaborate restructurings of character—from the comedic early plays to the later works featuring body parts or voices in the head—something defiantly frivolous, something essentially unserious: a hat cocked the wrong way, a disarming pun, a luxurious interest in pure aesthetic effect. Dehumanization in Beckett is oddly consoling;

his theater has been called a *commedia* of androids. But Fornes's *comme-dia* is darkened permanently by her sense of ethical crisis. The dissolution of individualistic characters in *The Danube* is not just an aesthetic experiment; it is a mode of dramatic realism. It emphasizes that the individual members of a society not only influence each other but create one another by processes of mimetic interaction. "Person" in this drama is regarded as a mythic concept, and "personality" never refers to private matters. In redefining the individual as a public phenomenon, the sum of a history of interpersonal involvements, Fornes in effect restores to character something of its ancient public context. *The Danube* asserts that intersubjective models for character may provide the only legitimate means to dramatize a world in which everything is seen increasingly as connected with everything else.

Abstract Art and the
Representation of Character

This book began as a series of separate essays that shared a single aim, namely, to account for the persistence of character (or something like it) on the stages of playwrights whose art seemed to be dominated in one way or another and for one purpose or another by abstraction. I do not mean to write in this epilogue a few thousand words that would condense the essays that precede it, and I certainly do not propose to tell a new version of modern drama, even one aspect of it, in these several final pages. Yet some tentative generalizations about the subject may be in order. Perhaps the most telling point at this stage to be made about the representation of character in modern drama is that, for all its apparent marginalization as a subject by critics, its death, as Mark Twain once quipped of his own, has been greatly exaggerated. "We need to confront the fact," writes Charles Lyons, "that the image of character in space and time constitutes an irreducible aesthetic unit. No critical system can erase the presence of the human image that occupies the space of the stage." [1]

If Lyons's words sound like a manifesto, perhaps the reason is that the criticism of character has all but vanished from critical disourse. No one, of course (and certainly not Lyons), would wish to return to nineteenth-century methodologies. [2] But to the extent that the playwrights in this study may be taken as representative of dramatists in general, it seems clear that the impulse to deny or to move beyond drama's essential medium, "the image of character in space," ends by affirming its relevance. To see this in something like a final perspective, I would like to turn once more to a specific text, in this case Marguerite Duras's *India Song*.

Despite its status as a postmodernist text, [3] *India Song* (1975) embodies many assumptions and techniques about dramatic representation that have inspired playwrights throughout the twentieth century, indeed from the earliest years of the modernist movement. As in the work of Craig nearly a full century ago, in Duras's art the basic assumptions of conventional stage realism seem artistically naïve if not dangerously inept. Yet introductory remarks such as Duras writes for *India Song* would be inconceivable without the continuing possibility of a realistic dramaturgy as well as the precedent of early modernist attitudes toward such realistic or referential dramaturgies. Duras writes her political and geographical fictions in the shadow of Craig's contempt for conventional realism and his concurrent fondness for any technique (even the "technique" of ineptitude) that mitigated against stage illusionism. ("The scenery," he wrote approvingly of the Reichers' staging of *Iphigenia in Tauris,* "to judge from the illustrated Journals, must have been appallingly bad, and the costumes seem to have been quite fairly incorrect" [*The Mask* 10 (December 1908), p. 203].) Her dramaturgy is indebted also to Brecht's more serious ideological objections to naturalism. In the work of all three artists the object is to reject conventional mimesis in order to stress the relationship of the elements of the work of art more for compositional or instructional than for representational or thematic purposes. Hence Duras's notes indicate,

> The names of Indian towns, rivers, states, and seas are used here primarily in a musical sense.
>
> All references to physical, human, or political geography are incorrect.
>
> You can't drive from Calcutta to the estuary of the Ganges in an afternoon. Nor to Nepal.
>
> The "Prince of Wales" Hotel is not on an island in the Delta, but in Colombo.
>
> And New Delhi, not Calcutta, is the administrative capital of India. And so on. (P. 5)

This insistence on geographical and political incorrectness seems aggressively artificial and calls attention to the fictiveness of the play's represented world. In one sense it is gratuitous, almost playful; it is a carefully distorted dream world reminiscent of surrealist whimsicality, where incongruous things may meet ("the fortuitous encounter of a sewing machine and an umbrella on a dissecting table"). In another sense, however, that whimsicality is modified by a more dignified, almost classical, melancholy. Duras's texts "chart landscapes of loss."[4] The drama of *India Song*—the narratives, respectively, of Anne-Marie Stretter, "wife of a French Ambassador to India and now dead,"[5] and of a Beggar Woman mad with grief whose story merges metaphorically with that of Anne-Marie Stretter—

occurs offstage, not in any real existential space but in intensely private and ultimately unreachable interiors dramatized mainly by silent actors and a host of offstage choral voices.

It is a play that questions the very limits of character and the adequacy of its linguistic representation, and many of the play's episodes include specifics of characterization or performance that recollect—as does the work of Bernhard, Beckett, and Fornes—the dramaturgies of Brecht or Craig. Within the second part of the drama, for example, as part of the dramatization of a reception at the French embassy, Duras specifies that *"the set should seem accidental—stolen from a 'whole' that is by its nature inaccessible, that is, the reception."* Overheard conversations are sometimes repeated with slight errors so as to stress spectators' remoteness from the original version of events, or, finally, that the voices themselves *"should not seem completely natural."* *"During rehearsals,"* Duras writes, *"some slight defect should be settled on, common to all voices"* (pp. 49, 50). *"One ought to get the impression of a reading,"* she says, *"but one which is reported, one which has been performed before"* (p. 50).

In all these ways, Duras follows well-worn paths of modernist dramatic figuration. The disjunction of the various elements of the theatrical performance, speech (lexis) from spectacle (opsis), recalls Brecht's "non-Aristotelian" or "alienated" dramaturgy,[6] but it may be linked also with Craig and an increased emphasis on the visual as a source of meaning in its own right. Spectacle no longer subserves the other elements of the play, and yet by detaching the text from its visual embodiment Duras paradoxically emphasizes the importance of the latter.

No doubt Duras wants to suggest that there are a number of possible scenarios (or subtexts) that might explain events. She conspicuously loads the drama, therefore, with contradictory or at least alternate possibilities that cause us to speculate about character rather than permit us clearly to discover it. Some of the various contradictions seem little more than decoys that throw the question of character (not to mention the possibility of its artistic representation or remembered retrieval) into doubt. For example, in part 2 The Women's repetition of Anne-Marie Stretter's conversation with The Young Attaché is deliberately contradicted by our next hearing her "original" words:

WOMEN *(low):*

———— Did you hear? *(Pause.)* She said to him: "I wish I were you, arriving in India for the first time during the summer monsoon." *(Pause.)* They're too far away . . . I can't hear any more . . .

Conversation between ANNE-MARIE STRETTER *(voice marvelous in its sweetness) and the* YOUNG ATTACHE:
A.-M.S. *(deliberate repetition with slight error)*:
   I wish I were you, coming here for the first time in the rains. *(Pause.)*
   You're not bored? What do you do? In the evenings? On Sundays?
   (P. 75)

The emphasis here is not so much on action as it reveals character, but rather on repetition as a means to prove the mystery and inaccessibility of character in the first place. As the ongoing disjunction between body image and sound source is disruptive for spectators who are accustomed to assume their unity in the production of character, so here the discrepancy between what is said and what is reported makes character seem almost inaccessible. We must acknowledge that The Voices, if they are inadequate in the transmission of relatively small matters, must lose something of great significance in their representation of Anne-Marie Stretter as a whole.

India Song covers a virtual spectrum of ways of representing character on the modern stage, from its haunting, disembodied voices or echolalic, poetic rhythms, to its visual artistry and formal, sometimes speechless pictorialism, to its insistent artifice or its impossible geographic reality, to its shifting among genres so that character openly varies according to the manner of its representation. In *India Song* and numerous other works Duras has indeed "opened up new dimensions in the possibilities offered by theater."[7] Yet her dramaturgy is surely indebted in many specific ways to the familiar abstractions of modernist art. Her affinities with the theaters of Beckett, or Fornes and Bernhard, and even with Brecht are obvious.[8] And in her instinctive preference for film over theater she has much in common with Craig, in particular his idiosyncratic bias against live actors.

India Song was conceived originally as a stage project to be done in collaboration with Peter Brook, but Duras chose instead to produce her work as a film, explaining her choice by saying that "film is more flexible (*malleable*) and less burdened by the weight of the actor."[9] Duras's preference for the relative "weightlessness" (therefore artfulness) of the filmic actor derives from the same artistic sensibility promulgated by Craig in his essays on the Übermarionette, the same sensibility that develops, mutatis mutandis, in the dramaturgies of Brecht, Beckett, Bernhard, and Fornes as a habitual preference for abstraction in the theater. All these playwrights must be understood, whatever their particular ambitions for theater, whether political or aesthetic or expressive, principally as the legitimate successors of that continuing modernist tradition—"an abstract, non-representational style of theater."[10] That is certainly not to say that this modernist tradition is the only tradition for representing character in twentieth-century theater, not even the only tradition of representation that matters, merely that abstraction not only survives as a tradition in theater art but may indeed—now that it is so clearly "traditional"—wield far more power than it ever did in its early, revolutionary phase.

Notes

Introduction

1. See Eric P. Levy, "*Mercier and Camier:* Narration, Dante, and the Couple," in *On Beckett: Essays and Criticism,* ed. S. E. Gontarski (New York: Grove Press, 1986), pp. 117–30.

2. Familiar alternatives would include theories of selfhood proposed for example by Marxists, social psychologists, certain anthropologists, Lacanians, and deconstructionists. For a brief but informative overview of recent thinking on the construction of character, see Wayne Booth, *The Company We Keep: An Ethics of Fiction* (Berkeley: University of California Press, 1988), pp. 237–40.

3. Joseph Wood Krutch, "*Modernism*" *in Modern Drama* (Ithaca: Cornell University Press, 1953), p. 84. The best single piece of criticism on "disappearing characters" is Elinor Fuchs's essay "The Death of Character," *TheatreCommunications* (March 1983), pp. 1–6.

4. See Stanley Cavell, "The Avoidance of Love: A Reading of *King Lear,*" in his *Must We Mean What We Say: A Book of Essays* (Cambridge: Cambridge University Press, 1976), pp. 267–72.

5. See Michael Cohen, "*Hamlet" in My Mind's Eye* (Athens: University of Georgia Press, 1989).

6. Harold Bloom, "The Analysis of Character," in *Major Literary Characters: Willy Loman,* ed. Harold Bloom (New York: Chelsea, 1991), p. ix.

7. Herbert Blau, *Take Up the Bodies: Theater at the Vanishing Point* (Urbana: University of Illinois Press, 1982), p. 278.

8. See Colin Falck, *Myth, Truth and Literature: Towards a True Post-Modernism* (Cambridge: Cambridge University Press, 1989), esp. chapter 4 ("Presence"). The fact that the fiction *Macbeth* omits Lady Macbeth's children does not make the question irrelevant. Falck answers L. C. Knights's famous attack on psychological criticism ("How Many Children Had Lady Macbeth?") in this way (p. 111): "A part of the problem here is precisely to determine what *is* contained 'within the fiction itself,' since the notion that such a question can be settled by any simple appeal to 'the words on the page' must obviously be unsustainable. The question would make perfect sense if it could be shown to be relevant to the play's drama (a new psychological theory might find unexpected relationships between the murderous propensities of parents and the numbers and ages of their children). Likewise we can quite sensibly talk about the kind of person that such a character as the J. Alfred

Prufrock of T. S. Eliot's . . . poem 'is,' even though the words on the page tell us little about him: it would be a pointless piece of critical abstinence to avoid constructing a context of life around such a character where the poem 'itself' seems more or less to invite us to do so."

9. See James Boswell's *Life of Johnson* (1904; rpt. London: Oxford University Press, 1960), p. 389.

10. See, for example, M. H. Abrams's influential *A Glossary of Literary Terms,* 4th ed. (New York: Holt, Rinehart and Winston, 1981), on "character" and "characterization": "*characters* are the persons presented in a dramatic or narrative work, who are interpreted by the reader as being endowed with moral and dispositional qualities that are expressed in what they say—the *dialogue*—and by what they do—the *action*" (p. 20).

11. André Gide, *Le Faux Monnayeurs* (1925); Arnold Bennett, *The Journals of Arnold Bennett* (1931); D. H. Lawrence, letter to Edward Garnett (June 5, 1914), *Letters* (1932). All citations are from Miriam Allott, *Novelists on the Novel* (New York: Columbia University Press, 1959), pp. 289–91.

12. Charles Child Walcutt, *Man's Changing Mask: Modes and Methods of Characterization in Fiction* (Minneapolis: University of Minnesota Press, 1966), p. 14.

13. Ingram Bywater, *Aristotle on the Art of Poetry* (1909; rpt. New York: Garland, 1980), p. v.

14. Charles Chamberlain, "From 'Haunts' to 'Character': The Meaning of *Ethos* and Its Relation to Ethics," *Helios,* n.s., 11 (1984): 97. I am indebted to Chamberlain's excellent essay for much of the following discussion of ethos.

15. Ibid.

16. Ibid., p. 99.

17. Ibid.

18. Ibid, pp. 102–3.

19. Seymour Chatman, *Story and Discourse* (Ithaca: Cornell University Press, 1978), p. 126.

20. William Gass, *Fiction and the Figures of Life* (New York: Random House, 1971), p. 45.

21. Bruce Wilshire, *Role Playing and Identity: The Limits of Theater as Metaphor* (Bloomington: Indiana University Press, 1982), p. 25.

22. John Locke, *An Essay Concerning Human Understanding,* ed. P. H. Nidditch (Oxford: Clarendon Press, 1975), book 2, chapter 27. In this instance Locke of course is arguing for the theoretical separability of the individual from the inner "person."

23. See Shlomith Rimmon-Kenan, ed., *Discourse in Psychoanalysis and Literature* (London: Methuen, 1987), introduction (pp. xi–xvi). Rimmon-Kenan writes that, "If in the near past, New Critics, Formalists and Structuralists all tended to avoid psychoanalysis because it seemed to them to lead the study of literature outside the domain of the specifically literary, today there is a renewed interest in psychoanalysis (not least on the part of New Critics, Formalists and Structuralists)

in an attempt to go beyond formalism without abandoning the formal aspects of literature" (p. xi).

24. See Mihai Spariosu, ed., *Mimesis in Contemporary Theory: An Interdisciplinary Approach* (Philadelphia and Amsterdam: John Benjamins Publishing Company, 1984).

25. See William V. Spanos, *Repetitions: The Postmodern Occasion in Literature and Culture* (Baton Rouge: Louisiana State University Press, 1987). Spanos writes that "[t]he literary revolution called modernism that occurred at the end of the nineteenth century . . . was ideologically a revolt against the Western humanistic tradition and aesthetically against its 'Aristotelian' poetics" (p. 14).

26. Brecht's relevance to postmodern theater (indeed literary criticism in general) is being increasingly documented: see, for example, Elizabeth Wright, *Postmodern Brecht: A Re-Presentation* (London: Routledge, 1989).

27. See Patrice Pavis, *Languages of the Stage: Essays in the Semiology of the Theatre* (New York: Performing Arts Journal Publications, 1982), pp. 100–101, and Una Chaudhuri, "The Spectator in Drama/Drama in the Spectator," *Modern Drama* 27 (1984): 285–87.

28. See Bert O. States, "Playing in Lyric Time: Beckett's Voice Plays," *Theatre Journal* 40 (1988): 453–67.

29. See Jonathan Kalb, *Beckett in Performance* (Cambridge: Cambridge University Press, 1989) on the dangers in applying to playwrights like Beckett the exclusive terms "modern" or "postmodern." Kalb writes that "almost all innovators in contemporary performance really represent new waves of the avant-garde . . . an established tradition in modernism" (p. 157).

30. Knights's celebrated analysis of *Macbeth* has been cited so often that further citation seems almost redundant; nevertheless, "How Many Children Had Lady Macbeth?" appeared first in 1933 and was reprinted and modified later in *Explorations* (New York: George W. Stewart, 1947).

Chapter 1. Gordon Craig's Depersonalized Stage

1. See Irène Eynat-Confino, *Beyond the Mask: Gordon Craig, Movement, and the Actor* (Carbondale: Southern Illinois University Press, 1989), pp. 191–92.

2. Theater and theory have a common history and a common etymology (*thea*, act of seeing). For a speculative reading of this linkage, see Michael Goldman, *The Actor's Freedom: Toward a Theory of Drama* (New York: Viking Press, 1975).

3. Julian Olf, "The Man/Marionette Debate in Modern Theatre," *Educational Theatre Journal* 26 (1974): 488–94.

4. Gordon Craig, *The Mask* 2 (1909–10, rpt. New York: Benjamin Blom, 1967), p. 75. Subsequent references to Craig's journal are included parenthetically in the text. Craig, who had dozens of pen names, published "A Note on Marionettes" in *The Mask* under the name "Adolph Furst."

5. See John Berger's provocative essay, "The Suit and the Photograph," in *About*

Looking (New York: Pantheon Books, 1980), pp. 27–36. Berger writes about the growing acceptance during the late nineteenth century of the suit as the only male costume appropriate for formal occasions, such as being photographed: "The working classes . . . came to accept *as their own* certain standards of the class that ruled over them—in this case standards of chic and sartorial worthiness. At the same time their very acceptance of these standards, their very conforming to these norms which had nothing to do with either their own inheritance or their daily experience, condemned them, within the system of those standards, to being always, and recognisably to the classes above them, second-rate, clumsy, uncouth, defensive. That is indeed to succumb to a cultural hegemony" (p. 35).

6. The phrase is from Wilshire, *Role Playing and Identity,* p. 97.

7. Ibid., p. 166.

8. See Lucy Gent and Nigel Llewellyn, introduction to *Renaissance Bodies: The Human Figure in English Culture c. 1540–1660,* ed. Gent and Llewellyn (London: Reaktion Books, 1990), p. 6.

9. See Laurence Senelick's comprehensive reconstruction of Craig's collaboration with Stanislavsky on a production of *Hamlet: Gordon Craig's Moscow "Hamlet"* (Westport, Conn.: Greenwood Press, 1982).

10. Martin Esslin uses this term to describe Beckett's plays for television; see his "A Poetry of Moving Images" in *Beckett Translating/Translating Beckett,* ed. Alan Warren Friedman, Charles Rossman, and Dana Scherzer (University Park: Pennsylvania State University Press, 1987), p. 74.

11. This is Senelick's description of nineteenth-century Romanticist theories of Shakespearean character (*Gordon Craig's Moscow "Hamlet,"* p. 80). According to Senelick, Craig (like the Decadents) "in essence" subscribed to Romanticist distortions of Shakespeare's characters.

12. Quoted in Senelick, *Gordon Craig's Moscow "Hamlet,"* p. 68.

13. Quoted in J. Michael Walton, ed., *Craig on Theatre* (London: Methuen, 1983), p. 88.

14. Gordon Craig, *Henry Irving* (London: J. M. Dent, 1930), p. 40.

15. See Olf, "The Man/Marionette Debate"; the entire essay is relevant.

16. William Shakespeare, *Hamlet,* 1.2.76–86, in *William Shakespeare: The Complete Works,* ed. Alfred Harbage (1969; rev. ed. New York: Penguin Books, 1977), p. 936.

17. Peter R. Schroeder, "Hidden Depths: Dialogue and Characterization in Chaucer and Malory," *PMLA* 98 (1983): 374–87.

18. Quoted in Senelick, *Gordon Craig's Moscow "Hamlet,"* p. 64.

19. See Senelick, *Gordon Craig's Moscow "Hamlet,"* esp. pp. 63–71.

20. Ibid., p. 67.

21. Ibid.

22. For example, in the Basilica of Constantine (c. A.D. 310–20), the well-known colossus of the emperor conveys many of the same effects Craig intends for his stage king. By modeling the emperor in a style that draws on features of an older period

(e.g., simplification of detail, reduction of facial features to resemble a mask), the artist subordinates the representation of individual personality to the representation of imperial authority. See *Gardner's Art through the Ages*, 8th ed., ed. Horst de la Croix and Richard G. Tansey (New York: Harcourt Brace Jovanovich, 1986), pp. 240–45.

23. See Christopher Innes, *Edward Gordon Craig* (Cambridge: Cambridge University Press, 1983), pp. 138–40.

24. Craig published his designs and commentary for *The Steps* in *Towards a New Theatre* (London: J. M. Dent, 1913), pp. 41–47.

25. Eynat-Confino, *Beyond the Mask*, p. 112.

26. Charles R. Lyons, "Character and Theatrical Space," in *Themes in Drama: The Theatrical Space*, ed. James Redmond (Cambridge: Cambridge University Press, 1987), p. 36.

27. Ibid.

28. Rudolf Arnheim, *To the Rescue of Art: Twenty-Six Essays* (Berkeley: University of California Press, 1992), p. 103.

29. See Eynat-Confino, *Beyond the Mask*, pp. 111, 117. Craig of course knew of Appia's work and praised it more than once, but on the significance of the staged figure they differed radically. See Richard C. Beacham, *Adolphe Appia: Theatre Artist* (Cambridge: Cambridge University Press, 1987), pp. 65–66, and Walter R. Volbach, *Adolphe Appia: Prophet of the Modern Theatre: A Profile* (Middletown, Conn.: Wesleyan University Press, 1968). Volbach summarizes the results of Craig's and Appia's extended conversations during their first (and only) meeting (Zurich, February 1914): Whatever their personal regard for each other's work, "their conflicting opinion about the actor's place let them go in opposite directions; while Appia had the actor dominate all the elements of staging, Craig considered him less essential. This is the decisive difference in their scenic concept" (p. 108).

30. Quoted in Beacham, *Adolphe Appia*, p. 49.

31. Volbach writes that "[i]n Craig's often monumental settings, the performers appeared like insignificant personnel, while Appia drew his sketches with the function of the actor in mind; his spatial surroundings were devised in scale to the size of human beings" (*Adolphe Appia*, p. 108).

32. See H. F. Garten, "Foreign Influences on German Expressionist Drama," in *Expressionism as an International Literary Phenomenon*, ed. Ulrich Weisstein (Paris: Didier, 1973), pp. 65–66.

33. Ibid., p. 65. On the history of the term *expressionism*, see John Willett, *Expressionism* (New York: McGraw-Hill, 1970), p. 75.

34. Ulrich Weisstein, introduction to *Expressionism as an International Literary Phenomenon*, p. 41.

35. Willett, *Expressionism*, p. 122.

36. John Willett, *The Theatre of the Weimar Republic* (New York: Holmes and Meier, 1988), p. 57.

37. To say that Craig's art is abstract (in contrast to that of the expressionists,

whose art was simply "abstractionist") does not mean it lacks meaning or expressivity or that it is merely decorative. "It is one of the principal doctrines of abstract art," writes W. J. T. Mitchell, "that although iconography and represented objects may disappear, content and subject matter do not." See Mitchell's informative essay, "*Ut Pictura Theoria:* Abstract Painting and the Repression of Language," *Critical Inquiry* 15 (1989): 348–71.

38. Eynat-Confino writes that the primary relationship in Craig's theater exists between stage and audience; once the actor is introduced this relationship is changed, "since it [the actor] belongs to a different semantic field" (*Beyond the Mask,* p. 118). The remarkable evocative power of Craig's sets recalls a primitive sense of the potency of actual spaces. See Steven Mullaney, *The Place of the Stage* (Chicago: University of Chicago Press, 1987), pp. 17–19.

39. Craig of course is not the first artist to paint with multiple perspectives; for example, in *The Virgin with the Canon van der Paele* (1436), Jan van Eyck employs different perspectives so as to direct attention equally to several figures—the Virgin, the infant Christ, Saint George, and the Canon. But the lack of spatial unification in the Van Eyck painting seems incidental, rather than intentional as with Craig: "Jan van Eyck and his generation still essentially conceive the organization of the two-dimensional picture surface in terms of shape, color, and symbol; they have not yet thought of it as a window into a constructed illusion of the third dimension, as the painters of the later Flemish schools will" (de la Croix and Tansey, *Gardner's Art through the Ages*), pp. 665–66.

40. Beacham, *Adolphe Appia,* p. 25.

41. Quoted in Senelick, *Gordon Craig's Moscow "Hamlet,"* p. 190.

42. Frederick J. Marker and Lise-Lone Marker, *Edward Gordon Craig and "The Pretenders": A Production Revisited* (Carbondale: Southern Illinois University Press, 1981), p. 37.

43. Ibid., p. 71. In *The Pretenders,* the Markers write, "Craig was concerned not with the depiction of a *place* . . . but with the living presence of *characters in an atmosphere*" (p. 71).

44. Ibid., p. 61.

45. Ibid., p. 78.

46. Ibid., p. 64.

47. Quoted in E. H. Gombrich, *Art and Illusion: A Study in the Psychology of Pictorial Representation* (Princeton: Princeton University Press, 1961), p. 274.

48. See Gombrich, *Art and Illusion,* pp. 291–329.

49. Hugo von Hofmannsthal's prologue was published in the *Tulane Drama Review* (1961), 117.

Chapter 2. Brecht and the Social Self

1. Timothy Garton Ash, *Times Literary Supplement,* 9 December 1983, p. 1365, quoted in Wright, *Postmodern Brecht,* p. 9. But see Roland Barthes, "The Tasks

of Brechtian Criticism," *Critical Essays* (Evanston, Ill.: Northwestern University Press, 1972). Anticipating much current interest in Brechtian poetics, Barthes observed that "Brechtian criticism is by definition extensive with the problematics of our time" (p. 71).

2. See, for example, Klaus Volker, "Brecht Today: Classic or Challenge," *Theatre Journal* 39 (1987). According to Volker, the solutions Brecht advocates in his plays are outdated and potentially dangerous: " 'Wagons to good drivers' is nonsense, since anyone can become a good driver and in industrial nations nearly everyone has a car, making driving itself a danger to the environment. This sentence reads like a Volkswagen slogan, written by a poet in 1940 who could not foresee the realities of the 1980s. . . . The times are not favorable for Brecht, and our well-known directors avoid producing his plays" (p. 429).

3. See Jonathan Dollimore, *Radical Tragedy: Religion, Ideology, and Power in the Drama of Shakespeare and His Contemporaries* (Chicago: University of Chicago Press, 1984).

4. Pavis, *Languages of the Stage*, pp. 37–49.

5. See Elin Diamond, "Brechtian Theory/Feminist Theory: Toward a Gestic Feminist Criticism," *The Drama Review* 32 (1988): 82–94.

6. Much of this paragraph summarizes an excellent article by George Lellis, "Brecht and *Cahiers du Cinéma*," in *Bertolt Brecht: Political Theory and Literary Practice*, ed. Betty Nance Weber and Hubert Heinen (Athens: University of Georgia Press, 1980), pp. 129–44.

7. See, for example, Herbert Blau's most recent work of theater theory, *The Audience* (Baltimore: Johns Hopkins University Press, 1990).

8. Brecht objected to "empathic" (or "Aristotelian") performances mainly because fully illusionist art effectively screened out the ideology that in reality produced it. In this aversion to theatrical performance, Brecht's position is remarkably close to Plato's notorious "antitheatricalism." For a full discussion of the links between the two men's theater theories, see my "Non-Aristotelian Theater: Brecht's and Plato's Theories of Artistic Imitation," *Comparative Drama* 21 (1987): 199–213.

9. John Willett, *Art and Politics in the Weimar Period* (New York: Pantheon, 1978), p. 105.

10. Quoted in John Willett, ed., *Brecht on Theatre: The Development of an Aesthetic* (New York: Hill and Wang, 1964), p. 54.

11. Bertolt Brecht, "Alienation-effects in Chinese Acting," *Gesammelte Werke* 7 (Frankfurt: Suhrkamp, 1967), p. 626. Translations of Brecht's works unless otherwise noted are mine. Brecht of course uses "realistic" to refer to his theater of social realism, not to conventional realist (i.e., illusionist) drama.

12. José Ortega y Gasset discusses a similar goal of modernism in *The Dehumanization of Art* (New York: Doubleday, n.d.), pp. 8–30.

13. Brecht, "Alienation-effects," *Gesammelte Werke* 7, p. 628.

14. Brecht, "Short Organon for the Theater," *Gesammelte Werke* 7, p. 689.

15. Quoted in Meg Twycross, " 'Transvestism' in the Mystery Plays," *Medieval English Theatre* 5 (1983): 148.

16. Ibid., p. 155.

17. Ibid., p. 157.

18. For the former view see for example Ronald Hayman, *Brecht: A Biography* (London: Weidenfeld and Nicolson, 1983), p. 229: "Because we identify with Courage more than Brecht intended, her cumulative sufferings come closer to tragedy than intended." For the latter, see Wright, *Postmodern Brecht*, p. 42. According to Wright, Brecht's twin protagonist in *The Good Person of Szechwan* "is the visible image of the objective contradictions of man/woman in the bourgeois capitalist world, an image of an alienated condition." For a useful overview of this recurring division in Brecht studies, see Siegfried Mews and Herbert Knust, eds., *Essays on Brecht: Theater and Politics* (Chapel Hill: University of North Carolina Press, 1974).

19. Quoted in Keith Dickson, *Towards Utopia: A Study of Brecht* (Oxford: Clarendon Press, 1978), p. 46.

20. Hayman, *Brecht*, p. 227.

21. I do not mean that Brecht's characters are acted incorrectly if they are acted passionately; surely Helene Weigel's representation of Mother Courage, screaming in silence upon learning of the death of her son Schweizerkas, stands with Lear's howling for Cordelia as one of theater's most awful moments. Even the description of her acting is almost intolerably moving (in George Steiner, *The Death of Tragedy* [New York: Oxford University Press, 1961], pp. 353–54). But the general history of productions of this and other Brecht plays suggests the difficulties many actors encounter in representing character without first supporting it with realistic personal motivations. Ironically, one of the most popularly successful Brecht productions I have ever seen was a version of *The Caucasian Chalk Circle* in which the action was reframed to occur during the American Civil War. By playing familiar stereotypes (Yankee soldiers, a Southern belle, and so on) in front of an Atlanta audience, actors had no need consciously to alienate themselves from their characters.

22. E. M. Forster, *Aspects of the Novel* (New York: Harcourt, Brace, & World, 1927), p. 78.

23. Ibid., pp. 75–76.

24. Roland Barthes assigns this function exclusively to proper names: "What gives the illusion that the sum is supplemented by a precious remainder (something like *individuality*, in that, qualitative and ineffable, it may escape the vulgar bookkeeping of compositional characters) is the Proper Name" (*S/Z*, trans. Richard Miller [London: Jonathan Cape, 1975], p. 191).

25. Jane Austen, *Mansfield Park*, quoted in Forster, *Aspects of the Novel*, p. 74.

26. I borrow here from Schroeder's essay on characterization in medieval narratives, "Hidden Depths," p. 381.

27. Jane Austen, *Mansfield Park*, in *The Complete Novels of Jane Austen* (New York: Random House, n.d.), p. 744.

28. Given Austen's description of Lady Bertram's state of mind, the word seems appropriate: "To talk over the dreadful business with Fanny, talk and lament, was all Lady Bertram's consolation. To be listened to and borne with, and hear the voice of kindness and sympathy in return, was everything that could be done for her. To be otherwise comforted was out of the question. The case admitted of no comfort" (ibid.).

29. Paul Ricoeur, *Time and Narrative*, vol. 3, trans. Kathleen Blamey and David Pellaver (Chicago: University of Chicago Press, 1988), p. 249.

30. Ibid., p. 246.

31. Bertolt Brecht, *Werke 6* (Frankfurt: Suhrkamp, 1989), pp. 83–84; my translation.

32. See David Richard Jones, *Great Directors at Work: Stanislavsky, Brecht, Kazan, Brook* (Berkeley: University of California Press, 1986), p. 135.

33. Ibid., p. 136.

34. George Orwell's essay "Shooting an Elephant" is widely anthologized; I cite from *The Norton Reader*, 7th ed., ed. Arthur M. Eastman et al. (New York: W. W. Norton, 1988), p. 771.

35. Dickson, *Towards Utopia*, p. 35.

36. Ralph Manheim and John Willett, eds., *Bertolt Brecht: Collected Plays*, vol. 2 (New York: Random House, 1977), p. 246.

37. Dickson, *Towards Utopia*, pp. 42–43.

38. Ibid., p. 45.

39. Manheim and Willett, eds., *Collected Plays* 2, p. 245.

40. George Herbert Mead, in *George Herbert Mead on Social Psychology*, ed. Anselm Strauss (Chicago: University of Chicago Press, 1964), p. 227.

41. Peter L. Berger and Thomas Luckmann, *The Social Construction of Reality* (Garden City, N.Y.: Anchor-Doubleday, 1967), p. 61.

42. Ibid., p. 103.

43. Aristotle, *Poetics*, trans. S. H. Butcher, in *Criticism: The Major Texts*, ed. Walter Jackson Bate (New York: Harcourt Brace Jovanovich, 1970), p. 24.

44. Ian McLachlan, "Ironic Tension and Production Techniques: *The Measures Taken*," in Weber and Heinen, *Bertolt Brecht: Political Theory and Literary Practice*, p. 101.

45. Rainer Steinweg, ed., *Auf Anregung Bertolt Brechts: Lehrstücke mit Schulern, Arbeitern, Theaterleuten* (Frankfurt: Suhrkamp, 1978), quoted in Wright, *Postmodern Brecht*, p. 23.

46. See James H. Spencer, Jr., and Leon Balter, "Empathy and the Analyzing Instrument," in *Empathy II*, ed. Joseph Lichtenberg, Melvin Bornstein, and Donald Silver (Hillsdale, N.J.: The Analytic Press, 1984), pp. 289–307. Psychoanalytic discussions of empathy often run parallel to Brechtian dramatic theory, as for example in the following passage from Spencer and Balter: "One of the controversies around the concept of empathy centers on the danger that the empathic response may be treated as an end rather than a means. . . . And the empathic response to a patient's

material, even when nothing is said aloud, may be experienced by the analyst as an end rather than a means toward further analysis. Viewed in this way, empathy becomes an interference to analyzing rather than an element in analytic methodology" (pp. 301–2).

47. John Fuegi, *Bertolt Brecht: Chaos, According to Plan* (Cambridge: Cambridge University Press, 1987), p. 71.

48. Ibid.

49. Blau, *The Audience*, p. 272.

50. See Dickson, *Towards Utopia*, p. 140.

51. Ibid.

52. See, for example, Bennett Simon, *Mind and Madness in Ancient Greece: The Classical Roots of Modern Psychiatry* (Ithaca: Cornell University Press, 1978), pp. 26–27.

53. See Bennett Simon, *Tragic Drama and the Family: Psychoanalytic Studies from Aeschylus to Beckett* (New Haven: Yale University Press, 1988), pp. 244–45.

54. Manheim and Willett, eds., *Collected Plays 6*, p. 368.

55. Wright, *Postmodern Brecht*, p. 42.

56. Manheim and Willett, eds., *Collected Plays 6*, p. 368.

57. Ibid., p. xxiii.

58. See, for example, Mary Douglas, *How Institutions Think* (Syracuse, N.Y.: Syracuse University Press, 1986). In the nineteenth century in Europe, for example, writes Douglas, "As fast as new medical categories (hitherto unimagined) were invented, or new criminal or sexual or moral categories, new kinds of people spontaneously came forward in hordes to accept the labels and to live accordingly. The responsiveness to new labels suggests extraordinary readiness to fall into new slots and to let selfhood be redefined. This is not like the naming that, according to nominalist philosophers, creates a particular version of the world by picking out certain sorts of things, for instance, naming stars, foregrounding some and letting others disappear from sight. It is a much more dynamic process by which new names are uttered and forthwith new creatures corresponding to them emerge" (p. 100).

59. Judith Butler, "Performance Acts and Gender Constitution: An Essay in Phenomenology and Feminist Theory," *Theatre Journal* 40 (1988): 520.

Chapter 3. Character Portraits/Portraying Character: *Krapp's Last Tape, Rockaby, Catastrophe*

1. August Strindberg, author's foreword to *Miss Julie*, trans. Elizabeth Sprigge, in *Masters of Modern Drama*, ed. Haskell Block and Robert Shedd (New York: Random House, 1962), p. 95. But given the unusual amount of coherent psychological baggage Strindberg supplies for Miss Julie and Jean, his comments seem inappropriate, or possibly prophetic, in that they apply more clearly to the characters in the later works.

2. Sam Shepard, *Fool for Love and Other Plays* (New York: Bantam Books, 1984), pp. 61–62.

3. Booth, *The Company We Keep*, p. 237.

4. Erving Goffman, *Frame Analysis: An Essay on the Organization of Experience* (Cambridge, Mass.: Harvard University Press, 1974), p. 573.

5. Billie Whitelaw in an interview by Linda Ben-Zvi, quoted in *Women in Beckett: Performance and Critical Perspectives,* ed. Linda Ben-Zvi (Urbana: University of Illinois Press, 1990), p. 9.

6. Dame Peggy Ashcroft, in an interview by Katharine Worth, in Ben-Zvi, *Women in Beckett*, p. 12.

7. Kalb, *Beckett in Performance*, p. 62.

8. For an excellent discussion of the ways in which mimesis and mimetic theory continue to dominate Western literature and literary creation, see Earl Miner, *Comparative Poetics: An Intercultural Essay on Theories of Literature* (Princeton: Princeton University Press, 1990), esp. pp. 34–81. According to Miner, a true alternative to Aristotelian mimesis would be an "expressive" poetics, not a "nonmimetic" one. By these standards, *Godot* and *Endgame* are clearly mimetic works.

9. Kalb, *Beckett in Performance*, p. 66.

10. Ibid., p. 57.

11. Michael Goldman, "Vitality and Deadness in Beckett's Plays," in *Beckett at 80/Beckett in Context*, ed. Enoch Brater (New York: Oxford University Press, 1986), p. 76.

12. Kalb, *Beckett in Performance*, pp. 61–64.

13. Kristin Morrison, *Canters and Chroniclers: The Use of Narrative in the Plays of Samuel Beckett and Harold Pinter* (Chicago: University of Chicago Press, 1983), pp. 4–5.

14. In this scene, a carrier enters early in the morning, talking about the time of day as Shakespeare's characters often do in order to frame a new scene: "Heigh-ho! an it be not four by the day, I'll be hanged. Charles' wain [i.e., the constellation Ursa Major] is over the new chimney, and yet our horse not packed" (2.1.1–3). Of this scene, A. D. Nuttall writes that "Here is a real shiver of Truth. One senses, across the intervening centuries the darkness, the inn yard without artificial illumination, the eyes straining upward, for a moment to pick out the known shape of the new chimney and the stars above it. This is what they must have done, in the cold time before the sun came up" (*A New Mimesis* [London: Methuen, 1983], p. 184).

15. Pierre Chabert, "The Body in Beckett's Theatre," *Journal of Beckett Studies* 8 (1982): 23.

16. Enoch Brater, "Light, Sound, Movement, and Action in Beckett's *Rockaby*," in *On Beckett: Essays and Criticism*, ed. S. E. Gontarski (New York: Grove Press, 1986), p. 392. But Brater sees in the few moments of live speech in *Rockaby* occasional moments of "psychological texturing" as well as an "emotional tenderness that greatly humanizes their meaning" (p. 390).

17. James Knowlson, "*Footfalls*," in Gontarski, *On Beckett,* p. 356.

18. And perhaps even to ignoring the text itself. See Kalb, who writes that "[t]oday there is taking place among artists a slow recognition of the cul-de-sac described by Pavis [*Languages of the Stage*]: that language cannot be merely one equipotent element among many in a composite stage language, as Artaud insisted, for it inevitably becomes more important than that in performance, constituting the very structure of the viewer's thoughts (Wittgenstein) and the object of our natural impulse to name experiences" (*Beckett in Performance,* pp. 160–61).

19. Ibid., p. 117.

20. I borrow the phrase from P. J. Murphy, *Reconstructing Beckett: Language for Being in Samuel Beckett's Fiction* (Toronto: University of Toronto Press, 1990). Murphy deals exclusively with Beckett's prose works, but much of his polemical re-appraisal of Beckett's fiction (he maintains the fiction is "realist") could be applied usefully to Beckett's works for the stage.

21. John Dryden, "An Essay of Dramatic Poesy," in *Criticism: The Foundations of Modern Literary Judgment,* ed. Mark Shorer, Josephine Miles, and Gordon McKenzie (New York: Harcourt, Brace, 1958) p. 232.

22. August Strindberg, *Miss Julia,* trans. Peter Watts (New York: Penguin Books, 1958), p. 83.

23. Stanton B. Garner, Jr., "Visual Field in Beckett's Late Plays," *Comparative Drama* 21 (1987–88): 349–73.

24. For a useful summary of the art of the early Christian era, see *Gardner's Art through the Ages,* ed. de la Croix and Tansey, pp. 248–58.

25. Ibid., p. 249.

26. Samuel Beckett, *Krapp's Last Tape,* in *The Collected Shorter Plays of Samuel Beckett* (New York: Grove Press, 1984), pp. 60, 57. References to *Krapp's Last Tape* and other plays by Beckett are to this edition.

27. See Steven Connor, *Samuel Beckett: Repetition, Theory, Text* (London: Basil Blackwell, 1988), p. 130.

28. Dougald McMillan and Martha Fehsenfeld, eds., *Beckett in the Theatre* (London: John Calder, 1988), p. 294.

29. Ibid., p. 292.

30. Ibid., p. 273.

31. Ibid., p. 257.

32. Ibid., p. 299.

33. Ibid., pp. 288–89.

34. For a very useful discussion from within a psychoanalytic frame of some of Beckett's short works for the stage, see Daniel Gunn, *Psychoanalysis and Fiction: An Exploration of Literary and Psychoanalytic Borders* (Cambridge: Cambridge University Press, 1988). Gunn writes that "Beckett's work pushes repeatedly against the fact that there is no first repetition, that 'Again' . . . is the order of the day, every day" (p. 5).

35. While "endopoetic criticism" of Beckett's characters rarely seems appropriate, in the case of *Krapp's Last Tape* there are suggestive parallels between Beckett's play and the narcissistic disorders psychoanalysts describe as typical of modern "protean" individuals. See Bennett Simon, *Tragic Drama and the Family,* pp. 271–89.

36. For a complete and convincing discussion of the play's Manichaean elements, see McMillan and Fehsenfeld, *Beckett in the Theatre,* pp. 242–54.

37. J. Laplanche and J.-B. Pontalis, *The Language of Psychoanalysis,* trans. Donald Nicholson-Smith (New York: Norton, 1973), pp. 26–27.

38. Beth Dawkins Basset cites the work of Stoudemire in "The Nature of Grief," *Emory Magazine* (March 1985), 18–23.

39. Enoch Brater, *Beyond Minimalism: Beckett's Late Style in the Theater* (New York: Oxford University Press, 1984), pp. 174–75.

40. The story of Beckett's dissatisfaction with Worth is widely reported; see Brater, *Beyond Minimalism,* p. 173.

41. Ibid.

42. This summary of Freudian terms appears in David Michael Levin, *The Listening Self: Personal Growth, Social Change and the Closure of Metaphysics* (London: Routledge, 1989), p. 153.

43. Freud, "Further Recommendations in the Technique of Psychoanalysis: Recollection, Repetition, and Working Through," in *Therapy and Technique,* ed. Philip Rieff (New York: Macmillan, 1963), p. 160.

44. Brater, *Beyond Minimalism,* p. 174.

45. Paul Schilders, *The Image and Appearance of the Human Body* (New York: International Universities Press, 1950), quoted in Wilshire, *Role Playing and Identity,* p. 169.

46. Brater, *Beyond Minimalism,* pp. 173–74.

47. Ibid., p. 174.

48. Arendt, *The Life of the Mind,* quoted in Levin, *The Listening Self,* p. xiv.

49. Interviewed by Lois Overbeck in Ben-Zvi, *Women in Beckett,* p. 51.

50. See Kalb on Beckett's refusal (or inability) to provide actors with plausible subtexts for their characters' situations: "One could interpret his almost complete refusal to discuss internal situations as a tacit admission that the actor's physical dilemmas onstage *are* the significant situations" (*Beckett in Performance,* p. 66).

51. Rosemary Pountney, *Theatre of Shadows: Samuel Beckett's Drama 1956–76* (Totowa, N.J.: Barnes and Noble, 1988), p. 228. See also S. E. Gontarski, "*Quad* and *Catastrophe,*" in *On Beckett.* Of *Quad,* Gontarski writes that "[t]he closing image suggests political defiance as well as the uncontrollability of art, art's tendency to exhibit its own Will, to reveal perhaps more than the artist intended" (p. 406).

52. Kalb says this of *Ghost Trio* and the Schiller Theater *Godot* (*Beckett in Performance,* p. 101).

53. Quoted in Kalb, *Beckett in Performance,* pp. 224–25.

54. De la Croix and Tansey, *Gardner's Art through the Ages,* p. 382.

Chapter 4. Mental Life in Thomas Bernhard's Comic Types

1. Claude Rawson, "Order and Cruelty," in *Essays in Criticism* 20 (1970): 24–56. Stephen Dowden, in *Understanding Thomas Bernhard* (Columbia, S.C.: University of South Carolina Press, 1991), reads Bernhard's work as "similar in nature" to that of Swift and other great satirists. Dowden's book in my opinion is the best work by far to appear on Bernhard in English, and while I disagree in many cases with his readings of individual works, I acknowledge his influence in this and the following several paragraphs.

2. Thomas Bernhard, *Der Italiener* (Salzburg: Residenz, 1971), p. 83; my translation.

3. Attributed often to Hermann Göring, but originally said by Hanns Johst, *Schlageter* (1933), cited in *Bartlett's Familiar Quotations,* 16th ed. (Boston: Little, Brown, 1992), p. 679.

4. Lyons, "Character and Theatrical Space," p. 30.

5. Dowden, *Understanding Thomas Bernhard,* p. 72.

6. Gitta Honegger, "Acoustic Masks: Strategies of Language in the Theater of Canetti, Bernhard, and Handke," *Modern Austrian Literature* 18 (1985): 64.

7. Dowden, *Understanding Thomas Bernhard,* p. 5.

8. Martin Esslin, "A Drama of Disease and Derision: The Plays of Thomas Bernhard," *Modern Drama* 23 (1981): 377.

9. Nicholas Eisner, *"Theatertheater/Theaterspiele:* The Plays of Thomas Bernhard," *Modern Drama* 30 (1987): 105.

10. Denis Calandra, *New German Dramatists: A Study of Peter Handke, Franz Xaver Kroetz, Rainer Werner Fassbinder, Heiner Müller, Thomas Brasch, Thomas Bernhard and Botho Strauss* (New York: Grove Press, 1983), p. 27.

11. Dowden, *Understanding Thomas Bernhard,* p. 7.

12. Ibid, p. 24.

13. Ibid., p. 32.

14. Thomas Bernhard, *Ein Fest für Boris* (Frankfurt: Suhrkamp, 1968), p. 34; translations of Bernhard's works unless otherwise noted are mine.

15. See Hans Wolfschütz, "Thomas Bernhard: The Mask of Death," in *Modern Austrian Writing: Literature and Society after 1945,* ed. Alan Best and Hans Wolfschütz (Totowa, N.J.: Barnes and Noble, 1980), pp. 214–35. Wolfschütz writes that "all Bernhard's characters are marked by such an 'event,' whether this takes the form of some personal misfortune or shock, or has been experienced as part of a general or historical 'catastrophe' " (p. 214).

16. Thomas Bernhard, *Histrionics,* trans. Peter Jansen and Kenneth Northcott (Chicago: The University of Chicago Press, 1990), pp. 218–19.

17. Nicholas J. Meyerhofer, "The Laughing Sisyphus: Reflections on Bernhard as (Self-) Dramatist in Light of His *Der Theatermacher*," *Modern Austrian Literature* 21 (1988): 108.

18. Calandra, *New German Dramatists*, p. 144.

19. Bernhard, *Histrionics*, p. 282.

20. In Ibsen's play, of course, the child is comforted by the parent. But Sarah's role in *Histrionics* is to minister to Bruscon's emotional needs, in effect a kind of mothering.

21. Amity Shlaes, "Thomas Bernhard and the German Literary Scene," *The New Criterion* 5 (January 1987): 30.

22. Quoted in Kurt Hofmann, *Aus Gesprächen mit Thomas Bernhard* (Vienna: Löcker, 1988), p. 79.

23. Martin Esslin says Bernhard is "a kind of Austrian Beckett," in "Beckett and Bernhard: A Comparison," *Modern Austrian Literature* 18 (1985): 67. Esslin also discounts any direct influence of one writer on the other.

24. Cited in Calandra, *New German Dramatists*, p. 145.

25. Esslin, "Drama of Disease and Derision," p. 374.

26. Bakhtin's "dialogic" (or "heteroglossic") self and Burke's "dramatistic" readings of behavior are well known; it should not be necessary to develop an extended comparison between their respective theories and Bernhard's models for character. Such an extended comparison would prove little, though of course the points of comparison are many. See M. M. Bakhtin, *The Dialogic Imagination: Four Essays*, ed. Michael Holquist, trans. Caryl Emerson and Michael Holquist (Austin: University of Texas Press, 1981), and Kenneth Burke, *Language as Symbolic Action: Essays on Life, Literature, and Method* (Berkeley: University of California Press, 1966).

27. Thomas Bernhard, *Eve of Retirement*, trans. Gitta Honegger (New York: Performing Arts Journal Publications, 1982), p. 204.

28. Robert Skloot, *The Darkness We Carry: The Drama of the Holocaust* (Madison: University of Wisconsin Press, 1988), p. 110.

29. Thomas Bernhard, *Der Spiegel*, 23 June 1980, quoted in Calandra, *New German Dramatists*, p. 149.

30. Text is *Der Präsident* (Frankfurt: Suhrkamp, n.d.), p. 140. My translation.

31. Bennett Simon, *Tragic Drama and the Family*, p. 237.

32. See W. R. Bion, "Attacks on Linking," *International Journal of Psycho-Analysis* 40 (1959): 308–15.

33. Robert Langbaum, *The Poetry of Experience: The Dramatic Monologue in Modern Literary Tradition* (New York: Norton, 1963), p. 182.

34. Ibid., p. 183.

35. Esslin, "Drama of Disease and Derision," p. 374.

36. Ibid.

37. Thomas Bernhard, *Force of Habit* (*Die Macht der Gewohnheit*, Frankfurt: Suhrkamp, 1974), pp. 9–12. All references to *Force of Habit* are to this text; translations are mine.

38. "Character-armor" is Wilhelm Reich's term for describing repeated defensive acts. For an application of the concept to stage characters, see Edward Burns, *Character: Acting and Being on the Pre-Modern Stage* (London: Macmillan, 1990), p. 228.

39. *Verscharren*, "to cover with earth secretly or hurriedly," implies shame.

40. Julien Bigras, "French Psychoanalysis," in *Psychoanalysis, Creativity, and Literature: A French-American Inquiry*, ed. Alan Roland (New York: Columbia University Press, 1978), pp. 15–16.

41. Ernest S. Wolf, "The Disconnected Self," in Roland, *Psychoanalysis, Creativity, and Literature*, pp. 104–6.

42. Freud, "Mourning and Melancholia" (1917), in *General Psychological Theory*, ed. Philip Rieff (New York: Macmillan, 1963), p. 173.

Chapter 5. The Characters of Maria Irene Fornes: Public and Private Identities

1. Jonathan Culler, *Structuralist Poetics* (Ithaca: Cornell University Press, 1975), p. 28.

2. The clearest example is the hero of Aristophanes' first play, *The Acharnians*, who is named "Dikaiopolis," or "just city." For a general discussion of Aristophanic heroes, see Cedric Whitman, *Aristophanes and the Comic Hero* (Cambridge, Mass.: Harvard University Press, 1964). The distinguishing feature of Aristophanes' protagonists, writes Whitman, is their "boundlessness" (p. 124). See also my own discussion of identity and role playing in Aristophanic comedy, *Comic Theaters* (Athens: University of Georgia Press, 1986), pp. 11–41.

3. Simon, *Mind and Madness*, p. 61.

4. Ibid., pp. 63–64.

5. Ibid., p. 284.

6. Ibid.

7. See, for example, Sue-Ellen Case, "From Split Subject to Split Britches," in *Feminine Focus: The New Women Playwrights*, ed. Enoch Brater (New York: Oxford University Press, 1989), pp. 126–46. Case identifies three types of characters in recent feminist drama: split subjects, metonymically displaced subjects, and collective subjects.

8. Pam Gems, *Three Plays* (London: Penguin Books, 1985), p. 50.

9. The reviews are collected in *New York Theater Critics' Reviews*, 42, ed. Joan Marlowe and Betty Blake (1981), pp. 340–46.

10. See, for example, Sue-Ellen Case, *Feminism and Theater* (London: Macmillan, 1988), and Diamond, "Brechtian Theory/Feminist Theory," pp. 82–94. Case describes feminist theatrical groups who use Brecht's gestural acting techniques to frame the process of gender construction, while Diamond argues that Brecht's theory has much potential relevance for feminism and that through application to

feminism Brecht's theory could be "re-radicalized." As I hope I have shown in my chapter on Brecht, it is misguided to think that a Brecht old enough to be familiar (quotable) needs to be updated; Brecht's theory (and theater) are despite their age already sufficiently radical. See Wright, *Postmodern Brecht*.

11. Here too (as with Brecht) "Aristotelian drama" seems to collect under a single term a great deal of incongruous material. In the extreme case, Aristotle is condemned for writing biology as if it were poetic theory. A character in Martha Boesing's *The Web* (1981), for example, carefully outlines a theory of dramatic form based on differential orgasmics: whereas Aristotle's theory of tragedy is kin to male orgasm, "women's plays could or should be multi-orgasmic in form, small mini-scenes, perhaps, coming in waves of emotions, crests and valleys, like the ebb and flow of changing tides and finally consummating in a sense of nourishment and plenitude, the creation of new life, birth" (cited in Elizabeth J. Natalle, *Feminist Theatre: A Study in Persuasion* [Metuchen, N.J.: The Scarecrow Press, 1985], p. 67). More common are objections to Aristotelian aesthetics, for example, to the linear plot or to "recognition scenes"; these and other feminist objections to Aristotle's poetics are summarized by Helene Keyssar in *Feminist Theatre: An Introduction to Plays of Contemporary British and American Women* (London: Macmillan, 1984).

12. See, for example, Elin Diamond, "Benmussa's Adaptations: Unauthorized Texts from Elsewhere," in *Feminine Focus: The New Women Playwrights,* ed. Enoch Brater (New York: Oxford University Press, 1989), pp. 64–78. Brecht, upon being criticized for cannibalizing others' writings, is said to have remarked that "in literature as in life I do not recognize the existence of private property."

A good example of Fornes's communal dramaturgy is a decreased emphasis on authority and on the uniqueness of the artwork. Even though most of her plays have been published, Fornes seems not to consider them finished. Her introductory notes typically specify which particular script appears on the page, but there is no indication that the published text is definitive or even authoritative. It is simply one of several versions that have been produced to date, part of an ongoing developmental sequence. For example, *Promenade* was first produced in April 1965 by the Judson Poets' Theatre (New York). An expanded version using different actors and a different set was produced four years later at the Promenade Theatre (New York). The published text is based mostly on this later production but omits a number of scenes. "Scenes performed in that production and subsequently omitted," Fornes writes, "may be found in an appendix following the text of the play" (*The Winter Repertory: Promenade and Other Plays* [New York: Winter House, 1971], p. 202). It is possible to object that this kind of developmental process occurs over the history of any staged production, but to do so overlooks the fact that for Fornes (as for Brecht) the repetitive or "process" script is itself a political rationale.

13. See Diamond, "Brechtian Theory/Feminist Theory": ideally, says Diamond, the "Brechtian-feminist body is paradoxically available for *both* analysis and iden-

tification" (p. 84). For a discussion of further implications of Brecht's mimetic theory, see my article, "Non-Aristotelian Theater," pp. 199–213.

14. See W. B. Worthen, "*Still Playing Games:* Ideology and Performance in the Theater of Maria Irene Fornes," in Brater, *Feminine Focus,* pp. 167–185.

15. Fornes, *Winter Repertory,* p. 8. Subsequent references to *A Vietnamese Wedding* and *Tango Palace* are to this collection of Fornes's plays and appear in the text, abbreviated as *WR.*

16. See Martin Meisel on the cultural broadening accomplished by Victorian popular domestic drama: *Realizations: Narrative, Pictorial, and Theatrical Arts in Nineteenth-Century England* (Princeton: Princeton University Press, 1983), p. 162. See also Wilshire, *Role Playing and Identity:* "The limits of transformation of self via mimetic response to others and diremptions from them cannot be set. If creatures from outer space should land on earth and should take toward us an attitude roughly comparable with that of adult teachers toward nursery pupils, the limits of our ability to follow them mimetically could not be determined by us in advance" (p. 233). There is plenty of evidence in the history of theater to suggest that representations of others are not ipso facto political or cultural suppressions.

17. At the risk of oversimplification, I follow here Freud's model for spectators' identification with the hero of a play. See "Psychopathic Characters on Stage," in Freud, *Standard Edition,* trans. James Strachey (1955; rpt. London: The Hogarth Press, 1978), vol. 7, pp. 305–10.

18. Levin describes "the listening self" in similar terms. See *The Listening Self,* pp. 205–23.

19. Conventional performances are sometimes marked by surprising, even shocking, tensions between actors and audiences, many explicitly sexual. See Stephen Aaron, *Stage Fright: Its Role in Acting* (Chicago: University of Chicago Press, 1986).

20. Quoted in Levin, *The Listening Self,* p. 221.

21. Aaron, *Stage Fright,* p. 42.

22. Fornes, *Fefu and Her Friends,* in *Word Plays: An Anthology of New American Drama* (New York: Performing Arts Journal Publications, 1980), p. 25.

23. Deborah R. Geis, "Wordscapes of the Body: Performative Language as *Gestus* in Maria Irene Fornes's Plays," *Theatre Journal* 42 (1990): 298.

24. Gitta Honegger, introduction to *Thomas Bernhard: "The President" and "Eve of Retirement,"* trans. Gitta Honegger (New York: Performing Arts Journal Publications, 1982), p. 11.

25. Barthes, *Critical Essays,* pp. 74–76.

26. Geis, "Wordscapes," pp. 299–300.

27. The definition of plot as involving causality is widely accepted; see Forster, *Aspects of the Novel.*

28. Douglas Robinson, "Henry James and Euphemism," *College English* 53 (1991): 404.

29. Even if the motives are not present actually (i.e., even if they are not literally "in" the text) we may infer their virtual presence; in the same way one may, upon discovering a man's left shoe, "wonder who lost it, and why he was not aware or troubled to lose it" (Miner, *Comparative Poetics,* p. 46).

30. P. F. Strawson, *Individuals: An Essay in Descriptive Metaphysics* (New York: Anchor Books, 1963), p. 108.

31. *Mud,* in *Maria Irene Fornes: Plays* (New York: Performing Arts Journal Publications, 1986), p. 40. Subsequent references to *Mud* are to this edition.

32. Geis, "Wordscapes," p. 301.

33. Ibid., p. 304.

34. I am thinking of Craig's reaction to a performance of Goethe's *Iphigenia in Tauris,* done in Esperanto and therefore presumably unintelligible for the majority of spectators. "It must have been an entrancing sight," Craig wrote, "to see Fraulein Reicher moving gracefully through the dramatic piece and to have heard the fine voice of Emanuel Reicher without having to follow the sense of the things they were saying. The scenery, to judge from the reproductions in the illustrated Journals, must have been appallingly bad, and the costumes seem to have been quite fairly incorrect" (*The Mask* I [1908], p. 203). Brecht's approval of "artless" performances is well known; see my "Non-Aristotelian Theater," esp. pp. 207–10.

35. Bonnie Marranca, "The Real Life of Maria Irene Fornes," *Performing Arts Journal* 22 (1984): 29.

36. Simon, *Mind and Madness,* p. 87.

37. For a full discussion of the differences between Brechtian "alienated" acting and the ironic self-consciousness sometimes observed in Beckett's characters, see Kalb, *Beckett in Performance.* Whereas for Brecht and Fornes, splitting off the actor from the character can give rise to productive tensions and insights, such splitting is, according to Kalb, "exactly what does *not* happen on Beckett's stage. His actors play characters who are fully aware that such self-irony is possible but who hold unappeasable doubts about whether it has any effect, whether it is worth their trouble, or whether they are 'as much as being seen'" (p. 45).

38. Susan Sontag, preface to Fornes, *Maria Irene Fornes: Plays,* p. 8.

39. An exception would be the 1983 Theater for the New City production of *Mud,* where (as Geis recounts the performance) "one could see the actors 'drop' their characters, then pick them up when the next scene was resumed" ("Wordscapes," p. 297).

40. Marranca, "Real Life," p. 30.

41. I borrow this example from Wilshire, *Role Playing and Identity,* p. 202.

42. Derek Parfit, *Reasons and Persons* (London: Oxford University Press, 1984).

43. *The Danube,* in *Maria Irene Fornes: Plays,* p. 44. Subsequent references to *The Danube* are to this edition and are included in the text.

44. See, for example, Fornes's comment on writing *Fefu.* In that play, she says, "the characters became more three-dimensional" and that "the style . . . dealt more

with characters as real persons rather than voices that are the expression of the mind of the play" (quoted in an interview by Scott Cummings, "Seeing with Clarity: The Visions of Maria Irene Fornes," *Theatre* 27 [1985]: 53).

45. Marranca, "Real Life," p. 30: "*The Danube* resounds with the unspeakable horror of nuclear death precisely because it is not named." As is well known, Fornes was asked by the Theater for the New City to write an antinuclear piece; *The Danube* is the result. But the play can point to an entirely different crisis. Fornes has told me in conversation that once, during rehearsals, one of the actors became visibly sick with AIDS, and the sores that appeared on his skin gave an appalling reality to the scenes in which some of the characters develop radiation burns. According to Fornes, it occurred to her then that *The Danube* was "about" AIDS.

46. Ross Wetzsteon, "Irene Fornes: The Elements of Style," *Village Voice*, 29 April 1986, p. 43.

47. Miner, *Comparative Poetics*, p. 74.

48. It is instructive to compare *The Danube* with another contemporary antinuclear drama, the "realistic"—or so it was advertised—television film *The Day After*. I am not troubled by the absurd sequence of closing images in that film—a campfire, the sharing of food, two heads touching—which convey an optimism that would be ludicrous if it were not so dangerous; what chills the bone is the very important formal possibility that cinematic realism (narrativity) itself might betray the subject by telling its story.

49. Worthen, *"Still Playing Games,"* p. 173.

50. Ibid., p. 172–73.

51. Wilshire, *Role Playing and Identity,* p. 97.

52. Worthen, *"Still Playing Games,"* pp. 172–73.

53. Wilshire, *Role Playing and Identity,* p. 192.

54. Ibid.

Afterword: Abstract Art and the Representation of Character

1. Lyons, "Character and Theatrical Space," p. 30.

2. As Lyons writes (ibid.), "I want to assert emphatically that I am not calling for a return to the methodologies of Edward Dowden or A. C. Bradley."

3. See, for example, Susan D. Cohen, "Fiction and the Photographic Image in Duras' *The Lover*," *L'Esprit Creatur* 30 (1990): 58–68.

4. Deborah N. Glassman, *Marguerite Duras: Fascinating Vision and Narrative Cure* (Cranbury, N.J.: Associated University Presses, 1991), p. 12.

5. Marguerite Duras, *India Song*, trans. Barbara Bray (New York: Grove Press, 1976), p. 146; all citations of *India Song* are from this edition.

6. See Liliane Papin, "Staging Writing or the Ceremony of Text in Marguerite Duras," *Modern Drama* 34 (1991): 128–37. Papin writes that "Duras's desire to create a process of 'distanciation,' her recommendation to actors to avoid inter-

pretation, inevitably calls to mind Brecht, who had similar preoccupations. Brecht wished to break with the Aristotelian tradition and the process of identification. Duras's goal, however, is different. Whereas Brecht wanted an estrangement that would enable the spectator to keep a clear mind and integrate the performance in a process of political awareness, Duras refrains from political 'messages' or lessons" (p. 134).

7. Ibid., p. 136.

8. See, for example, Papin, for whom Duras's "desire to create a process of 'distanciation' . . . inevitably calls to mind Brecht" (p. 134). See also Mary Kay Martin, "Space Invasions: Voice-Over in Works by Samuel Beckett and Marguerite Duras," in *The Theatrical Space,* ed. James Redmond (Cambridge: Cambridge University Press, 1987), pp. 239–46.

9. Martin, "Space Invasions," p. 128.

10. Ibid., p. 136.

Works Cited

Aaron, Stephen. *Stage Fright: Its Role in Acting*. Chicago: University of Chicago Press, 1986.

Abrams, M. H. *A Glossary of Literary Terms*. 4th ed. New York: Holt, Rinehart and Winston, 1981.

Allott, Miriam. *Novelists on the Novel*. New York: Columbia University Press, 1959.

Arendt, Hannah. *The Life of the Mind*. New York: Harcourt Brace Jovanovich, 1978.

Aristotle. *Poetics*. Translated by S. H. Butcher. In *Criticism: The Major Texts*, edited by Walter Jackson Bate. New York: Harcourt Brace Jovanovich, 1970.

Arnheim, Rudolf. *To the Rescue of Art: Twenty-Six Essays*. Berkeley: University of California Press, 1992.

Austen, Jane. *Mansfield Park*. In *The Complete Novels of Jane Austen*. New York: Random House, n.d.

Bakhtin, M. M. *The Dialogic Imagination: Four Essays*. Edited by Michael Holquist, translated by Caryl Emerson and Michael Holquist. Austin: University of Texas Press, 1981.

Barthes, Roland. *Critical Essays*. Translated by Richard Howard. Evanston, Ill.: Northwestern University Press, 1972.

———. *S/Z*. Translated by Richard Miller. London: Jonathan Cape, 1975.

Basset, Beth Dawkins. "The Nature of Grief." *Emory Magazine* (March 1985): 18–23.

Beacham, Richard C. *Adolphe Appia: Theatre Artist*. Cambridge: Cambridge University Press, 1987.

Beckett, Samuel. *The Collected Shorter Plays of Samuel Beckett*. New York: Grove Press, 1984.

Ben-Zvi, Linda, ed. *Women in Beckett: Performance and Critical Perspectives*. Urbana: University of Illinois Press, 1990.

Berger, John. *About Looking*. New York: Pantheon Books, 1980.

Berger, Peter L., and Thomas Luckmann. *The Social Construction of Reality*. Garden City, N.Y.: Anchor-Doubleday, 1967.

Bernhard, Thomas. *Eve of Retirement*. Translated by Gitta Honegger. New York: Performing Arts Journal Publications, 1982.

———. *Ein Fest für Boris*. Frankfurt: Suhrkamp, 1968.

————. *Histrionics*. Translated by Peter Jansen and Kenneth Northcott. Chicago: University of Chicago Press, 1990.

————. *Der Italiener*. Salzburg: Residenz, 1971.

————. *Die Macht der Gewohnheit*. Frankfurt: Suhrkamp, 1974.

————. *Der Präsident*. Frankfurt: Suhrkamp, n.d.

Best, Alan, and Hans Wolfschütz, eds. *Modern Austrian Writing: Literature and Society after 1945*. Totowa, N.J.: Barnes and Noble, 1980.

Bigras, Julien. "French Psychoanalysis." In *Psychoanalysis, Creativity, and Literature: A French-American Inquiry*, edited by Alan Roland. New York: Columbia University Press, 1978.

Bion, W. R. "Attacks on Linking." *International Journal of Psycho-Analysis* 40 (1959): 308–15.

Blau, Herbert. *The Audience*. Baltimore: Johns Hopkins University Press, 1990.

————. *Take Up the Bodies: Theater at the Vanishing Point*. Urbana: University of Illinois Press, 1982.

Bloom, Harold. "The Analysis of Character." In *Major Literary Characters: Willy Loman*, edited by Harold Bloom. New York: Chelsea, 1991.

Booth, Wayne. *The Company We Keep: An Ethics of Fiction*. Berkeley: University of California Press, 1988.

Boswell, James. *Life of Johnson*. Reprint. London: Oxford University Press, 1960.

Brater, Enoch. *Beyond Minimalism: Beckett's Late Style in the Theater*. New York: Oxford University Press, 1984.

————. "Light, Sound, Movement, and Action in Beckett's *Rockaby*." In *On Beckett: Essays and Criticism*, edited by S. E. Gontarski. New York: Grove Press, 1986: 385–403.

————, ed. *Feminine Focus*. New York: Oxford University Press, 1989.

Brecht, Bertolt. *Collected Plays*. Vols. 2 and 6. Edited by Ralph Manheim and John Willett. New York: Random House, 1976.

————. *Gesammelte Werke*. Vols. 1 and 7. Frankfurt: Suhrkamp, 1967.

————. *Werke*. Vols. 6 and 12. Frankfurt: Suhrkamp, 1989.

Burke, Kenneth. *Language as Symbolic Action: Essays on Life, Literature, and Method*. Berkeley: University of California Press, 1966.

Burns, Edward. *Character: Acting and Being on the Pre-Modern Stage*. London: Macmillan, 1990.

Butler, Judith. "Performance Acts and Gender Constitution: An Essay in Phenomenology and Feminist Theory." *Theatre Journal* 40 (1988): 519–31.

Bywater, Ingram. *Aristotle on the Art of Poetry*. Reprint. New York: Garland, 1980.

Calandra, Denis. *New German Dramatists: A Study of Peter Handke, Franz Xaver Kroetz, Rainer Werner Fassbinder, Heiner Müller, Thomas Brasch, Thomas Bernhard and Botho Strauss*. New York: Grove Press, 1983.

Case, Sue-Ellen. *Feminism and Theater*. London: Macmillan, 1988.

———. "From Split Subject to Split Britches." In *Feminine Focus,* edited by Enoch Brater, 126–46. New York: Oxford University Press, 1989.

Cavell, Stanley. *Must We Mean What We Say: A Book of Essays.* Cambridge: Cambridge University Press, 1976.

Chabert, Pierre. "The Body in Beckett's Theatre." *Journal of Beckett Studies* 8 (1982): 23–28.

Chamberlain, Charles. "From 'Haunts' to 'Character': The Meaning of *Ethos* and Its Relation to Ethics." *Helios,* n.s. 11 (1984): 97–108.

Chatman, Seymour. *Story and Discourse.* Ithaca: Cornell University Press, 1978.

Chaudhuri, Una. "The Spectator in Drama/Drama in the Spectator." *Modern Drama* 27 (1984): 281–98.

Cohen, Michael. *"Hamlet" in My Mind's Eye.* Athens: University of Georgia Press, 1989.

Cohen, Susan D. "Fiction and the Photographic Image in Duras' *The Lover."* *L'Esprit Creatur* 30 (1990): 58–68.

Connor, Steven. *Samuel Beckett: Repetition, Theory, Text.* London: Basil Blackwell, 1988.

Craig, Edward Gordon. *Henry Irving.* London: J. M. Dent, 1930.

———. *The Mask: A Journal of the Art of the Theatre.* Florence, 1909–29. Reprint, New York: Benjamin Blom, 1966.

———. *Towards a New Theatre.* London: J. M. Dent, 1913.

Culler, Jonathan. *Structuralist Poetics.* Ithaca: Cornell University Press, 1975.

Cummings, Scott. "Seeing with Clarity: The Visions of Maria Irene Fornes." *Theatre* 27 (1985): 51–56.

de la Croix, Horst, and Richard G. Tansey, eds. *Gardner's Art through the Ages.* 8th ed. New York: Harcourt Brace Jovanovich, 1986.

Diamond, Elin. "Benmussa's Adaptations: Unauthorized Texts from Elsewhere." In *Feminine Focus,* edited by Enoch Brater, 64–78. New York: Oxford University Press, 1989.

———. "Brechtian Theory / Feminist Theory: Toward a Gestic Feminist Criticism." *The Drama Review* 32 (1988): 82–94.

Dickson, Keith. *Towards Utopia: A Study of Brecht.* Oxford: Clarendon Press, 1978.

Dollimore, Jonathan. *Radical Tragedy: Religion, Ideology, and Power in the Drama of Shakespeare and His Contemporaries.* Chicago: University of Chicago Press, 1984.

Douglas, Mary. *How Institutions Think.* Syracuse, N.Y.: Syracuse University Press, 1986.

Dowden, Stephen. *Understanding Thomas Bernhard.* Columbia: University of South Carolina Press, 1991.

Dryden, John. "An Essay of Dramatic Poesy." In *Criticism: The Foundations of Modern Literary Judgment,* edited by Mark Shorer, Josephine Miles, and Gordon McKenzie. New York: Harcourt, Brace, 1958.

Duras, Marguerite. *India Song.* Translated by Barbara Bray. New York: Grove Press, 1976.

Eisner, Nicholas. "*Theatertheater/Theaterspiele:* The Plays of Thomas Bernhard." *Modern Drama* 30 (1987): 104–14.

Esslin, Martin. "Beckett and Bernhard: A Comparison." *Modern Austrian Literature* 18 (1985): 67–78.

———. "A Drama of Disease and Derision: The Plays of Thomas Bernhard." *Modern Drama* 23 (1981): 367–84.

———. "A Poetry of Moving Images." In *Beckett Translating/Translating Beckett,* edited by Alan Warren Friedman, Charles Rossman, and Dana Scherzer. University Park: Pennsylvania State University Press, 1987.

Eynat-Confino, Irène. *Beyond the Mask: Gordon Craig, Movement, and the Actor.* Carbondale: Southern Illinois University Press, 1989.

Falck, Colin. *Myth, Truth and Literature: Towards a True Post-Modernism.* Cambridge: Cambridge University Press, 1989.

Fornes, Maria Irene. *The Danube* and *Mud.* In *Maria Irene Fornes: Plays.* New York: Performing Arts Journal Publications, 1986.

———. *Fefu and Her Friends.* In *Word Plays: An Anthology of New American Drama.* New York: Performing Arts Journal Publications, 1980.

———. *The Winter Repertory: Promenade and Other Plays.* New York: Winter House, 1971.

Forster, E. M. *Aspects of the Novel.* New York: Harcourt, Brace, 1927.

Freud, Sigmund. "Further Recommendations in the Technique of Psychoanalysis: Recollection, Repetition and Working Through." In *Sigmund Freud: Therapy and Technique.* Edited by Philip Rieff, 157–66. New York: Macmillan, 1963.

———. "Mourning and Melancholia" (1917). In *Sigmund Freud: General Psychological Theory.* Edited by Philip Rieff, 164–79. New York: Macmillan, 1963.

———. "Psychopathic Characters on Stage." In *The Standard Edition of the Complete Psychological Works of Sigmund Freud.* Vol. 7. Translated by James Strachey. London: Hogarth Press, 1978.

Friedman, Alan Warren, Charles Rossman, and Dana Scherzer, eds. *Beckett Translating/Translating Beckett.* University Park: Pennsylvania State University Press, 1987.

Fuchs, Elinor. "The Death of Character." *TheatreCommunications* (March 1983): 1–6.

Fuegi, John. *Bertolt Brecht: Chaos, According to Plan.* Cambridge: Cambridge University Press, 1987.

Garner, Stanton B., Jr. "Visual Field in Beckett's Late Plays." *Comparative Drama* 21 (1987): 349–73.

Garten, H. F. "Foreign Influences on German Expressionist Drama." In *Expres-*

sionism as an International Literary Phenomenon, edited by Ulrich Weisstein, 59–68. Paris: Didier, 1973.

Gass, William. *Fiction and the Figures of Life*. New York: Random House, 1971.

Geis, Deborah R. "Wordscapes of the Body: Performative Language as *Gestus* in Maria Irene Fornes's Plays." *Theatre Journal* 42 (1990): 291–307.

Gems, Pam. *Three Plays*. London: Penguin Books, 1985.

Gent, Lucy, and Nigel Llewellyn, eds. *Renaissance Bodies: The Human Figure in English Culture c. 1540–1660*. London: Reaktion Books, 1990.

Glassman, Deborah N. *Marguerite Duras: Fascinating Vision and Narrative Cure*. Cranbury, N.J.: Associated University Presses, 1991.

Goffman, Erving. *Frame Analysis: An Essay on the Organization of Experience*. Cambridge, Mass.: Harvard University Press, 1974.

Goldman, Michael. *The Actor's Freedom: Toward a Theory of Drama*. New York: Viking Press, 1975.

———. "Vitality and Deadness in Beckett's Plays." In *Beckett at 80 / Beckett in Context*, edited by Enoch Brater, 67–83. New York: Oxford University Press, 1986.

Gombrich, E. H. *Art and Illusion: A Study in the Psychology of Pictorial Representation*. Princeton: Princeton University Press, 1961.

Gontarski, S. E. "*Quad* and *Catastrophe*." In *On Beckett: Essays and Criticism*, edited by S. E. Gontarski, 404–6. New York: Grove Press, 1986.

Gruber, William E. *Comic Theaters*. Athens: University of Georgia Press, 1986.

———. "Non-Aristotelian Theater: Brecht's and Plato's Theories of Artistic Imitation." *Comparative Drama* 21 (1987): 199–213.

Gunn, Daniel. *Psychoanalysis and Fiction: An Exploration of Literary and Psychoanalytic Borders*. Cambridge: Cambridge University Press, 1988.

Hayman, Ronald. *Brecht: A Biography*. London: Weidenfeld and Nicholson, 1983.

Hofmann, Kurt. *Aus Gesprächen mit Thomas Bernhard*. Vienna: Löcker, 1988.

Honegger, Gitta. "Acoustic Masks: Strategies of Language in the Theater of Canetti, Bernhard, and Handke." *Modern Austrian Literature* 18 (1985): 57–66.

———. Introduction to *Thomas Bernhard: "The President" and "Eve of Retirement,"* translated by Gitta Honegger. New York: Performing Arts Journal Publications, 1982.

Innes, Christopher. *Edward Gordon Craig*. Cambridge: Cambridge University Press, 1983.

Jones, David Richard. *Great Directors at Work: Stanislavsky, Brecht, Kazan, Brook*. Berkeley: University of California Press, 1986.

Kalb, Jonathan. *Beckett in Performance*. Cambridge: Cambridge University Press, 1989.

Keyssar, Helene. *Feminist Theatre: An Introduction to Plays of Contemporary British and American Women*. London: Macmillan, 1984.

Knights, L. C. *Explorations: Essays in Criticism Mainly on the Literature of the Seventeenth Century.* New York: George W. Stewart, 1947.

Knowlson, James. *"Footfalls."* In *On Beckett: Essays and Criticism,* edited by S. E. Gontarski, 350–59. New York: Grove Press, 1986.

Krutch, Joseph Wood. *"Modernism" in Modern Drama.* Ithaca: Cornell University Press, 1953.

Langbaum, Robert. *The Poetry of Experience: The Dramatic Monologue in Modern Literary Tradition.* New York: Norton, 1963.

Laplanche, J., and J.-B. Pontalis. *The Language of Psychoanalysis.* Translated by Donald Nicholson-Smith. New York: Norton, 1973.

Lellis, George. "Brecht and *Cahiers du Cinéma.*" In *Bertolt Brecht: Political Theory and Literary Practice,* edited by Betty Nance Weber and Hubert Heinen, 129–44. Athens: University of Georgia Press, 1980.

Levenson, Michael. *Modernism and the Fate of Individuality: Character and Novelistic Form from Conrad to Woolf.* Cambridge: Cambridge University Press, 1991.

Levin, David Michael. *The Listening Self: Personal Growth, Social Change and the Closure of Metaphysics.* London: Routledge, 1989.

Levy, Eric P. *"Mercier and Camier:* Narration, Dante, and the Couple." In *On Beckett: Essays and Criticism,* edited by S. E. Gontarski, 117–30. New York: Grove Press, 1986.

Locke, John. *An Essay Concerning Human Understanding.* Edited by P. H. Nidditch. Oxford: Clarendon Press, 1975.

Lyons, Charles R. "Character and Theatrical Space." In *Themes in Drama: The Theatrical Space,* edited by James Redmond, 27–44. Cambridge: Cambridge University Press, 1987.

Manheim, Ralph, and John Willett, eds. *Bertolt Brecht: Collected Plays.* Vols. 2, 6. New York: Random House, 1977.

Marker, Frederick J., and Lise-Lone Marker. *Edward Gordon Craig and "The Pretenders": A Production Revisited.* Carbondale: Southern Illinois University Press, 1981.

Marranca, Bonnie. "The Real Life of Maria Irene Fornes." *Performing Arts Journal* 22 (1984): 29–34.

Martin, Mary Kay. "Space Invasions: Voice-Over in Works by Samuel Beckett and Marguerite Duras." In *The Theatrical Space,* edited by James Redmond, 239–46. Cambridge: Cambridge University Press, 1987.

McLachlan, Ian. "Ironic Tension and Production Techniques: *The Measures Taken.*" In *Bertolt Brecht: Political Theory and Literary Practice,* edited by Betty Nance Weber and Hubert Heinen, 100–105. Athens: University of Georgia Press, 1980.

McMillan, Dougald, and Martha Fehsenfeld, eds. *Beckett in the Theatre.* London: John Calder, 1988.

Mead, George Herbert. *George Herbert Mead on Social Psychology.* Edited by Anselm Strauss. Chicago: University of Chicago Press, 1964.

Meisel, Martin. *Realizations: Narrative, Pictorial, and Theatrical Arts in Nineteenth-Century England.* Princeton: Princeton University Press, 1983.

Mews, Siegfried, and Herbert Knust, eds. *Essays on Brecht: Theater and Politics.* Chapel Hill: University of North Carolina Press, 1974.

Meyerhofer, Nicholas J. "The Laughing Sisyphus: Reflections on Bernhard as (Self-) Dramatist in Light of His *Der Theatermacher.*" *Modern Austrian Literature* 21 (1988): 107–15.

Miner, Earl. *Comparative Poetics: An Intercultural Essay on Theories of Literature.* Princeton: Princeton University Press, 1990.

Mitchell, W. J. T. "*Ut Pictura Theoria:* Abstract Painting and the Repression of Language." *Critical Inquiry* 15 (1989): 348–71.

Morrison, Kristin. *Canters and Chroniclers: The Use of Narrative in the Plays of Samuel Beckett and Harold Pinter.* Chicago: University of Chicago Press, 1983.

Mullaney, Steven. *The Place of the Stage.* Chicago: University of Chicago Press, 1987.

Murphy, P. J. *Reconstructing Beckett: Language for Being in Samuel Beckett's Fiction.* Toronto: University of Toronto Press, 1990.

Natalle, Elizabeth J. *Feminist Theatre: A Study in Persuasion.* Metuchen, N.J.: The Scarecrow Press, 1985.

Nuttall, A. D. *A New Mimesis.* London: Methuen, 1983.

Olf, Julian. "The Man/Marionette Debate in Modern Theatre." *Educational Theatre Journal* 26 (1974): 488–94.

Ortega y Gasset, José. *The Dehumanization of Art.* New York: Doubleday, n.d.

Orwell, George. "Shooting an Elephant." In *The Norton Reader,* edited by Arthur M. Eastman, et al., 768–75. New York: Norton, 1988.

Papin, Liliane. "Staging Writing or the Ceremony of Text in Marguerite Duras." *Modern Drama* 34 (1991): 128–37.

Parfit, Derek. *Reasons and Persons.* London: Oxford University Press, 1984.

Pavis, Patrice. *Languages of the Stage: Essays in the Semiology of the Theatre.* New York: Performing Arts Journal Publications, 1982.

Pountney, Rosemary. *Theatre of Shadows: Samuel Beckett's Drama 1956–76.* Totowa, N.J.: Barnes and Noble, 1988.

Rawson, Claude. "Order and Cruelty." *Essays in Criticism* 20 (1970): 24–56.

Ricoeur, Paul. *Time and Narrative.* Vol. 3. Translated by Kathleen Blamey and David Pellaver. Chicago: University of Chicago Press, 1988.

Rimmon-Kenan, Shlomith, ed. *Discourse in Psychoanalysis and Literature.* London: Methuen, 1987.

Robinson, Douglas. "Henry James and Euphemism." *College English* 53 (1991): 403–25.

Roland, Alan, ed. *Psychoanalysis, Creativity, and Literature: A French-American Inquiry.* New York: Columbia University Press, 1978.

Schilder, Paul. *The Image and Appearance of the Human Body.* New York: International Universities Press, 1950.

Schlaes, Amity. "Thomas Bernhard and the German Literary Scene." *The New Criterion* 5 (January 1982): 26–32.

Schroeder, Peter R. "Hidden Depths: Dialogue and Characterization in Chaucer and Malory." *PMLA* 98 (1983): 374–87.

Senelick, Laurence. *Gordon Craig's Moscow "Hamlet."* Westport, Conn.: Greenwood Press, 1982.

Shakespeare, William. *Hamlet.* In *William Shakespeare: The Complete Works.* Edited by Alfred Harbage. 1969. Rev. ed. New York: Penguin Books, 1977.

Shepard, Sam. *Fool for Love and Other Plays.* New York: Bantam Books, 1984.

Simon, Bennett. *Mind and Madness in Ancient Greece: The Classical Roots of Modern Psychiatry.* Ithaca: Cornell University Press, 1978.

———. *Tragic Drama and the Family: Psychoanalytic Studies from Aeschylus to Beckett.* New Haven: Yale University Press, 1988.

Skloot, Robert. *The Darkness We Carry: The Drama of the Holocaust.* Madison: University of Wisconsin Press, 1988.

Spanos, William V. *Repetitions: The Postmodern Occasion in Literature and Culture.* Baton Rouge: Louisiana State University Press, 1987.

Spariosu, Mihai, ed. *Mimesis in Contemporary Theory: An Interdisciplinary Approach.* Philadelphia and Amsterdam: John Benjamins, 1984.

Spencer, James H., Jr., and Leon Balter. "Empathy and the Analyzing Instrument." In *Empathy II,* edited by Joseph Lichtenberg, Melvin Bornstein, and Donald Silver, 289–307. Hillsdale, N.J.: The Analytic Press, 1984.

States, Bert O. "Playing in Lyric Time: Beckett's Voice Plays." *Theatre Journal* 40 (1988): 453–67.

Steiner, George. *The Death of Tragedy.* New York: Oxford University Press, 1961.

Steinweg, Rainer, ed. *Auf Anregung Bertolt Brechts: Lehrstücke mit Schulern, Arbeitern, Theaterleuten.* Frankfurt: Suhrkamp, 1978.

Strawson, P. F. *Individuals: An Essay in Descriptive Metaphysics.* New York: Anchor Books, 1963.

Strindberg, August. *Miss Julia.* Translated by Peter Watts. New York: Penguin Books, 1958.

———. *Miss Julie.* Translated by Elizabeth Sprigge. In *Masters of Modern Drama.* Edited by Haskell Block and Robert Shedd. New York: Random House, 1962.

Twycross, Meg. "'Transvestism' in the Mystery Plays." *Medieval English Theatre* 5 (1983): 123–50.

Volbach, Walter R. *Adolphe Appia: Prophet of the Modern Theatre: A Profile.* Middletown, Conn.: Wesleyan University Press, 1968.

Volker, Klaus. "Brecht Today: Classic or Challenge." *Theatre Journal* 39 (1987): 425–33.

von Hofmannsthal, Hugo. Prologue for *Baal* (1926). In *Tulane Drama Review* (1961) 111–22.

Walcutt, Charles Child. *Man's Changing Mask: Modes and Methods of Characterization in Fiction.* Minneapolis: University of Minnesota Press, 1966.

Walton, J. Michael, ed. *Craig on Theatre.* London: Methuen, 1983.

Weber, Betty Nance, and Hubert Heinen, eds. *Bertolt Brecht: Political Theory and Literary Practice.* Athens: University of Georgia Press, 1980.

Weisstein, Ulrich, ed. *Expressionism as an International Literary Phenomenon.* Paris: Didier, 1973.

Wetzsteon, Ross. "Irene Fornes: The Elements of Style." *Village Voice* (29 April 1986): 42–45.

Whitman, Cedric. *Aristophanes and the Comic Hero.* Cambridge, Mass.: Harvard University Press, 1964.

Willett, John. *Art and Politics in the Weimar Period.* New York: Pantheon, 1978.

———. *Expressionism.* New York: McGraw-Hill, 1970.

———. *The Theatre of the Weimar Republic.* New York: Holmes and Meier, 1988.

———, ed. *Brecht on Theatre: The Development of an Aesthetic.* New York: Hill and Wang, 1964.

Wilshire, Bruce. *Role Playing and Identity: The Limits of Theater as Metaphor.* Bloomington: Indiana University Press, 1982.

Wolf, Ernest S. "The Disconnected Self." In *Psychoanalysis, Creativity, and Literature: A French-American Inquiry,* edited by Alan Roland, 103–17. New York: Columbia University Press, 1978.

Wolfschütz, Hans. "Thomas Bernhard: The Mask of Death." In *Modern Austrian Writing,* edited by Alan Best and Hans Wolfschütz, 214–35. Totowa, N.J.: Barnes and Noble, 1980.

Worthen, William B. "*Still Playing Games:* Ideology and Performance in the Theater of Maria Irene Fornes." In *Feminine Focus,* edited by Enoch Brater, 167–85. New York: Oxford University Press, 1989.

Wright, Elizabeth. *Postmodern Brecht: A Re-Presentation.* London: Routledge, 1989.

Index